FIRST AMONG UNEQUALS

THE AUTOBIOGRAPHY

FIRST AMONG UNEQUALS

The Autobiography

Viv Anderson MBE
with Lynton Guest

FullBack
Media

First published in Great Britian 2010 by Fullback Media Ltd

Fullback Media Ltd
26 Eton Close,
Datchet,
Berks,
SL3 9BE

ISBN 978 184226 015 9 HB Arsenal

ISBN 978 184226 016 6 HB Manchester United

ISBN 978 184226 017 3 HB Notts Forest

ISBN 978 184226 018 0 HB England

ISBN 978 184226 019 7 PB

ISBN 978 184226 021 0 HB Sheffield Wednesday

Typeset by: Bookcraft Ltd, Stroud, Gloucestershire

Printed by Dolman Scott
www.dolmanscott.com

Front cover design by: PR3

TO:

Mam, Dad, Donald, Nichole, Debra, Charlie,
Gabrielle, Freddie and our new baby due soon

CONTENTS

ACKNOWLEDGMENTS

Very Special Thanks To:

Bill Hill, Les Molloy, John Kaufman, Roger Grime, Dean Morter, Chris Lloyd and his team, Orca Distribution, Richard Chalmers, David Landau, Harriet Lester, John Speer, Dave Clarke, David Wood, Graham Bell, Tony Stanley, Brian Longmuir, Alex Fynn, Lynton Guest, David Wood, Peter Law, Nottingham Forest F.C., Brian Clough, Gordon Taylor, Trevor Braithwaite, Danny Lynch, Arsenal F.C., Manchester United F.C., Sir Alex Ferguson, Sheffield Wednesday F.C., Bryan Robson, Tony Woodcock, Barnsley F.C., Middlesbrough F.C., The Alex Stepney Fund, Paul McGarvey at JP3, Norman Whiteside, John Sumpter @ PA Action Images, Danny Wilson, Steve Bruce, Martin O'Neill, John Robertson, Kevin Keegan, Bob Latchford, Shelagh Aitken, Debra Anderson, Nichole Burton, Bert Bowery, Michael Wykes, Glyn Saunders, Peter Wells, Michale & Kevin Byrne, Trevor Kershaw, Colin Wragg, Kevin Rodgers, John & Paula, Bert Johnson, Trevor Brooking, Pedro Richards, Robin Fox, Sacit and Monica Amorim Molloy.

PHOTO
ACKNOWLEDGEMENTS

All photographs are from the author's personal collection.

The Author would like to thank the following photographers:

Bob Thomas, H. Barlow, *Manchester Evening News*, AllSports Photographic, County Press, Charles A. Noble, Doug Poole, Steve Ellis, P. Spencer, Ken Prater, Barnsley F.C., Middlesbrough F.C., Getty Images

Every effort has been made to contact the copyright holders of the photographs used in this book, unfortunately some were not reachable. The publishers would be grateful if those concerned would contact Fullback Media.

PREFACE

It is now more than thirty years since I became the first black footballer to be capped by England. I was the first among unequals! In those days the number of black players was limited and we – the original generation – had to fight every step of the way to be recognised. How that has changed. Today, you would be surprised to see an English professional side without a full complement of ethnic minority players. What a difference from when I started.

With the approach of the thirtieth anniversary itself, in the 2008–09 season, a raft of celebrations were planned. It was pointed out to me that there were huge numbers of people out there who wanted to mark the occasion. It was fantastic to realise that my milestone meant so much to so many. One of the events suggested to me was an all-star charity football match, featuring some of the greatest players over the last thirty years. Another was for me to write a book about my experiences both in the game and in life. The match didn't take place in the end, for reasons you will see as you read on. The book, however, was completed and this is the result.

The first thing you need to know is that my memory

for detail is not the best in the business. Anyone who knows me will tell you that. Dates, times, even years are a mystery to me sometimes. Because of that I have tried to check all the facts in this book to make sure they are correct. If one or two fall outside that boundary, well I apologise but I'm sure you'll find your enjoyment of my story is in no way diminished.

In these pages you will read tales of some of the great footballers and managers I have worked with and played against. I've tried to give a proper opinion of them, for good or ill. I'll tell you about my time with England and my unique contribution to World Cup history. I have also written about being made an ambassador for our bid for the 2018 World Cup. I think you'll find that my views on our efforts to date are forthright, to say the least.

The clubs I played for form a large part of the book. Most of you will know the list: Nottingham Forest, in the most successful period they've ever had, under the incomparable Brian Clough; Arsenal, at the very beginning of the George Graham revolution which put the club back on top of the pile; Manchester United, where I was Sir Alex Ferguson's first signing; Sheffield Wednesday with Big Ron Atkinson in his pomp and Trevor Francis in the wings; Barnsley, the family club which gave me my first experience as a player-manager alongside Danny Wilson; with Bryan Robson at Middlesbrough, when we brought some of the world's greatest stars to the Riverside. All of these and more come under my microscope.

Rather than write a comprehensive account of my life,

I've included stories and incidents which I hope will keep you entertained and tell you a story about football. Many of them you will not have heard about before. There is a huge cast of characters in this book and I have tried to bring them all to life. At the same time I offer you my thoughts and opinions on the players and the events. What I haven't written is a compendium of games and seasons; you can get that elsewhere. Instead, I want to tell you about those personalities who shaped the world of modern football, most of whom I knew personally.

Much of my adult life has been lived in the public eye. In *First Among Unequals* I talk about what that's like and the effects it can sometimes have. I have also included aspects of my personal life which have made headlines over the years. I set the record straight wherever I can.

The most important element I have tried to sustain throughout the book is honesty. I've done my very best to tell it like it is. I've not gone out of my way to criticise anyone unnecessarily but I make no apologies for giving my views where appropriate. Parts of this book will be controversial, there's no question about that. But I think overall you will find it a riveting account of the life of a professional footballer in the today's world. I hope you enjoy it.

Viv Anderson MBE: Manchester, 2010

Chapter One

ENGLAND MY ENGLAND

As the day broke on Monday, May 18 2009, I was feeling pretty good. Making my way to Wembley was a joy I had felt many times before when I played at the old ground. I also loved attending matches there after my retirement. But this time was different. It wasn't a game I was going to see, nor was I simply visiting the new Wembley – probably the best stadium in the world – with its fantastic arch that you can see from miles away. It was none of these things. I was to be present at the public launch of England's bid to stage the 2018 World Cup. But what should have been a memorable occasion soon turned into a disaster and, as far as I am concerned, shows exactly why we have more to accomplish in this country, even though we have already achieved so much.

I couldn't fail to notice there were no black or Asian faces in the main group. That led me to remember my invitation had not come direct from the Football Association (FA) or the bidding committee. I didn't think about it too much at the time but I was there, if you like, by default. I had been asked if I wanted to attend by one of the companies for whom I carry out promotional work. They had been allocated a number of tickets. Maybe the fact that my invitation hadn't arrived direct from the FA should have alerted me but, to be honest, I never really gave it a second thought. I was pleased to be included, whatever route the invite took. But there was Prince William, along with the Prime Minister, Gordon Brown; there was David Beckham; there was Wayne Rooney for God's sake. But of black England players, there was not a sign. No Rio Ferdinand, no Ashley Cole, no Emile Heskey. It was the same with the speeches, which were broadcast and commented on throughout the media.

Now I know David and Wayne are box-office, I've got no problem with that. They should have been there and prominently displayed. But surely room could have been found at the main table for some of the black footballers who have contributed to England's cause over the years. It was not the only sour note. Hardly commented upon in the next morning's back pages was the fact that the England manager, Fabio Capello, was also noticeable by his absence. It seemed to me a strange way to announce our bid to the waiting world. Yet again, just like a previous attempt to secure the 2006 tournament, when the English delegation committed just about every mistake in the book, our nation got off on completely the wrong foot.

Suddenly, as I was taking everything in, a murmur went around the assembled dignitaries near where I was sitting. I didn't realise it at the time but it turned out that the FA had invited a London Assembly member from the racist British National Party to the event. How this happened I really don't know. I don't think the FA knows either. In fact the FA was caught cold. The next day, the stories in the press were as much concerned with the BNP member as they were about the bid. To me, it was sad and the truth is the whole thing left a nasty taste.

Those people who know me would tell you I am an optimistic, humorous, happy-go-lucky kind of person. Alex Ferguson once attempted to buy me back from the club he sold me to – Ron Atkinson's Sheffield Wednesday – because I was such a positive influence in the dressing room. Fergie felt he needed my presence for Manchester United's first European campaign in many years. For someone like me to say what I have about my experience at Wembley tells you that something about our 2018 bid is seriously wrong.

The debacle was felt well beyond our shores. The influential FIFA Vice President, Jack Warner, who is also the controversial President of the Central American Football Federation, Concacaf, and who has often been a thorn in England's side in the past, could hardly have been any clearer, when he said: "I'm quite sure the FA will recognise an error when one is made and they will correct it. I hope they will do it quickly." My old mate Garth Crooks was even more forceful when he declared: "What I find so desperately sad is that whatever your views (are) about the BNP being there, there is a bigger view. If it had been a really diverse event, if there had been a selection of black multi-ethnic groups there, we could have got over this. We've spent twenty years trying to drive the

BNP out of football and they are getting an invitation to the launch of our World Cup bid." Now Garth, who I played against many times, takes some stick for the length of his pronouncements, but here I think everyone would agree that he was absolutely spot on. At the time of writing this, the FA has made some efforts to right its terrible wrong but I remain worried that the damage has already been done.

Soon afterwards, a football conference took place at Stamford Bridge, during which Jack Warner again made his feelings known. Among other observations, he said the England bid was "lightweight". This was an implied criticism of the bid leader, Lord Triesman (who is also Chairman of the FA), and his bid team. Since Warner, as a close ally of FIFA President Sepp Blatter, wields some considerable influence on the votes to decide who gets World Cups, this was as bad as it could get. Later, it turned out that Australia, which is also bidding for 2018, had stolen a march on England by providing those attending the conference with goody bags promoting its bid but there was no sign of any English equivalent. For this, the England bid team were derided in the press.

As you will see later in this book, I have some experience in the ways of the press. One aspect of what I have learnt is that if the media has decided something is a shambles, everything that happens from then on is reported in that light. So when it became known that England had spent £24,000 buying expensive Mulberry handbags to give away to FIFA delegates' wives (including Mrs. Jack Warner), the same papers that had taken the FA to task for not providing goody bags at Stamford Bridge blasted the organisation for its extravagance over the handbags. The point is that the FA, in its desperate attempts to respond to the negative comments in the press, merely made everything worse. The association's expensive PR machine should have realised this way before it got out of hand.

In response to the unfavourable publicity, the FA decided to recruit fifty "ambassadors" to help promote the 2018 bid. Huge dossiers were sent to each ambassador explaining the party line. I was one of those chosen. I still have the 100 page email. I was happy to accept the invitation. I want to do all I can to bring the World Cup to my country. That is part of the reason why I believe far more transparency is required on the part of the bid team. The good thing about the ambassadors is that we are made up of many different nationalities, all of us having made an impact on the English game at one time or another. However, I do not feel that our role has been properly thought through or developed over time. What was a good idea in principle is, in my view, in danger of being squandered.

I want to say right here that I am fully committed to helping England win the right to stage the 2018 World Cup. Like every other Englishman, I desperately want this country to host the tournament once again. It's been far too long. However, as one who accepted the role of ambassador for the bid I believe I should speak freely, both to the powers that be and the public at large. With the matter to be decided in December 2010, time is running out. The

FA has made mistakes and continues to make them. The belated move to create the panel of ambassadors might have been honourably meant but – since little has been asked of us – it appears to be a case of both tokenism and a failure to understand the nature of the beast they are dealing with. Sending out David Beckham is an obviously good move. He is a global icon. He will woo crowds and delegates wherever he goes anywhere in the world. We need him. But we ambassadors are not being used to anything like the same effect. I am ready to talk to anyone, anytime to help my country. But I only get the occasional email with requests to perform an ambassadorial duty. The role is undefined. As one of the players who was at the centre of England's change from an all-white game to a game of all the talents, I would have thought the FA would have found a way to use my status – and that of the others who came afterwards – to promote the bid, particularly around the world. The bid team needs to resolve these issues – and fast – if we are to stand any chance of bringing the World Cup back to these shores.

As if to vindicate my position, I heard from a colleague one day in November, 2009, that there were serious disagreements within the bid committee and that Jack Warner would soon be back to haunt us. Within a couple of days the Warner story was public knowledge and it wasn't very pretty. Mr. Warner decided to return his wife's Mulberry handbag, accusing the FA of giving her a present which was "a symbol of derision, betrayal and embarrassment for me and my family." Accepting the handbag had, according to Warner, caused him to suffer all manner of "indignities" from "all kinds of persons". It seemed he was objecting to negative coverage in the media which implied his wife's acceptance of the gift and the FA's giving of it was somehow evidence of corruption. He went on, in a letter to Lord Triesman, to say, "When these insults touch my wife, it represents an all time low." As if that wasn't enough damage to inflict in one day, Warner directly accused Lord Triesman of failing to stand up to those who were making the allegations of wrong-doing.

However much we might not agree with the interpretation put on the Mulberries by either the press or Warner, we must respond to the criticisms of those who have the vote. Not capitulate, but learn. I am told that panic ensued at the FA after the series of terrible articles and broadcasts following Mr. Warner's outburst. Again my information proved correct and by the middle of November the whole bid committee had been restructured. I was pleased to see the former Chelsea player, Paul Elliot, drafted in. Paul has long campaigned against racism and is a welcome addition. The question is: will he be deployed in a way that will best use his talent? The rest of the restructuring exercise smacked of indecision.

Sometimes I think there is a sense of entitlement in this country (or at least in those that run football). It goes like this: because we haven't had the World Cup here since 1966 and we are the home of football, it is our right to have it now. Others, we point out, like Germany, have hosted two World Cups since it was last held here. Frankly, this kind of thing cuts no ice with FIFA and the notion needs to be rapidly abandoned if we are to have any hope of winning. If we don't grasp these issues and deal with them, our bid will go the same way as our attempt to get the 2006 tournament. Nowhere!

After the experience of Wembley and its aftermath, my mind went back to earlier times; to growing up a black kid in Nottingham. I can't say I particularly suffered from racism in my youth but of course I knew it was out there. I spent the whole of my energy trying to make it in the cut and thrust world of professional sport. In those days casual racism did exist in the dressing room and on the training pitch. It was the 1970s, remember. Life on Mars and all that! And there weren't many professional black players back then. I remember Clyde Best at West Ham and Albert Johansson of Leeds, that's about it. But I just didn't have the space, mentally, to deal with the world's prejudices. I'm not saying I was oblivious to it all, just that if I'd have let it get to me, my career would have been that much harder and may not have happened at all. Even when I won my first England cap I refused to be sucked into the media frenzy that came with it. Well, not too much anyway!

Whether I like it or not, I will always be remembered as the first black player to be capped by England. The accolade is an honour and I will always treasure the memory of my achievement. The match, against Czechoslovakia on a freezing cold night in November 1978, was a run-of-the-mill friendly, so the emphasis placed by the media on my appearance was magnified. I don't recall too much about the game to be honest, except that I had a hand in the solitary goal which brought England victory. I remember that alright. I thought I did well on the night, particularly when I spotted Tony Currie ahead of me down the right and played the perfect pass to release him. Tony, one of the most skilful players I ever saw but who never really had enough chances at international level to show what he was capable of, put in a great cross for Steve Coppell to score. Despite the hysteria, for me, that night wasn't a case of me being the first black England player, no matter what the media said. I was a professional footballer and I wanted to reach the very top. I had just won the First Division Championship with Nottingham Forest, now I was an international. I was really pleased with my progress.

Many people at my club thought I would get my England chance earlier than I did. They felt that the player who occupied the position, Liverpool's Phil Neal, was no longer the best. But I had to bide my time. Phil was still a great full-back, no question, and it was up to me to dislodge him. When the call came, I was determined to show I could be a fixture in the England team. That's what I was thinking about. I wanted to lay down a marker. It would be some years before I could seriously consider the wider issues that were undoubtedly raised by my elevation to the national team. At the time I thought about my mother and father, hoping they would be proud of me. Like everybody, I wanted their approval. As fate would have it, on the day after the game my mother was involved in a car accident that required a stay in hospital, so my celebrations were cut short. I was at first worried sick about her condition and only perked up when it was explained to me that her injuries were not too serious. Nothing, however, could take away the inner glow I felt over my achievement.

Like everybody else, I didn't get to choose the era in which I played. I always regarded myself as a footballer, not a black footballer, and I wanted to be judged on my ability and performances, not the colour of my skin. However, as a player who helped open up football to black players, I suppose it was inevitable that the race issue would be uppermost in many people's minds, even if not in mine. I can say now that I am proud of the role I played. It helped pave the way for the huge improvements in football that have occurred since then. I am also pleased to have helped the game move away from the prejudices that stood in the way of black footballers when I started.

Of course, in those days, crowds at games were often blatantly racist. Nowhere was free from the scourge. I suffered as much as anyone from the hate but most of the time I was able to shut it out and concentrate on my game. Perhaps it even spurred me on to be a better player. There was no room for complacency, certainly, because you never knew what was around the corner. The next away game could bring the most disgusting chants by the crowd and racist comments from individual supporters. I learned this lesson early. In only my second game for Forest I was subjected to a mass taunt – and that was before the game even started. It was a League Cup tie away to Newcastle. Now the St. James' Park regulars could be intimidating to any footballer but what I experienced that night went way beyond the boundaries of acceptable behaviour. Before the match, the then Forest manager, Dave Mackay, took us pitch-side to get a flavour of the atmosphere. As soon as the crowd got a glimpse of me the baiting started. I froze. As a teenager I must admit I was totally unprepared for the taunting. I told Dave Mackay I didn't want to play. He took me aside and gave me a good talking to. He didn't mince his words. "If you want to be a footballer, son, you've got to learn to cope with stuff like this," he said. I played.

It was only with the support of the management and the other Forest players that I came through it. Maybe it was better to have that experience so early on in my career. It probably made me a stronger person. In the future I would always refuse to be intimidated. My tactic was to concentrate even harder on my game. But it should never have happened in the first place. No player should have to deal with that. To be fair to the Geordies, Newcastle was one of the first grounds where this kind of thing was eradicated. I have since found the Geordie supporters nothing but fair in the way they give me stick.

I don't think the reaction of the Newcastle crowd on that day was any different to what went on at other grounds. It was simply that at St. James' Park the noise was deafening and the antagonism immense. I shut it out. I had to, otherwise my career would have been over there and then. Of course I shouldn't have had to do that but I found out that night that I could cope. No crowd ever really got to me again, even as things turned nastier when eighties hooliganism took hold of the game and almost destroyed it.

After my first appearance against Czechoslovakia the media gave me rave reviews for my performance. The manager, Ron Greenwood, also praised my contribution, saying he was "very pleased" with me. His assistant, Don Howe, was even more impressed and told me I could become a fixture in the England team. This was all I wanted to hear. However, I wasn't picked for the next match or the five after that. Footballers have to learn quickly that no matter how well you think you have done you can suddenly be out of the team. By the time I first played for England I had already learned the lesson. In my short time in the game I had been rejected by the club I had always supported, Manchester United, and been ignored by the great Brian Clough when he first arrived at Forest. I had come back from those disappointments to more than prove my worth. You just have to believe in yourself and work your way back any way you can. The higher you go the more this applies. In my case, Phil Neal came in for me in the England team and when he wasn't available for one match, Trevor Cherry of Leeds got the nod before me. I could have been forgiven for thinking my England career was over almost as soon as it had started.

Happily, this proved not to be the case, although I had to wait until the following June before I got another chance to show what I could do for the national team. Seven months! Today, I can look back with satisfaction on my record for England. I won over thirty caps at right-back in an era when there were quite a few exceptional full-backs about. That's a pretty good return. Not only that, I managed to score two goals in my international career, one against Turkey, one against Yugoslavia.

When he first selected me for England, the manager, Ron Greenwood, didn't really give me any individual advice as to how to approach the game. He just briefed the team as a whole. It was as if he kind of expected you to know what you were about because he had selected you. He sort of floated above it all, smiling. I will always be grateful to Kevin Keegan and Bob Latchford, who took me aside for a chat.

"Just remember you wouldn't be playing if you weren't good enough," Kevin said, while Bob told me to "make sure you do what you do for your club every Saturday." While what they said might seem a cliché, let me tell you that their intervention made all the difference to me. So much so it's something I tried to pass on to younger players when I was established, both for club and country. These are the incredible values that do exist in the world of football. Beyond the cynicism, there are people prepared to take time out to reassure a newcomer; to let him know he is accepted for what he is. Kevin Keegan and Bob Latchford were living examples of this tradition.

Until then, I had only known the training and management team at my club, Nottingham Forest. With England I was finding out that Brian Clough and Peter Taylor were not typical. This was brought home to me, not only through the methods of Ron Greenwood and his assistant, Don Howe, but also in the stories I heard from the other players. I had sampled something of this when I had been called up to the "B" team or age-based squads previously. But nothing compared to the education I received with the senior boys. Management, media interest and competitive instinct fuelled a completely different atmosphere. I discovered that other managers and coaches had very different ideas from Clough, including hard physical training during the season, something Clough thought pointless. That's why he often used to take us off to Mallorca or somewhere where relaxation was the objective and precious little training was carried out. I was soon disabused of the notion that this was the norm.

As time went on, more black players were called up for England, first Laurie Cunningham, who so tragically died in a car crash in Spain some years later, then Cyrille Regis and bit by bit, many, many others. I think I can speak for all of us when I say we are pleased we blazed the trail in the way we did. Today, it would be inconceivable for any English team – whether club or country – not to field its fair share of black players. Nothing is so eloquent a testament to the way our country can respond to change as that.

There is no question that throughout the game and its supporters the issue of racism has improved immeasurably since I began playing. But resting on our laurels should not be the order of the day. While the launch bid for England 2018 was going on under the full glare of publicity at Wembley, other events were unfolding, much more personal to me and relevant to every decent football follower, which showed just how much further the game has yet to travel. Nothing of what was happening found its way into the media. I am going to tell everything in this book, but that incident, which really shows where the game is at in this country, will come later.

First, I want to tell you about my involvement – if you can call it that – in a couple of previous World Cups.

Chapter 2

WORLD CUPS

It is every footballers dream to play in a World Cup.
It's the pinnacle of the game and the summit of any
career. But those highs don't just arrive after a few good
performances for your club. Before I made it into the
full England team I played in the under-21s and the "B"
team. Before I got into a World Cup squad I played in
friendly games, various qualifiers and one match in the
European Championships. What I found was that international football is at best unpredictable, as you'll see
from my experience.

After my initial appearance in the England first team
in 1978 and my seven month wait for another cap, I
was in and out of the side. However, as the 1980 Euro
Championships in Italy approached, I played in the
qualifying games and considered myself the number
one choice. I had, after all, just won the European
Cup for the second time. In the event I was included
in the squad for Italy but I was only selected for one
game, the last group match against Spain. By that time
we were already out of the tournament so it was a dead
match. It was, however, the only game we won, by two
goals to one. This wasn't the progress I had hoped

for following my performance against Czechoslovakia two years before. Still, I was an international novice in 1980, so when I thought about it later I realised that playing in the one game wasn't too bad. I obviously would have preferred more minutes on the pitch. But then I thought I should have been in the team for every game. I decided it was all part of learning about the international set-up.

When we qualified for the 1982 World Cup in Spain I was hopeful of getting more of a chance than I had received in Italy. Four years on from my debut I really felt I was at the top of my game. I was finally established as Greenwood's right-back, or so I thought. It soon began to dawn on me, however, that things were not going my way. They were not going my way at all.

International football is nothing like playing for your club, where you can get in the team, do reasonably well, and be fairly sure you will keep your place. It was different with the national team. For instance, England international managers in my time were notorious for chopping and changing the side. There were always lots of players withdrawing from England squads in those days – not always through genuine injury but often at the request of their managers, who wanted to keep them ready to play for their clubs. This unnerved England's managers. They rarely seemed to know what their best eleven was. So it was no real surprise to me when Liverpool's Phil Neal would sometimes be drafted in by Ron Greenwood. But now, with the World cup approaching, I felt it was my time. With Nottingham Forest, I had won promotion from the old division two, the First Division title, and two European Cups back-to-back. It was time to go to the next level.

But I wasn't selected for the first game. I had to sit and watch as, after a great start to the tournament, things started to go horribly wrong.

Two of our most creative players, Kevin Keegan and Trevor Brooking, were injured going into the campaign. I think any side which had those two fit could have achieved great things. Without them, we were severely lacking in the playmaker department and up front. We had Glenn Hoddle, who could unlock opposing defences, but he was never really trusted in the role by either Greenwood or his successor, Bobby Robson. Keegan became a great player through commitment and determination and he was one of the few English players at the time who had played on the continent. In his time at Hamburg it was obvious he had developed an under-standing of the European game. Brooking, who played under Greenwood at West Ham, was simply top-draw, all silky skills and great passing. Without those two, it was always going to be tough.

Ron Greenwood got the England job when just about everyone thought my boss at Forest, Brian Clough, should have been given the crown. And if Clough had been appointed I'm pretty sure I would have been in his first eleven. Instead, in Spain, Greenwood's preferred right-back was Mick Mills of Ipswich. Now don't get me wrong, but at that time – good though they were

– Ipswich had hardly reached the heights that I had achieved with Forest. Mick Mills was effective but I had stopped some of the greatest wingers in the world. In truth I was devastated. I couldn't understand the manager's decision and he didn't explain it to me. Mr. Greenwood was not always the best communicator, especially when there was bad news to be broken. I tried to stay optimistic and be a good member of the squad. But it still hurt.

Despite the injuries to Brooking and Keegan, things looked good after the first game. We beat the French 3–1, with Robbo scoring the fastest-ever World Cup goal, 27 seconds after we kicked off. I watched with the dawning realisation that the manager was unlikely to want to change a winning team. What was worse and what really filled me with foreboding was that with Kevin Keegan injured, Mick Mills had not only taken my position, Greenwood made him captain.

To be fair, the win against the French had been a good performance. We had beaten the side which would get to the semi-final in this tournament then win the European Championships two years later. From the French game, England's performances looked to have got even better as the team triumphed in their two remaining group matches. It was looking bad for me as we beat Czechoslovakia and Kuwait without conceding a goal.

The injuries meant an awful lot of hopes rested on the shoulders of Bryan Robson and Ray Wilkins, with occasional support coming from Glenn Hoddle. Hoddle, however, played in just one and a half matches, a full game against Kuwait and half a game against the Czechs. Brooking and Keegan, both obviously unfit, only managed appearances as substitutes in our final game against Spain, when it was a case of either score or go home. I kept my natural optimism, though, and I was hopeful I would be included at some stage.

But it didn't happen. It turned out to be worse than Italy. I didn't get to play in even one game. I didn't get on the pitch at all. Not one minute of one game. This kind of disappointment became a recurring feature of my time in international football. I loved being an England player. That's why I would get dejected when I was left out. In Spain, just as in Italy, the worst thing about my omission was that the team was not pulling up any trees. Apart from a very good first match and a reasonable showing in the group, we were nothing more than average. It wasn't as if we won the tournament or even got close. Yes, the defence was solid but ...

The problems for England and Greenwood came in the next round when we failed to score a goal in two games, against West Germany and the hosts, Spain. In the Spanish World Cup, the second round was not a knockout stage as it is today. The teams emerging from the first round entered a second group phase. Each group contained three teams with only the winners progressing. England's performances, which had at first stirred hope, began to fade badly. The defence looked rock-solid but we couldn't score goals. Both of England's matches in the second round ended

0–0. This meant we were out – without losing a match and I never got to kick a ball in anger.

After Spain, Ron Greenwood's tenure as England manager came to an end. He was a man who often couldn't make up his mind, as in the famous rotation of the two goalkeepers, Peter Shilton and Ray Clemence. Maybe he just wanted to keep both of them happy, I don't know. This indecision hindered us at the highest level. But he was also a man who believed football should be played in the right way and he earned the trust of the players. I certainly learned a lot from him. As I mentioned earlier, he was sometimes reticent. When he omitted me from the team in Spain, he hardly offered a word of encouragement. That was left to the coaching staff, especially Don Howe, who told me that he thought I was the best right-back around. Still, I remember Greenwood with fondness. He may not have found room for me in his stab at winning the World Cup but he was the man who gave me my big opportunity for England. For that I owe him an awful lot.

I was selected in the squad for new manager Bobby Robson's first big match, a friendly against the old enemy, West Germany. Robson had been recruited after performing heroics for Ipswich over many years. They may not have matched Forest's epic feats but they had gradually become more impressive under Robson, eventually winning the UEFA Cup. Like all players when a manager is replaced, I was apprehensive at first. I needn't have worried. Robson made it clear he rated me and said I would be in the team for his first game.

However, in football, just as you think you've got it worked out, fate can take a hand, for better or worse. In my case it was definitely for the worse. In training on the day before the West Germany game I was marking a promising young winger called John Barnes. I attempted to tackle him, landed badly and dislocated my knee. I was out for four months. After I recovered and made it back for my club, it took me a further year to get back into the England team. During my absence, qualification for the 84 Euros went badly and we didn't make it to the tournament in France. Today that would not be tolerated, as Steve McClaren discovered to his cost when he failed in his attempts to qualify for the 2008 tournament.

But after the disaster of the 1984 Euro-qualifiers, Bobby Robson kept his job, despite mutterings in the press. The FA was more tolerant of failure back then. I was fit again and back in favour under the new man. Going into the Mexico World Cup of 1986 I really thought my time had come. I had put the disappointment of Spain behind me and played regularly throughout the qualifying competition. We won our group with something to spare and as is often the case when England are about to enter a big tournament, the nation's expectations were high and the team was performing well. It didn't turn out as we would have liked, both for me and the team.

I saw Mexico as an opportunity to put matters right after the experience of Spain. I was also desperate to put my injury behind me. However, exactly the same thing happened in Mexico as in Spain. This time it was Everton's Gary Stevens who became a fixture in what I thought should have been my position. I might be bigging myself up here but I think I could have made a good fist of stopping Maradona when he went on that mazy run through the England defence for Argentina's second goal in the quarter-final. Well! Maybe!

I stopped George Best once and he was the closest thing to Maradona this country has ever seen. In the seventies I was a youngster at Forest when we went to Craven Cottage to play a resurgent Fulham, who boasted the combined talents of Best, Bobby Moore and Rodney Marsh in their team. I've got to admit that as the game drew closer I got more and more nervous. I have never been one to suffer with nerves, either before or since, but the thought of facing the legendary Best was getting to me. He may have been at the fag-end of his career but he was still the man. He was the player most people regarded then and still believe now to be the best footballer the British Isles has ever produced.

By the time we went onto the pitch I was a nervous wreck. I just didn't want George to make a fool of me like he had so many full-backs all round the world. That was what was in my mind. "Don't let him make a fool of you ... . Don't let him make a fool of you." I kept repeating the phrase to myself. For just about the only time in my whole career, the old red mist came down. When, as half-time approached, Besty received the ball at his feet I steamed in. I creamed him. He almost went into orbit. When he landed he gave me a rueful smile but to his credit he got up and got on with the game. He didn't trouble us too much for the rest of the match, though, and eventually had to limp off the pitch. I almost felt guilty.

There was no doubt it was a bad tackle. As a defender you always want to be hard but fair. But at the same time you do everything you can to make sure the winger doesn't get past you. You might try to send him outside or force him to go inside, depending on how good he is with his left or right foot. Or the manager's tactics might dictate which way you tried to shuffle your winger. With George (and Maradona) it didn't matter, he had a hundred ways of going past you and was equally good with both feet. He could also ride a tackle better than anyone I have played against. I suppose my extreme youth is my excuse for mullering him. In subsequent years I tried to stop the opposition in a more stylish fashion. But the fact is, as everyone knows, there are bad tackles in football, plenty of them, and I'll describe one or two more during the course of this book. That one of mine against Best stands out, though, as the crudest chop I ever meted out. But back to Mexico 86. In that one run, Maradona made a fool of virtually the whole England team. Someone should have creamed him like I did Besty.

There were many excellent full backs around during the time I played. Initially, there was Phil Neal, Mick Mills and myself competing for one place in the national side. Later we were joined by Gary Stevens, a good defender in a very good Everton team, and others, including Mike Duxbury from Manchester United. I thrived on this sort of competition. I thought I could more than hold my own. But I suppose it didn't help my cause that by the time the World Cup came round I was experiencing turmoil at my club. I had been playing for Arsenal for two seasons, having been transferred from Forest in the summer of 1984. Arsenal had not done as well as expected under Don Howe and a new manager was liable to be appointed in the summer of the Mexico World Cup. We were a club in transition and had won nothing, which did little to advance my case with England.

Just as my thoughts were turning to Mexico, Arsenal were parting company with Don Howe and installing George Graham in his place. Graham had been making a name for himself as manager of Millwall but we didn't know much about his managerial style beyond that. Although Arsenal had not made much of an impact in the League under Don Howe, I felt sure my performances over the season had been good enough for me to get the nod for England. Also, I had been selected for our two warm-up games and felt I had played really well. But no, when we got to Mexico, Robson decided to go with Stevens. Surely this couldn't be happening again. I was gutted. I went back to my hotel room and took it out on my room-mate, Terry Butcher. Normally, I roomed with Bryan Robson but in Mexico I was teamed up with Terry. He took the brunt of my outburst.

I railed against the manager to Butch, telling him that Robson was "fucking useless" and "didn't know what he was doing." I didn't really believe this, of course, but players just can't help reacting badly when things like that occur. It's part of the competitive instinct. Butch – who was the first choice centre-half and therefore always in the team – told me to "get over it and go to sleep." It was probably the best advice I could have got. The experience produced an odd combination of emotions. I was pleased for Butch that he was in the team, yet annoyed and despondent because I wasn't. I felt the determination to compete and win back my place and I wanted to help the team win. It's the strangest feeling.

Like Greenwood, Robson said nothing to me about the reasons I was left out. He just muttered "this is the team." Any bad feeling this kind of thing might bring about is stopped in its tracks because, at the end of the day, all players are in it together. And nothing is more important than the England team doing well. So you are saved from your self-pity by the camaraderie and the desire for the team to win.

Unlike Spain, England's start in Mexico was disastrous – a 1–0 loss to Portugal and a terrible 0–0 draw against Morocco, when Bryan Robson injured his shoulder (it was an injury he had sustained previously) and Ray Wilkins was sent off. I thought there might be wholesale changes to the team to face Poland in a must-win last game. Well, there certainly were changes, but not at right-back. In defence, the only player to come in was

Alvin Martin for Terry Fenwick. Most of the changes were in midfield and up front, two of them enforced because of Robbo's injury and Butch Wilkins's sending off.

Before the Poland encounter some of the senior players, particularly Peter Shilton and Peter Reid, argued for a change of formation. Until then we had been playing four in the middle of the park but it wasn't working and we were often overrun. Bobby Robson listened and a general discussion took place involving the whole squad and the management. Eventually, Robson agreed that we needed a change. So half-way through the tournament the manager altered his team and his tactics. It didn't make any difference to my situation. For me, there was still no place in the starting line-up.

No-one was more overjoyed than me that England notched up a brilliant win against Poland courtesy of a Gary Lineker hat-trick, but I realised it meant I was now unlikely to be considered for the rest of the tournament. And so it proved. I still say that if I had been on the pitch against Argentina I would at least have anticipated and come across when Maradona went on his run for the second goal. If I had been there ... who knows. As it was, England failed to reach the country's expectations and couldn't get beyond the quarter-final.

Although Maradona's second goal was brilliant by any standard, I got a good view of the so-called "Hand of God" goal. I wasn't even on the subs' bench so I was positioned in a different part of the stadium, right on top of the area where Maradona was operating when he handled the ball. It was just on the edge of our penalty box. I don't think I've ever seen anything so blatant on a football field as Maradona's cheating that day. How none of the officials saw it is beyond belief. To this day most of us, players and fans alike, believe that had it not been for that terrible mistake by the referee and his assistants, we could have beaten Argentina and progressed to the semi-final. But then football is often a case of what might have been.

If I was upset when I didn't get a game in Spain, I was totally traumatised by my experience in Mexico. At first I thought my time was up with England. Although it's always an honour for any footballer to play for his country I kind of lost faith in the whole thing after that. However, a footballer cannot harbour those types of thoughts for too long. Football is always about the next game, not the last. So I moved on and decided to knuckle down and try to win back my place. In England's first game post-Mexico, I came in for the injured Gary Stevens in a 1–0 defeat to Sweden. Despite the loss I felt I had put in a good display. Once again I was proud when both the press and the manager singled me out for praise. Robson said I was "the one real plus" and described my performance as "terrific". Maybe I was back.

But football being football, nothing is that simple. I made a dream move to Manchester United in the summer of 1987 (I loved my time at Arsenal and I can honestly say there was no other club I would have joined except United). But I picked up an Achilles injury early on and struggled for most of my first and second seasons. The injury just wouldn't heal properly and I played many times when I probably shouldn't have. Despite the injury, in that last stage of my England career I went on to gain another nine caps. I was playing well enough to be first choice once again during the qualifying stage for the 1988 European Championships in Germany. I had done more than enough to be selected in the squad. This time, though, I realised I wasn't really fit enough for tournament football. I didn't think my heel had recovered enough to stand up to three matches in the first week. However, Bobby Robson said he wanted me in the squad anyway, even if I could only make a limited contribution. Being someone who has always been ready to answer my country's call, I agreed to Robson's request and once again packed my bags for a major tournament. But yet again I didn't make an appearance, although this time I wasn't too displeased. In the event, England crashed out in the first round, losing every game, including the first match against Jack Charlton's Republic of Ireland. In my whole career as an England international, the only tournament fixture I actually played in was that final group game of the 1980 Euro competition in Italy, after we were eliminated.

I was with Sir Bobby Robson for his first six years of international management. He was a lovely man and he knew how to fill you with his enthusiasm. It is well known that he mangled the English language from time to time, particularly when it came to people's names. He used to call Mark Hately "Tony." Mark would reply, "that's my dad," but it didn't seem to make any difference. Once he was reading out the team. "Bluther's number nine," he said. "Who the fuck's Bluther?" someone asked from the back. It turned out he meant Luther Blissett. I've left the best one till last. I was chatting to the Newcastle player Shola Ameobi not long after Robson became manager. "How's everything going with Bobby?" I asked him. "Great," came Shola's reply. "Except that he thinks I'm Carl Cort."

Before our first game in Mexico, Robson organised a screening of a qualifying match that one of our opponents – Portugal – had won. They were playing Turkey. After about 40 minutes watching Portugal destroy the Turks, Robson opened the curtains and said "Those Turkey's are chickens." He didn't mean it as a joke, of course, but the whole room collapsed in laughter.

Following Euro 88, it was time to retire from international football. I had never been one to suffer too many injuries and was not what you'd call injury-prone. But during my time at Old Trafford I seemed to suffer injury after injury and my heel continued to be a problem. This turn of events certainly impacted on my international career. It was also the case that by then my knees were taking longer to recover. It was time to recognise that World Cups were a thing of the past. But my contribution to England's World Cup history is unique. I went to two consecutive tournaments and didn't play for one single minute. If you include the Euros, I went to four tournaments and played one game. Still, nothing, let me tell you, feels like playing for your country.

There would be plenty more amazing experiences for me in football before I hung up my boots. Before I tell you about some of those, however, I would like to say a thing or two about how I got there in the first place.

Chapter Three

IN THE BEGINNING

My Dad, Audley Anderson, arrived in the UK from Jamaica in 1954. He was part of the first big wave of immigration to this country from the Caribbean. How the people who came to these shores in those days had the courage to leave everything behind and travel halfway round the world in search of a better life is something for which I have the greatest respect and admiration. Dad, for some reason I still don't fully understand, decided not to follow most immigrants from the West Indies to Notting Hill, Brixton or towns where there was an established Jamaican population. Instead, he made his way to Nottingham, where he was one of the first arrivals in the city from that part of the world. It must have been unbelievably hard for him but to this day I have never heard him complain. Not once.

Before long, he managed to secure a job as a porter at a local hospital in Nottingham. He was on his way. My mother, Myrtle, arrived from Jamaica a few months later to join him. She was a nurse and, like a number of her compatriots, a mainstay of the National Health Service for decades to come. The NHS might well have collapsed without their contribution. While Dad was quite philosophical about the different life here, Mam was intensely homesick. She had been used to land and space in Jamaica, as well as fine weather. In England she had to make the best of life in cold, cramped accommodation in the city. And what was worse for her was that – in the days before regular transatlantic calls, let alone mobile phones – she missed her friends and family terribly. Many were the nights she cried.

I arrived in this world in 1956. My brother Donald came two years later. I think, although I have never been told, that our births made our parents really happy and helped them become totally committed to their new homeland. Ours was a Christian family and for my brother and me, our early years were centred round the church, especially Sunday school. Although I never admitted it to my team-mates when I became a professional footballer, I was also something of a choirboy in my youth. It was, with some ups and downs, a great upbringing.

Perhaps the most difficult event I had to come to terms with in my childhood years was the serious illness which overtook Donald. I am not looking for sympathy here, not least because Donald was the one who really suffered. But I saw the pain on the faces of my mother and father, much as they tried to hide it. I had come down with a cold or the flu, which I recovered from quite easily. Donald then started to display similar symptoms. To this day I wonder if he caught it from me. But instead of getting better as I had done, Donald's condition got worse. My lovely younger brother's life was in the balance. He had, in fact, contracted a condition that was the scourge of Britain in the 1950s and 60s, Poliomyelitis. Now, polio was a killer until a vaccination was invented. Donald was lucky to be alive but was extremely unlucky to be left disabled. I don't know how I would have coped with that. Yet Donald has always remained an optimist, an outlook on life which I think I gained from him. Not only that, he refused to go into his shell like many would have done. To this day he has asserted his independence. Maybe he could have been a sportsman too. As it was, through no fault of his own, he was denied the possibility of finding out.

Perhaps it was this experience which later led me to question many of the certainties with which I was brought up. I'm no expert but I asked myself time and again over the years how this could happen. How could Donald to be so struck down? I don't know what I think or believe today to be honest, but the memories can haunt me still. It was such a cruel suffering to be inflicted on both Donald and my parents.

I was always more interested in sport than anything else. If my parents had stayed in the Caribbean, maybe I would have been a cricketer or a track and field athlete. Or maybe not! I've played other sports over the years and I have to say that football was made for me. I played for my school, for local clubs around Nottingham and when I wasn't playing matches or with my mates I was kicking a ball against the wall that occupied one side of our house. Although my mother made sure I worked at school, my heart wasn't really in it. I wanted to be a footballer, pure and simple. As a youngster I was a striker, scoring goals for fun. If you had told me then I would become a full-back I would have questioned your sanity. If you'd told me I would become a pro footballer, I'd have believed you totally.

For whatever reason – and I don't know to this day what it was – I turned away from my two local teams, Forest and County, and decided to support Manchester United. In those days United fielded the Best, Law and Charlton team and they captivated my imagination to the point that it overwhelmed any real interest in the Nottingham clubs. In those days most kids tended to support their home-town team. I was the odd one out being a United fan in Nottingham. I dreamed of playing for United, of course. But so did thousands of others. Little did I know it would become a reality for me before too long.

When I was fourteen or so the unimaginable happened. The family had gone to Bridlington for our summer holidays. One day I was playing football on my own on the beach. This bloke approached me and said he was a scout for Sheffield United (life was more innocent in those days). Was I interested, he said, in a trial at Bramall Lane? My parents didn't really want me to go, they thought I was too young and needed to pay more attention to schoolwork. And anyway a professional footballer lived a precarious and not very well-paid life. It wasn't what parents would want for their kids. But I had a desire to be a footballer, I think they knew that deep down. We eventually came to an agreement: if I did another year at school I could then go for the trial. I didn't like it but there was nothing I could do.

In the meantime, I played football whenever and wherever I could. I won trophies in schoolboy competitions and honed my skills against the wall while I tried to keep up in school. I wasn't bad at English but I had to work hard at most other subjects. Then, out of nowhere, Manchester – not Sheffield – United came knocking. One of their scouts saw me playing at a soccer camp and recommended me to Old Trafford. My parents made sure I went to these summer camps for kids, so you can see how they really did encourage me. I enjoyed the trips away and the games of football, around which everything was organised. I'm told there were always a few scouts from League clubs on the look-out for promising youngsters at the camps. Thrilled to have been singled out, I now had the chance to go to what I thought was the centre of the football universe, Manchester – and United's youth set-up. Even my parents were impressed and said I could go. It was there that they turned me into a proper footballer, and a defender at that.

I had a wonderful time in the year I spent at United. I loved it. I remember watching those great players train. I can see them now if I shut my eyes. They were an inspiration to the young guys. This was a dream come true. Every time I travelled up to Manchester from Nottingham I was full of anticipation. There was suddenly nothing I couldn't achieve. And when I stayed in Manchester, I lived with the parents of John Aston, the brilliant United winger. It was the experience of a lifetime. Many years later, Garry Birtles was transferred from Forest to Manchester United. At Forest he was on fire and scored bundles of goals, many against world-class defences, but for United he could hardly get a kick, let alone score a goal. I think part of his problem was that he was homesick. He didn't enjoy life in the big city. He loved getting back to Nottingham whenever he could to be with his old mates, playing snooker and going to pubs. Even at my young age, I never suffered that type of homesickness. I took in everything I could in Manchester, both at the club and in the city.

But when I reached sixteen, the powers at United decided I was not good enough to be offered a contract and they let me go. I don't know who made the actual decision or why. Maybe I hadn't asserted myself enough. I certainly didn't feel that I was way behind the other kids in footballing ability. I was as good as any of them. But with that decision going against me I felt all my dreams of being a professional footballer were shattered. I wasn't told and therefore I didn't realise, that this was only one club, no matter how big. Nor did anyone point out that the majority of those in the youth set-up would eventually be let go. I simply believed I had no future in the game. I returned home to Nottingham with my tail between my legs. My mother was right. I should get a 'proper' job. My world had collapsed. I looked at what I might do for a while. For some reason I still can't fathom I decided to become an apprentice silk screen printer. That's what my life would be from now on. A solid trade! I would play football for fun.

Yet within six months I was offered a second chance, and this time I told myself to really go for it. Once again I was spotted by a scout, this time while I was playing amateur football in Nottingham. I was invited into the Forest youth programme. It was a lifeline that would shape my destiny. I made friends early on with another aspiring youngster, Tony Woodcock. Woody and I struck up an instant friendship which has lasted to this day. I'm certain we helped each other achieve the success that came our way. Along with Kevin Keegan, Woody was one of the first English players of the modern era to ply his trade in Europe. Like Keegan, Woody went to Germany. He learned the language and immersed himself in German culture. When he later played in the same Arsenal side as me and whenever he turned out for England he brought all that to his game. In my opinion should have won many more caps than he eventually did. He scored his fair share of goals at all levels but probably not quite enough to become England's long-term centre-forward. But he was a fantastic footballer with great vision.

I had been long-time childhood friends with a couple of other kids in the youth scheme at Forest. There was goalkeeper, Peter Wells and defender, Glyn Saunders. We all lived on the same council estate in Clifton and played for the same school team. They went to Forest before me and tipped me the wink about how I should behave. I was the new kid on the block and they helped pave the way for me. Peter, Glynn, Woody and me all became apprentices together.

The trouble for all of us was that in the early seventies Forest were going nowhere. They were a run-of-the-mill second division side which had known better days. The first team showed no signs of being able to challenge for promotion back to the top flight under the manager, Matt Gillies. It seemed the committee members who ruled the club at the time were content with mediocrity. Gillies soon departed, to be replaced by the legendary Dave Mackay, who, after a great career as a player, was making his way in management. Mackay only lasted a year, however, during which time the club drifted further into obscurity. Allan Brown took over from Mackay and initially the team picked up. But it was soon facing a dogfight against relegation once more.

This period for me, however, was the end of the rainbow, the possibility once again of realising my dream. No, no, no! I was a silk screen printer, I was bound, surely, for a life in that solid trade. But gradually I progressed through the ranks alongside Woody, until I ended up in the reserves. I still have a copy of the written invitation which tells me I was selected for the Forest "A" team to play Coventry "A". At last I had a chance. This was it. Do or die!

I must have done something right because I soon came to attention of the manager. He brought me, along with Woody, into the senior set-up. I made my debut for the Nottingham Forest first team in August 1974, in a pre-season friendly at Walsall. The 1–1 draw was played out in front of only 1700 spectators. I didn't think I performed particularly well but then neither did anyone that day. Martin O'Neill was in the team and Tony Woodcock was a substitute. It may not sound much but to me it could have been a Wembley Cup Final. The feeling was electric. I realised at that moment that I was in my element, this was what I was here for.

I didn't make my full League debut for another six weeks. During that period the team made a poor start to the season, winning just twice in our first nine games. We drew a fair number, including a 2–2 at Old Trafford in front of 40,000 people. Manchester United had suffered the unthinkable the previous season when they were relegated from Division One. It had shocked their fans and the nation to the core. They were still drawing huge crowds to Old Trafford, though, and would eventually run away with Division Two to make an immediate return to the top flight. My turn came in the tenth game of the campaign. It was an away match at Sheffield Wednesday which we won 3–2. Wednesday was a club I would come to love many years later when I was part of Ron Atkinson's and Trevor Francis's successful spells in charge. I kept my place for the next three matches but they brought two defeats – against Newcastle and Aston Villa – and a 1–1 draw with Sunderland. It was no wonder I was dropped and Liam O'Kane made it back into the team in my position.

No matter what I said about my feelings when I was left out of various England teams, actually, being dropped is experienced at some point by 99% of footballers. You have to work out a way of dealing with it and come back stronger. I have since found out, of course, that young players often lack the consistency to maintain a high level of performance week in, week out. I probably fell into that category.

But sometimes poor management or coaching plays its part. Whatever combination the manager, by then Allan Brown, sent out, the team just couldn't put any kind of run together and the relegation places were staring us in the face. The low point came in a massive Christmas game played at the City Ground against our neighbours by the Trent, Notts County. Now Forest fans don't even consider matches against County to be proper derbies, since County are supposed to be far inferior to Forest. Our derbies are against Derby or Leicester, not County. But as the end of 1974 beckoned County came to our place ahead of us in the division. In front of a 20,000 crowd, in a complete debacle of a game, they beat us 2–0. It proved to be Allan Brown's last match in charge. It could have been far worse. We were lucky to get nil. I didn't play in the match but I shared the terrible feelings with the rest of the squad. The result was too much even for the Forest committee to bear and they were forced to act. Brown was sacked before the New Year and a new manager installed. That manager was, of course, Brian Clough.

Clough arrived following his disastrous 44 days in charge of Leeds, a time made famous recently in the book and film, *The Damned United*. His exploits at Derby, when he won the League and reached the semi-final of the European Cup were no more than a distant memory after the Leeds business. He was still a big name, though, the first Forest had employed for quite some time. We weren't too sure what to expect. Looking back, I can see that the pressure was actually on him. The Forest job was probably his last chance to really prove himself again. But at the time he appeared to be oozing with confidence and knowhow. If he ever had doubts about his ability to make us the best he never, ever showed it.

I can't quite remember if Clough was in place when we played in the third round of the FA Cup, at home against First Division Spurs. He certainly selected the team for the replay, which was necessary after we somehow managed to draw the first game 1–1. I had to come off with cramp. I couldn't train afterwards but was fit to play when the replay was due. I wasn't included in the squad that went to London. We won the game, incredibly, 1–0. I wondered if Clough thought I was any good as he had left me behind. I said to myself: "if the great man doesn't fancy me, I'll soon be on my way."

But we had beaten the mighty Spurs. At that moment, the legend that was Clough was up and running again. He showed no bias against me in training, even encouraging me from time to time, so I began to believe I had a future. And if someone with such a massive name as Brian Clough thought so, it must be true. It took another six weeks before the boss decided I was ready for an extended run in the side. However, from the end of February I was more or less a fixture in the team. At last I was a real footballer.

We managed to pull ourselves clear of the threat of relegation and finished 16th in the table, two places behind County. Manchester United won the division at the first time of asking, nine points ahead of the second placed team, Aston Villa. Norwich City secured the third automatic promotion spot (there were no play-offs then).

For the new season, the manager brought in two players who had been with him at Derby and Leeds, John McGovern and John O'Hare. His plan, he told us, was to put his faith in youngsters like myself and Tony Woodcock, and ally us to the experience of McGovern and O'Hare. Both of the old boys relished the new challenge Clough presented to them. For us, they knew exactly how Clough worked, what he wanted from players and they could pass all that information on. For Clough, his old boys would reinforce his beliefs to the younger generation while he hollered at all and sundry from the sidelines.

That next season was one of consolidation. Clough stabilised the team and we finished a creditable but unspectacular eighth. It was far better than the threat of relegation, though. Sunderland were top, with Bristol City and West Bromwich Albion filling the other promotion positions. That season was notice-able for the emergence of John Robertson on the left wing. John Robbo had been in and out of the side in midfield before Clough came. I think even he would admit that he was overweight and his game was going nowhere. But the manager saw something no-one else had seen and converted John to a wide man. He became a classic winger, not of the type that goes past defenders with speed. John Robbo could shift the ball a yard to create space behind the full-back. He would then put in a succession of pin-point crosses. Near post, far post, you name it, he did it. At the same time Clough got on Robbo's case to lose weight and get fit, which, to his credit, he did.

Also coming into his own was Martin O'Neill, who operated along the right in front of me. Martin always claimed that the work he put in up and down the line made me the player I was. It is a feature of Martin that he can make ironic, tongue-in-cheek comments which are both humorous and wrong but contain a tiny bit of truth. It doesn't surprise me that Martin has become such a spectacularly good manager. Mind you, Clough used to really get on his case sometimes, telling him he didn't like him because he had a law degree and he was Irish. In truth I was lucky to have someone like

Martin playing in front of me. But equally, he was lucky to have someone like me playing behind him. Martin is a lovely man. In later years, both he and his wife, Geraldine, were very kind to me at a very difficult time.

During that first full term under Clough I played for the first half of the season but lost my place to Colin Barratt for the second. As I said before, I think I was an example of how young players often struggle to maintain their form in their first and second seasons. But back then I was inconsolable. I told myself it was temporary but I could see the Manchester United experience repeating itself. By now I had thoroughly joined the world of the professional footballer. I did not want to go back to being a silk screen printer. The only way out was to do enough to convince the great Brian Clough that I was worth a place in his team. I wanted to be crucial to his plans. I was not going to be a printer ... I was not going to be a printer.

The defining season for the players and the club was not when we won the League. It wasn't even when we won the European Cup. No! What decided all our futures was the season we won promotion to the First Division. The seventies! For me, the year 1976–77 was the year of all years. It was the year that made everything else possible.

First, and most important, I was back in contention for the team. I must have done something right in preseason. Again though, it was some time before I really nailed down my place. Clough insisted that pre-season was about getting the players fit and ready to accept his every word and decision without question. It was psychological moulding as much as it was about getting fit for football. Once he made us run through stinging nettles. We did it without question. After pre-season, Clough didn't believe in anything other than light training and five-a-sides. With lots of walks. And some drinking. And some trips to Mallorca. He never paid much attention to the opposition. We went into the season ready.

And yet it came so close to going wrong. We were there or thereabouts for most of the campaign but we were not playing well enough be sure of our place in the promotion mix. No-one was tipping us to go up, that was for sure. We had some good results but had setbacks too. However, changes were taking place which later made promotion seem inevitable. Of course nothing in football is inevitable, it just seems like that now. Clough was increasing his influence in all areas. But perhaps the most important of these changes was the arrival of Peter Taylor as Clough's assistant.

Taylor had been Clough's right-hand man at Derby but had stayed at Brighton when Clough went to Leeds. Now the great duo were reunited. Taylor brought an immediate contrast to the boss. Where Clough was aloof, Taylor was your friend. And Taylor, it was reputed, could spot a player like no other. He drafted in three who would make a huge difference to our prospects. First there was the uncompromising centre-forward, Peter Withe, who grabbed sixteen goals that season; then there was Larry Lloyd, who was massive at the centre of the defence; finally, there was the surprising figure of Frank Clark, the grizzled pro deemed too old by Newcastle but who graced the City Ground for the next four seasons. Frank was never happier than when he spent time telling us youngsters a hundred stories from his hundred years in the game.

So although we didn't take the division by storm, we were now a team to be reckoned with, we thought. As the season came to its business end we began to get more consistent. We scraped into third place, behind Wolves and Chelsea. That was enough for promotion. We finished one point in front of both Bolton and Blackpool, both of whom missed out. For us, it was a massive achievement. No-one had thought we were promotion material. But the momentum was ours and it was to stay that way for many a year. I didn't get a game until the middle of October, when I scored in a 6-1 rout of Sheffield United. I had actually scored a goal. In the professional game! I was walking on air. I began to feel times were changing.

And even better, after that October victory over Sheffield United, I stayed in the team for the rest of that momentous season. Of our last four games, we won three, while the other was drawn. Most of our goals in the run-in were supplied by Woody, Martin and Peter Withe. We could at last feel we were going places. Never in our wildest dreams could we have known exactly how far we would get. The stage was set. We didn't know it yet but we were about to tear up the script of football and write our own. It wouldn't have made it past the first editor if it was fiction. It was too ridiculous.

Chapter Four

YEARS OF BLISS

No-one: not the media, not the Forest fans, not the players, thought that we would or could win anything in our first season back in Division One. The only exception to this opinion was Brian Clough, who told us we were winners. Mind you, he said it through his schoolboy smile.

There were some new arrivals in the dressing room, both in the close season and during the campaign itself. One of them was Peter Shilton in goal, who the manager described to anyone who would listen as the best keeper in the world. No-one was prepared to disagree with Clough's statement, but no-one had Shilts in the frame for a top club either. Clough said that Peter would win us points. This is what we wanted to hear. In training he would point to Shilton and say that he "frightened the life" out of opposing centre forwards. I think it is fair to say that Peter himself gained considerably from the manager's faith in him and his performances just got better and better. At last he began to fulfil the potential he had showed when he first broke into the Leicester side as a sixteen-year-old (at the expense of Gordon Banks). To me, that was entirely due to Brian

Clough's influence and Peter's recognition that he at last had someone to believe in him, not just as a goal-keeper but as a person.

Archie Gemmill also arrived to add some bite to the midfield. But perhaps the most surprising acquisition was the Bad Boy of Birmingham, Kenny Burns. Burns started out as a forward but was converted into a centre half. His fiery Scottish temperament got him into all sorts of trouble on the pitch. His stock in trade was getting sent off. All told, he had been dismissed seven or eight times in his career. Somehow, Clough and Taylor believed, they could keep the best of Kenny, who was a very good defender, and eliminate the worst, his habit of violently assaulting opponents. Virtually the whole of the football world thought Clough had lost it when he signed Kenny. Once again, the manager had not only brought someone to the club who could play, he also knew how he could garner massive publicity at the same time. Clough and controversy walked hand in hand. He loved it. I was still a young lad, I didn't appreciate many of these things at the time, understanding only came with experience, both of football and of life. Then, I just wanted to please the manager and keep my place in the team.

For our return to the top flight, our pre-season went well. We were undefeated on a tour of Germany. Our first game in the League was a real test, however, away to Everton, who would finish the season in third place. They were a good side who would get better and better over the next ten years. The match at Goodison Park, in front of over 38,000 fans, went better than we could have dreamed. We won 3–1 with goals from Peter Withe, Martin O'Neill and John Robertson. We were off and running.

The high that everyone felt after that beginning was just unbelievable. In some ways it defined our whole season. John Robbo and Martin were a revelation. Football reporters everywhere gave them rave reviews. The triumph over Everton was followed up with three straight wins, including a 5–0 thrashing of West Ham in the League Cup. To say we were on a roll would be an understatement. We were flying. So were Clough and Taylor and that made them even better at what they did.

As summer turned to autumn we kept up with the pack. Liverpool, the country's leading club by far in the seventies and eighties, were up there, as they always were. Bill Shankly and Bob Paisley had created a giant out of nothing. What we at Forest got annoyed by, though, was that Liverpool had become a machine which was expected to win all the big match-ups as if it were their right. Clough didn't like that. Everton and Manchester City posed a threat and Arsenal were showing signs of resurgence. But no-one looked any further than the Scousers for the eventual title winners.

In what was by any measure a most remarkable season, perhaps the match that really made us believe we could topple Liverpool came just before Christmas when we went to Old Trafford to face Manchester United. Going back to the club that had rejected me just a few years earlier was emotional for me. I had missed the game in Manchester when we met in the second division. Stepping out at the Theatre of Dreams was certainly a dream to me. A dream come true. I was now firmly established as the number one right-back in Clough's scheme of things.

What was totally unexpected was that by the time we visited Old Trafford, Forest were top of the table. We had already beaten United at the City Ground. But what was about to unfold was something really special. We produced our best display of the season, filmed by the *Match of the Day* cameras, and ran out 4–0 winners. Now, even though United were not the force they had been previously or would become again, it was still an incredible result and from there, we never looked back. To beat them in their own lair was one thing, to win by four goals was unprecedented.

Confidence just flooded through the team after that. It came in the middle of a period when the manager could do no wrong. The result at Old Trafford only served to magnify the mystique of Brian Clough and what he could drive his side to achieve.

Kenny Burns was a sensation, curbing his excesses and becoming an extremely accomplished defender, indispensible even. He didn't get sent off once. The press couldn't believe the transformation that took place before their very eyes. The Clough magic was working again. Looking back I can see that with every game, the ghost of Clough's disastrous time at Leeds was receding. Even his exploits with Derby might be bettered. Nottingham Forest was the project of his life. This was his - and therefore our - destiny.

After a 1-0 defeat to Leeds in November, we didn't lose another match all season and the title was ours. To write that now hardly conveys the immensity of our achievement. That season has been talked and written about ever since. It is the stuff of fantasy that in these days of the Premier League and its riches seems about as real as Harry Potter. I don't think anything like our League campaign that year could happen again. The game has changed so much. A provincial side storming to the title the season after promotion - you couldn't make it up. Forest weren't the only team to do it in that era. I must give respect to a club that paved the way over fifteen years before. In the early sixties, Ipswich Town managed the same feat. Having said in an earlier chapter that Ipswich didn't reach the heights of Forest, I am happy to give their earlier side the credit they are due. That team was managed by Alf Ramsey and it was enough to make him the only candidate for the England job when it came up. Ramsey, of course, went on to win the World Cup. Shouldn't Brian Clough have been similarly rewarded for his Herculean effort? I think so. Anyone who can achieve such success from such modest beginnings - and only Ramsey and Clough have done it in the modern era, although Bill Shankly came close - is an obvious candidate for higher things. Ramsey won the

World Cup, something no other England manager has come close to. I think Clough would have done the same. It is to the eternal shame of the FA that they snubbed Clough and I believe it set the England cause back for more than a generation.

Even though our League campaign that season was immense, I think you can see what the team was all about by looking at our Cup runs. Clough and Taylor wanted to win every match, there was no let up. In the FA Cup we beat Swindon, Manchester City and Queens Park Rangers (in a second replay). We went out of the competition in the sixth round with our worst display of the season, losing to West Brom 2-0. The Ipswich side of Bobby Robson won the trophy when they beat Arsenal in the final.

For all our success over the next few years, the FA Cup always eluded us. Funnily enough, the FA Cup was the one trophy Brian Clough couldn't win, either as a player or manager. In the last years of his time in football and long after our great team had broken up, Clough finally got a Forest team to the final – the 1991 showpiece against Spurs. But somehow the gods were against him in the FA Cup. The match was bizarre, with Gazza's reckless tackle early doors which put him out of the game. Stuart Pearce gave Forest the lead with an incredible free-kick. But we somehow contrived to lose 2-1, with Spurs' winning goal coming from Des Walker's head. In all the years I was with Forest – and for years after I left – the FA Cup was always just beyond our reach.

If we floundered in the FA Cup, we more than made up for it in the League Cup. It was our run to the final of this competition that sealed our growing reputation. In our amazing story, this was the first trophy the team won. The success set us up for the rest of the season. And it taught us to win. These days, the League Cup is often devalued by the top clubs, except for Jose Mourinho when he was in charge of Chelsea. Mourinho decided that it was important for his side to win a trophy as soon as possible and it is no coincidence that in his first season in the Premier League his Chelsea side won the League Cup. It set them up for the league title, as it did us twenty-five years earlier. It seems strange to me that more managers don't seem to understand the importance of trying to win the League Cup. Bryan Robson and I gave it a good go in the nineties with Middlesbrough. The only modern top division manager I know who really takes it seriously is Martin O'Neill, who won the competition twice as manager of Leicester. And where was it that he learned of its importance?

We overcame West Ham, Notts County, Aston Villa, Bury and Leeds on our way to Wembley. Our opponents, Liverpool, were hot favourites, as they always were in those days. No-one could beat them, let alone the upstarts of Nottingham Forest. But we snuffed them out and took them to a replay. The second game was as tight as they come. A John Robertson penalty, which, to be honest, was a bit dubious, won it. Liverpool beaten! Yes!

In the first game our star performer was our goal-keeper: not Peter Shilton, but the young Chris Woods, who was playing because Shilton was cup-tied. Brian Clough made Woods feel as if he were second only to Shilts in the world, not just Nottingham Forest. I have to say, if Chris felt any nerves going out at Wembley he didn't show it. Shilts helped gee him up before the game, while Clough just kept telling him that if he were in any other team he would be first choice. Chris's performance guaranteed us the replay. The replay was ours. We now knew how to win.

We were unstoppable. Clough was in his element. He was, once again, the talk of the nation. We won the League before April was out, with an anticlimactic 0-0 draw at Coventry. Technically, Liverpool could have caught us if they won a game in hand due to be played on the Monday. We had a midweek game against Ipswich on Tuesday. But Liverpool failed to win and Nottingham Forest were League Champions. We spent the next few hours celebrating like it was 1999. Needless to say, there was very little in the way of training for the Ipswich game (which we won 2-0). In the event, we ended up seven points clear of Liverpool, which in the days of two points for a win was an immense gap. It was an achievement of the most incredible proportions. Brian Clough was God.

We had done the impossible. Throughout that season, our exploits were marvelled at. Woody and I were just on cloud nine. We thought football would always be like this. Woody scored 27 goals. What a return that was. It was an unbelievable season for him. He was without doubt the top English goalscorer. Our other striker, Peter Withe, scored 20 goals and his partnership with Woody was the most potent in the country. Brian Clough, of course, was worshipped. The media could not get enough of him. His estimation of his own worth, high enough previously, went through the roof. Trips to Mallorca were planned.

However much praise was heaped upon our achievements, it was still Liverpool that the country looked to as the best team in the English game. While we triumphed in the League and the League Cup, Liverpool somehow managed to retain the European Cup they first won in 1977. I think it was someone called Dalglish who got the winner. Looking ahead to the next season, few pundits could see beyond Liverpool to find the likely European Champions. Yet again, we were the upstarts who would soon be 'found out' and put in our place. And the reason for that view was that Forest had no tradition in Europe and because few people realised how desperately Brian Clough wanted to win European Cup.

On the eve of the following season – 1978-9 – Clough called us together. We were going to retain the League title, he said. We would win both domestic cups and move heaven and earth to win the European Cup. Provided, of course, we listened to no-one else but him. It was him who had brought us to this place and it would be him who would take us to even greater deeds. Once again he mesmerised us. It was like a religion, with us players as the apostles and the fans as the followers. I was brought up in the church. Brian Clough was like the fiery preacher. When he spoke, we listened.

Our statement of intent came in the Charity Shield at Wembley against the Cup winners, Ipswich. Bobby Robson's team had out-thought and out-fought Arsenal in winning the Cup 1–0. In the Charity Shield we swotted them aside, beating them 5–0. Martin O'Neill grabbed two goals, while John Robbo, Larry Lloyd and Peter Withe scored one each. In the space of a year, we had gone from second division nobodies to the only side in the land that could really challenge Liverpool. Clough told us we shouldn't worry about any other team. We were going to make history.

After that, surprisingly, Peter Withe only played in the first League game before he was shipped out. He was replaced in the beginning by local boy Garry Birtles. Before long Garry and Woody were joined by the country's first player to command a transfer fee of one million pounds, Trevor Francis. Clough caused another sensation when he announced that he had paid the massive fee. We were a bit put out when Withey left. He not only notched up goals, he was a great player to be around as he took on the burden of roughing up opposing defences and making space for everyone else. But Birtles and Woodcock were altogether more refined and began to forge another great partnership. Garry ended the season our top scorer. Trevor Francis, however, was on another plane. He was not only naturally gifted, he also scored goals at the most important moments.

Despite Clough's predictions, there would be no repeat League title that season. The crown went back to .... damn it .... Liverpool. We finished a distant second, eight points adrift, with West Bromwich Albion third. Nevertheless, it was a superb campaign in many ways, consolidating our position and ensuring we weren't one season wonders. We notched up notable wins, especially in the two games against Chelsea in March, which we won 6–1 and 3–1. It is difficult to conceive today, but that season Chelsea finished bottom, fourteen points from safety. I managed to score four goals that year, the best return of my career so far. Clough wasn't always pleased when I scored. "Good goal young Mr. Anderson", he would say. "But it's defending I pay you for." It wasn't that I didn't have a licence to get forward. I like to think I was one of the first English full-backs to make driving runs into the opposition's half. I tried to model that part of my game on Terry Cooper, the left-back of the great Leeds team of Don Revie and the brilliant Celtic full-back, Danny McGrain. I think the manager didn't want me to get ahead of myself. He wanted to remind me of what my primary duty was: to stop the opposing winger.

Once again, the FA Cup proved a step too far. At first we looked good, with convincing victories in the third and fourth rounds, against Aston Villa and York City. We were well set up for our fifth round tie at home to

Arsenal. But the Gunners stifled the life out of us and knocked us out 1-0. They did to us what we had done to Liverpool in the League Cup Final.

It was in the League Cup that we again showed our mettle. We won it. Again! Now no-one could dismiss us as a flash in the pan. Our best win in terms of performance in that season's competition came at Goodison Park, against Everton in the fourth round. As usual, the manager refused to let us train too much before the game. Not only that, he never said anything at all, except that we had to go for a walk along the banks of the River Mersey. Still, we won 3-2. We defeated Southampton in the final by the same score. Again, training before the game was banned. Garry Birtles loved this non-training stuff; he scored two in the final with the other coming from Woody.

We returned to Nottingham as heroes. It was nothing compared to what we were about to achieve. We would soon be bigger in Nottingham than Robin Hood.

Yes, we might have been tearing up the domestic script but, so went the accepted wisdom, we did not have the resources to make waves in the European Cup. British teams had suffered in Europe over the years and in the major competition, the European Cup, it was only in the last two years that Britain had punched its weight. I remember the great, great Celtic team. I was a young football fanatic when they became the first British side to win the Cup in 1967. Manchester United had also won it with the great side of 68 but for nine years after that the country floundered in the major European competition. Until Liverpool, with Kevin Keegan rampant, destroyed Hamburg in 1977 and retained the Cup the following year with a 1–0 win in the final against Bruges. But that was because they were Liverpool. Wasn't it? There was no club like Liverpool, the way they did things, the continual record of success, even when managers departed. Shankly to Paisley, it made no difference. If anything, Liverpool got better. As Manchester United discovered when Matt Busby left Old Trafford, maintaining success is no easy task when an icon departs. Not at Liverpool. Liverpool, Liverpool, Liverpool!

It was a simple equation. Only a country's champions played in the European Cup plus the holders. There was no seeding, no groups, just straight knockout ties played over home and away legs. You could draw anyone from the first round on. We, of course, drew Liverpool. From the moment that improbable draw took place the players, like the fans, couldn't help but talk about it. I remember Peter Shilton saying he thought we would win it but most of us were somewhat apprehensive. We might have beaten Liverpool to the title and in the League Cup Final but this was Europe, where they reigned supreme and untroubled. We had not managed to beat them in League matches in our title-winning season, with both games ending in draws. If we read the press, it told us that Liverpool were overwhelming favourites. Strangely, Bob Paisley was one of the few who gave us a chance, saying Forest were the one club who could prevent Liverpool from emulating Bayern Munich and Ajax and win three European Cups in a row.

Brian Clough hardly mentioned Liverpool as the first leg at the City Ground approached. He did, however, let us know in no uncertain terms that he expected nothing less than for us to win the European Cup. If we listened to him, we would realise we were more than good enough to reach that objective. Peter Taylor told us how their Derby side had reached the semi-finals, only to be thwarted by poor refereeing and official corruption. There was, we realised, really good European experience in our management team. Just about the only thing that Clough had to say was that "Liverpool couldn't beat you in four matches last season. You beat them in a final (the League Cup). There is no way for them to win." In the absence of Peter Withe – and before the arrival of Trevor Francis – we were a bit light up front. That's when Clough pulled his masterstroke and threw Garry Birtles into the team. Birtles was a completely unknown player who was signed from Long Eaton. The first leg against the Scousers was only his second game in Forest colours. I remember seeing him with a grin from ear to ear when he realised he would be playing.

The tie against Liverpool has passed into folklore. It was Forest's first ever game in Europe, Liverpool's one hundredth. For one of the only times during Clough's reign, he dropped Martin O'Neill for the game. All of us were shocked. Martin had come to display all of the things that were the hallmark of Clough and Taylor at Forest: industrious, skilful and prepared to adapt his game to the boss's wishes. In his place was Archie Gemmill, on the face of it to hamper Liverpool's progress down our right side. I think it was one of the manager's eccentricities, designed first to throw us off-guard, then to bind us as a team in the belief that he could do no wrong. We were also pleased – and Clough knew this – that it was none of us that had been dropped.

Woody instigated the breakthrough. We were playing the ball on the left side of Liverpool's defence when he took the ball beyond the defenders in the inside-right channel. I watched as he put in a pass to Garry Birtles and Garry did the rest. 1-0. We were unim-pressed by Liverpool's response. They didn't seem too bothered about going back to Anfield losing by a goal. It was a fatal mistake. It spurred us on. We talked to each other throughout the game and told ourselves that at this rate, we could get another and kill the tie stone dead. Sure enough, in the 87th minute, the most junior player on the field, the Long Eaton dead-eye, Garry Birtles, went past a couple of defenders. He found Woody, who headed the ball back across the goal for Colin Barrett, playing at left-back in place of Frank Clark, to conjure a volley and make it 2-0 on the night. That goal gave Liverpool a mountain to climb.

Fourteen days later we went to Anfield for the return. Clough had a way to prick the balloon of hype that often overcame away teams at Liverpool before the match even started. "You know that sign – the one you see when you run onto the pitch saying 'This is Anfield,'" he said. "Well, so fucking what."

Chapter Five

SLAYING DRAGONS

If Manchester United were the Red Devils, Liverpool were the dragons, breathing fire and invincible on their own patch. English pretenders or European giants – it didn't matter – they all came to grief at Anfield. It needed someone like St. George to slay them. For St. George read Brian Clough. He sent us into the cauldron believing we were about to dispatch the European champions. Without that, even a 2–0 lead might not have been enough. That was the measure of how Liverpool unnerved their opponents. Ever since our victory at the City Ground, the press and television, both at home and across Europe, were forced to reassess their analysis of Forest. It was an upset to them, that's for sure. Still they couldn't see beyond Liverpool. To us, that win was one more fact to prove there was nothing we couldn't achieve. It was bred into us by the manager and reinforced by the results his methods were bringing. As long as we remained loyal and committed to his way of doing things, we thought we were invincible.

His way of doing things in the return game was unbelievable. First, he refused to let the bus leave the hotel until the last possible moment. His excuse was that he wanted the traffic to clear so we could have a "nice ride" to the ground. Then, once on board, he produced wine and beer and told us to get stuck in. It was only a friendly, he assured us. Clough was showing us that he would be the only one to decide when we were under pressure. Not the press; not the opposition; certainly not the Anfield hordes. Only Clough! This wasn't pressure, this was the European Cup.

The return match against Liverpool was a damp squib as we intended it to be. To be honest, we were happy for the game to stay at 0–0. If Liverpool scored one, it would only inflame the Kop and pass the advantage to the opposition. If we scored it might do the same thing. No! 0–0 was perfect.

I was involved in the game's two talking points. The one player we – and anyone else who faced Liverpool – were concerned about was Kenny Dalglish. That night he was perfectly played by Larry Lloyd, a former Liverpool player with something to prove to his old team-mates. Larry was outstanding all game, ensuring Kenny could not employ his trademark turn which often left defenders for dead. Then, for one moment, Kenny got the better of Larry. I saw it coming and decided to retreat to give the rest of the defence some cover. Kenny got his head to the ball and it looped towards our goal. I was in the right place at the right time and managed to head the ball off the line. It was the last time Kenny came anywhere near getting a goal. Later in the match, I saw the opportunity to break forward. The Liverpool defence backed off so I let fly. I'm sure, even to this day, that the ball was heading into the Liverpool net. Then the arm of Phil Thompson came out. It was like slow motion. I watched with delight as the ball struck his hand inside the box. I was sure it was a stick-on penalty. His hands were so far away from his body it looked like a crucifixion scene. But the referee waved it away. A home decision! The danger for Liverpool had been averted but it showed they could take nothing for granted – except gifts from the referee. No problem! We were hardly in trouble at all towards the end of the game and won the tie embarrassingly easily.

We had sent a message to the whole of Europe. None of them could halt the Liverpool march but we had done it. The Scouse dragon was vanquished. The English as a football nation, not just Liverpool, were back. It gave us a massive psychological advantage over the rest of Europe. We must be some team. We were.

In the next round we were drawn against the Greek team, AEK Athens. If the Liverpool tie was an unusual pairing, this was uncanny. The reason was we had already played Athens on their own ground in a pre-season friendly, which ended in a 1–1 draw in front of a partisan crowd numbering some 30,000 Greeks. We therefore knew exactly what to expect in the first leg, which was at their ground. We knew what the pitch played like, what the crowd sounded like. It was a huge advantage. Martin O'Neill was back in the side and we attacked them from the start. We ran out 2–1 winners. Garry Birtles scored again, along with John McGovern.

The return at the City ground was a goal-fest. It was a party. We won 5–1. Yet again, Garry Birtles was the scourge of Europe with two well-taken goals. Woody grabbed one for himself and David Needham, coming up from centre-back, scored another. But this was my night. It belonged to me. I picked the ball up just inside their half, found no-one barring my way, so off I went forward. The Greek defence seemed to ignore me. As I advanced towards the penalty area I looked for a pass. None was available so I hit it from twenty-five yards. It screamed into the net. I had scored in the European Cup. For those of you not lucky enough to have played professional football it is difficult to find the words to explain the feeling that goal gave me. It was, simply, indescribable. Some great banter went around the dressing room afterwards, most of it started by me, talking about my incredible goal again and again.

Results elsewhere in the competition went in our favour. It was as if the destination of the trophy was pre-ordained. Was our name on the Cup? Juventus, the Italian champions, were already out at the hands of Rangers, while Bruges, who had reached the final the year before, when they lost to that Kenny Dalglish winner at Wembley, were also removed from the competition. Perhaps most important, Real Madrid, who would have been the most difficult of opponents, were knocked out in the first round by the minnows from Switzerland, Grasshoppers of Zurich. We drew Grasshoppers in the third round and saw them off quite comfortably with a 4–1 win at home and a 1–1 draw in Switzerland. Garry Birtles yet again scored a goal in the first leg, Martin O'Neill securing the draw in Zurich. Of the teams that remained, only the West German champions, Cologne, were a side to be feared. It goes without saying that we drew them in the next round, the semi-final.

I missed the first game against the Germans. I had been booked in the second leg against Grasshoppers for a nothing foul, which meant I was banned for one match. It was hell watching when I should have been playing. We were also without Trevor Francis, who was injured. Among a number of talented players, Cologne boasted the brilliant Bernd Schuster, a player who could really hurt any side. It proved to be an incredible game.

It was the only time we underestimated our opponents. Brian Clough often used to belittle the opposition in team meetings. The way he did it, though, made you understand that you could only exploit the opposition's weaknesses if you worked to implement what Clough told you to do. Before the home tie against Cologne, Clough decided to hand over the team talk to Peter Taylor. Taylor tried the same tactics as Clough, telling us Cologne were basically useless. But, great though Taylor was in his own sphere, he was not Clough when it came to the psychology of playing. He made the side feel that all they had to do was turn up. Knowing I was not playing, I took the time to look at our players and I could see the overconfidence.

Twenty minutes into the first half we were 2–0 down and facing a rout. I watched aghast from my seat in the stands. But our success was built on some intangible quality that you might call spirit or belief. Gradually, Ian Bowyer and John Robbo began to get a hold of the midfield. They hauled us back into contention. Both of them scored, as did Garry Birtles and suddenly we were 3–2 up. Maybe if Cologne hadn't scored their goals so early on in the match they might have beaten us. As it was we had both the time and the ability to come back. We couldn't hold on to the lead, however. With ten minutes to go, Cologne's substitute, the Japanese player, Okudera, hit a speculative shot from distance. For one of only a very few times that I witnessed, Peter Shilton made a mistake and let the ball go under his body and into the goal. The match ended 3–3 and the general view was that we would be defeated in the return leg and be out of the European Cup.

Within the camp, we were not so pessimistic. Clough was convinced we would win and told us in no uncertain terms that nothing but a win would do. He informed the press that we would win the tie. The players were quietly confident. Our defending was poor in the first leg, which was unlike Forest under Clough. We felt we would not play so poorly again and we would certainly not gift them any goals this time.

My suspension over, I came back in for the second leg, which we had to win (or gain an improbable 4–4 draw) to go through. As usual, the management refused to overplay the importance of the game and we spent most of our time in Cologne walking round the old city, looking at the cathedral, things like that. We were also encouraged to have a few, but not too many, beers. We did a little light training and that was it.

"What I want you to do," went Clough's team talk, "is to ensure they don't score in the first half. Then in the second half you will score the winning goal. End of story." The game went exactly as Clough demanded, with Ian Bowyer getting the winner. In the dying moments, Peter Shilton redeemed his mistake in the first leg with interest when he pulled off an incredible save which prevented a certain equaliser. We had dumbfounded British critics and the whole of European football, just as we had done in winning the League the previous season and in knocking Liverpool off their pedestal.

The final in Munich against Malmo of Sweden was a bit of an anticlimax in terms of the football. But it meant everything to us. In many ways it was the minnows' final. Neither Malmo nor Forest possessed any European tradition. For once, we weren't underdogs but we weren't favourites either. No-one was more pleased with the prospect of playing in a European final than Trevor Francis. He was the wonder-kid at Birmingham but he had come to Forest with a million pound price-tag round his neck. As John Robbo put in one of his immaculate crosses from the left, which bamboozled the entire defence and the goalkeeper, Trevor stole in on the blindside and headed home from two yards. Never can one goal have justified such a high transfer fee.

Champions of England! Champions of Europe! I must admit those phrases have a certain ring to them. Hundreds of thousands of people turned up to watch us return to Nottingham. We had put the club and the city on the map and we had shown that you didn't have to be one of the big boys to win the glittering prizes. What you did need, if you were good players in the first place, was a manager like Brian Clough, whose determination to succeed overcame all obstacles, provided he had compliant players who were in awe of him, as we were. It turned out there was no mystery as to why he had failed so miserably at Leeds. The players there had already enjoyed unbelievable success under Don Revie. Brian Clough's methods just left them cold and he could never use the argument that all they had achieved was due to him, as he could with us.

These days, when managers are asked to account for success, they generally say it's down to 'hard work', as if the opposing side did not work so hard. Don't get me wrong, we worked as hard at Forest as anyone, particularly in pre-season, but during the regular season, Clough recognised when to put in the hard yards and when to keep the training light and interesting. Sometimes, as you will have gathered, it was weird. Most of the time when we were away from home, the only training we did was by way of walking past local beauty-spots and enjoying the odd recreational drink. Some of today's managers might do well to take a leaf out of Clough's book and go to Mallorca on a whim. Trips to foreign resorts these days are usually part of some pre-planned strategy when there is an international week or something. The trouble is, too many confuse 'hard work' with a lack of talent. To Clough, football was simple: you passed it to a player in a red shirt and the rest would take care of itself if you had good players.

As the new season – 1979–80 – approached, there was only one thing anyone could say: follow that! Clough and Taylor had already answered that to their own satisfaction. They were now ploughing their own furrow and they had the once-sceptical media eating out of their hands. I was to miss only two games throughout the season, which pleased me no end. In a move which left the rest of football reeling, the boss signed the legendary Stan Bowles. Now for anyone who saw him, Stan Bowles was the most naturally gifted footballer you could wish to see. In his heyday at Queens Park Rangers he was a revelation in what was anyway a good team. The trouble with Stan was, as everyone knows, he had an off-field lifestyle which wasn't compatible with that of a professional athlete. With Stan, his particular vice was gambling. He would bet on anything. He probably would have made a great bookmaker, so extensive was his knowledge of odds. He could give you odds on anything. As they say, if he could have passed a betting shop the way he passed a football he'd have been an all-time great.

Having experienced Clough and Taylor over some years by then, I got the feeling they were making a statement when they signed Stan. They had rehabilitated Kenny

Burns and got the best out of him when others scoffed. They had told anyone who would listen that Peter Shilton was the best in the world while others wavered. They had shown their intent when they became the first in this country to splash out a million on a single player. Now they would get the best out of one of England's most talented but wayward post-war footballers. They soon added to their reputation for left-field decisions by bringing in another veteran, Charlie George, on loan.

Unfortunately, Stan never really reached the level he was capable of at Forest. He was sporadically brilliant, that's for sure, and when he turned it on he was fantastic. But I think Stan would be the first to admit that his days at Forest were inconsistent at best. His behaviour was also often erratic. Stan being Stan, one game when he really turned it on was in the away leg of the European Super Cup, when we faced the mighty Barcelona in front of 90,000 fanatical supporters. Stan hadn't played in the first leg at the City Ground. We edged it 1-0 with a goal from, you've guessed it, the on-loan Charlie George. Yet again our chances were written off. We might have performed amazing feats but Barcelona were an entirely different proposition.

Clough found us plenty of entertainment and walks in the Catalan capital but didn't want us to do too much training. He wanted us "nice and relaxed". His masterstroke was to tell Stan Bowles that this was his stage and he brought him in for Ian Bowyer. To select a flair player in place of a solid performer when you are defending a 1-0 lead in such circumstances was a staggering move.

It was typical of Clough's readiness to make bold decisions which went against football wisdom. He was busy creating a new wisdom all his own.

Running out at the Camp Nou was one of the highlights of my career. The emotion streams from the crowd in a way that Liverpool can only dream of. It comes in waves from those mile-high stands. But it was us who were in heaven. We were underdogs in the home of our opponents, just like Cologne, just like Liverpool. Stan ran the second leg. Responding to the occasion he was like some returning matador. He was absolutely brilliant. He was responsible for us getting a 0–0 draw and we were applauded off the pitch. We had won the European Super Cup in one of Europe's most iconic stadiums. Incredible!

Our League form was not what any of us wanted. It is amazing to think that only a couple of years before we were happy with second division respectability. Now, we were disappointed to finish fifth in Division One. Yet again, Liverpool won it. In the FA Cup, we were as bad as ever, flattering to deceive. We smashed Leeds at Elland Road 4–1 in round three, then we were drawn at home to ... Liverpool.

It wasn't as simple as that, though. We had already been paired against the Scousers in the semi-final of the League Cup, the first leg of which came three days before the FA Cup tie. Two of the three games before the Anfield leg of the League Cup tie were the Super Cup matches against Barcelona. "This is what success means", was what the manager had to say about it all.

We saw off Liverpool 1–0 in the first leg of the League Cup semi-final. So far so good! That gave us confidence for the FA Cup game the following Saturday. There was little in the way of rotation then. Pretty much the same team turned out in all competitive matches with a couple of exceptions like Stan Bowles at the Camp Nou. All us regulars played in one game in the sequence which could have been a chance to give some hard-pressed players a breather. It was a home League match against Bristol City. Clough would have none of that. He approached the game against Bristol in exactly the same way as the matches against the more illustrious opponents. However, that old FA Cup demon still had it in for us no matter what Clough did. Liverpool beat us on our own turf 2–0.

We had won the League Cup two years running. We almost felt it belonged to us. There was no way we would surrender that to Liverpool, particularly after the FA Cup reverse. We managed a 0–0 in the second leg, to go through to our third Wembley final in a row. We were favourites but not by much. Our opponents, Wolves, finished only a point behind us in the League and were a more than decent side. For the first time in a major final, we failed to function properly at Wembley and Wolves beat us 1–0. None of us liked the taste of defeat. Clough liked it least of all.

Over the previous few months, in fact it was probably longer than that when I look back on it, Woody had been talking about going abroad. It wasn't that he was fed up with Forest or had anything against the manager.

He just wanted to lift his sights to other challenges. We used to get together a lot and he would tell me how he wanted to experience more than Nottingham had to offer, more than England had to offer. I didn't try to talk him out of it, his mind was made up. Much as I enjoyed his company and what he brought to the team, I understood his ideas even if I didn't share them. Then all of a sudden, the deal was done and Woody was gone. To Cologne, would you believe!

The defeat by Wolves was even worse for us and our fans because ten days earlier we had been beaten by Dynamo Berlin in the home leg of the third round of the European Cup. Was our campaign to defend our most treasured trophy about to founder so early? The game in Berlin was only four days after the League Cup Final, which of course we had lost. We went to Germany for the return, our European status hanging by a thread.

Lots of praise has been heaped on the quality of our victories over Liverpool and Cologne in our glory years. But our performance in Berlin is to me the greatest of them all. We were on the floor. The manager refused to accept that the two defeats we had suffered at the hands of Berlin and Wolves had occurred at all. He acted as if nothing were any different to usual. He took us for walks, gave us history lessons about Berlin and wouldn't let us train too much. We won 3–1. Trevor Francis got two of the goals. I felt I put in one of my best ever performances that night. Their winger never got a kick. We had confounded our critics one more time.

To be fair to the pundits – and someone needs to be – that win in Berlin turned us from upstarts to a team with genuine European pedigree. You would have thought winning the European Cup and the Super Cup would have achieved that. But no, it took that comeback against Berlin to establish our place among the greats of Europe. Now even the media finally took Clough at his word when he told them how good we were.

That win pitched us against the Dutch masters, Ajax, in the semi-final. Ajax had won the trophy three times in a row in the seventies, with the legendary Johan Cruyff pulling the strings. True, the 1980 vintage might not have been as good as that team but they were still a force to be reckoned with. In the first leg, played at our place, we ran out good winners, 2-0. It was the same score as our famous first leg against Liverpool the previous season and we knew how to defend it. In Amsterdam, Clough took us for a walk by the canals and then to the city's famous red-light district. About half-an-hour into the trip, the manager stopped us and announced that "if anyone wants a quick one the club's paying". We didn't know how serious he was and to my knowledge no-one took him up on the offer. Instead, we had a few drinks. One thing we didn't do too much was train.

In front of a crowd of 65,000, we lost the return leg 1-0, taking a bit of a battering in the process. That meant we were in the final. Again! Only the dreaded Liverpool among English clubs had managed that, two appearances on the spin. Now, we had to win.

1980 was more of a glamour final than the previous season. The game was to be staged in the incredible Bernabeu Stadium in Madrid, home of Real, the club who are a byword for European greatness. Clough waxed lyrical about Spanish culture and tried to tell us about a civil war or something. We were housed in a lovely hotel in the hills outside the city. Our wives and girlfriends were in 5-star accommodation in downtown Madrid, quite close to the stadium. It was not often that those in charge of Forest were so generous. We were a bit put out, though, that our spouses were in a hotel which was quite a distance from us. Any time we spent with them would be controlled by the manager.

We were up against SV Hamburg, a top team of the time. Kevin Keegan was their most famous player, Felix Magath their best. They had disposed of Real Madrid in the semi-final. Clough hardly mentioned Keegan or Magath. He took us to Mallorca before the game. Stan Bowles, in one of his more inexplicable bouts of erratic behaviour, didn't show up for the flight. So he missed what could have been a reprise of his display in Barcelona, a chance of glory on the ultimate stage. If Clough was put out by Stan's non-appearance, he didn't let on. He ensured we stayed relaxed. Not much training took place. Playing at the Bernabeu was another milestone. If the Camp Nou was inspiring, the Bernabeu was the ultimate. The match itself was a tight encounter. John Robertson provided the only moment of class. Weaving his way forward he cut in from the left and passed the ball into the net. If winning the European Cup once was immense, this was beyond awesome.

It was a magnificent climax to the season. We were now among the greats. Nothing could ever diminish this achievement. However, after the game, the manager delayed our reunion with our wives and girlfriends by keeping us in the mountain retreat for the night. It was a strange way to reward us for our efforts. Some of us, including myself, Martin and John Robbo, decided to defy the manager and slip out of the hotel. In the end, John Robbo bottled out, for which he took some serious stick. The rest of us made our way to Madrid. We weren't caught, thank God. We did celebrate with the management but something didn't feel right. In many ways, it was never the same again at Forest. The great team had already lost Withey and Woody. Soon it would begin to break up completely.

Chapter Six

THAT MAN

When Brian Clough arrived at Forest, the whole world wondered if he could recapture the magic he had performed at Derby. At the Baseball Ground he had won the League and reached the semi-final of the European Cup. He felt he was cheated of the opportunity to reach the final by corrupt administrators and referees. That was an issue which would impact on us further down the line, as you'll see later. Clough's Derby side was the most successful in the club's history. At first sight, it didn't seem likely he would be able to regain that kind of success ever again, especially not with us. Many thought his experience at Leeds had worn him down. He was, it was said, a busted flush. Some busted flush.

We soon found out that with Clough, we should always expect the unexpected. I have played under some great managers. And I really mean great. Each of them possessed special characteristics that marked them out. If they had anything in common it is that they all seemed as if they were born to be in football. But you got the impression with Brian Clough that he would have been just as successful whatever he had done in life. And he would have ended up a celebrity even if he'd been a chartered accountant. His fame spread way beyond our shores and the world of football. It's fair to say that the players at Forest, used to the more conventional approaches of coaches like Allan Brown and Dave Mackay, were immediately blown away.

On the first day, the new boss called us together and told us we were hopeless. He went on to say that we could do well or we could be also-rans. We would only get anywhere, he said, if we listened to him and followed his instructions to the letter. If he had been in any way humbled by his time at Leeds it didn't show. He took great pains to make it clear that he wasn't there just for an easy pay day and neither were we. He was there to win. He was mesmerising.

It's a bit of a riddle how footballers respond to managers. If you are winning games, then of course players think their boss is brilliant. But what about when a manager first arrives? If he has been successful elsewhere as the main man, an assistant or a coach, he has a head start. If he has been a top player, won championships, cups or international caps, he automatically gets respect from the players. But footballers are a funny bunch. Unlike many jobs, the integrity of the group is the most important thing. One or two disaffected guys can cause all kinds of problems for the team and when it comes down to it, football is about winning games as a team. The trouble is, there is no set method for success, nor is there just one type of manager who can inspire the necessary loyalty and level of performance. Some managers gee you up, tell you how good you are or could be if you did things their way. The trouble is, for most of them, 'their way' is not that different to lots of others. Believe it or not, the vast majority find it difficult to deal with even simple issues, such as the fact that some players react to a bollocking while others need to be cajoled.

Brian Clough was most definitely a one-off among managers. You couldn't fit him into any category. I think everyone knows that. His short spell with Leeds had been an unmitigated disaster, no question. But he had created that Derby side. His reputation for strange behaviour had, of course, preceded him. We were, I think it's safe to say, a bit wary when he pitched up. The difference between him and the manager who had been sacked to make way for him, Allan Brown, was immense. Whereas Brown was an old-school coach who was good on the training ground but somehow couldn't motivate the group beyond second division mediocrity, Clough was like a whirlwind.

I hadn't been in the first team squad for long when he arrived so I didn't have too much experience of how managers operate. I soon discovered from players at other clubs that Clough was different. He was adamant from day one that his ambitions reached the stratosphere and yours had to be the same. Otherwise you would be out. He would often stoop to insults, which he repeated again and again. John Robertson was "too fat and lazy", Martin O'Neill "had no skill" and so on. He rarely, if ever, praised you directly. Or if he did, it was either to make a wider point (as when he named Peter Shilton the 'Best Goalkeeper in the World' in order to intimidate his own players and opponents alike) or to pave the way for a sometimes savage put-down.

In fact, you never knew where you were with Brian Clough. Sometimes he would talk to you, sometimes he wouldn't. When I was left out of the team for that cup replay at Spurs there was no explanation. On other occasions he went out of his way to explain himself. The fact that I was injured in the first leg of the Spurs FA Cup game gave him ample opportunity to tell me that because I hadn't trained, he couldn't risk me in such an important match. But no! There was nothing. Just a great big empty silence. I thought I had been doing quite well up to then but there I was left behind in Nottingham for the Spurs match. Mind you, in hindsight, that was better than what happened to Tony Woodcock.

As I've already said, Tony and I came up through the ranks together. We remain the best of friends to this day. Then, we were both young teenagers who broke into the side at more or less the same time. Tony thought he was in favour when he was included in the squad for the cup replay against Spurs and naturally thought he had a good chance of playing. Clough didn't let on what the actual team would be but that only increased Woody's expectations. After all, why would the manager take him if he wasn't going to throw him into the game at some point.

That was Woody's reasoning. But no-one realised at that time quite what Clough was really like. As it happened Woody came back to Nottingham from London without making an appearance in the game. He told me what happened.

When the squad arrived in London, the new manager called everyone together, seemingly for a team talk. First, he turned to Woody.

"I've got a special job for you, young man," he began. Woody's expectation level went up another notch. Then Clough delivered the punch-line. Handing Tony a small package, he continued: "There's a brush and polish, go and clean my shoes." Tony looked blank but Clough was deadly serious. Woody was there to clean his shoes. And that was the closest Woody came to the action that night. It did, however, establish the way things were going to be from then on.

We were soon to find out that it was best never to try and second guess Clough. You had no idea what he was going to do. This carried on throughout my time with him. If anything, that aspect was intensified when Peter Taylor arrived as Clough's assistant. Clough and Taylor used to egg each other on. I don't know which of them came up with this little wheeze. In one of many, many examples of Clough's unique approach to football management, we were staying at a hotel near London the night before a big game. It was a very big game indeed. It was the League Cup Final. We enjoyed a good meal and were sent to bed at 8pm. Soon afterwards, we each got a phone call from the manager summoning us to a private room downstairs. Clough stood up and banged his spoon on a plate to shut us all up and get our attention.

"Right you lot," he said (this was a favourite phrase of Clough's). "Everyone here is going to have a drink. I've got champagne laid on for you. But not one of you leaves this room until you have all told us a joke." So one by one we each had to deliver a gag. I was never that good at telling jokes and really struggled. But the boss persisted and I managed to mumble some rubbish. That was pretty much the extent of the pre-match talk. I finally made it to bed around midnight. Needless to say I woke up with a hangover, as did quite a few of the other players. At the game the next day Clough hardly said a word. Wolves beat us 1–0. Andy Gray scored the only goal. Clough never asked us to tell any jokes again.

There was never too much talk about tactics or the opposition with Cloughie. There were certainly no dossiers on the strengths and weaknesses of opposing players. Nonetheless, you wanted to play for him, you would do anything to please him. If he put a hand on your shoulder after a match you knew he was bestowing high praise and you walked on air for days. Just a hand on your shoulder! It didn't mean you would be in the team for the next game, though.

I've never experienced, before or since, the kind of training sessions which Clough and his trainer, Jimmy Gordon employed (Peter Taylor was rarely involved in coaching. Come to think of it, Clough didn't do much coaching either. It just seemed like he did). As you will have already seen, during the season there wasn't much training at all. There were walks, there was eating and a bit of drinking, but very little training beyond five-a-sides. Clough always liked his players to work with the ball if they were working at all. Anything else, to him, was a waste of time. It came as a shock when I moved to other clubs and found out first-hand how most coaches approached training, with work-outs and endless talk about tactics.

One thing Clough did spend time telling us, especially defenders, was his ownership of the goal. By this I mean he would point to the goal in training and say: "That there is MY net. Keep the ball out of MY net, that's what I pay you for." That was Clough's coaching method. He had this knack of coming up with a phrase – like 'MY net' or 'just pass the ball to someone in a red shirt' – which was so memorable it imprinted the idea on your mind. There may have been little in the way of what could be called team talks but somehow his insistence on passing the ball and keeping possession were instilled until they became second nature. And Clough made it abundantly clear that we were never, ever to argue with referees or question their decisions. A knock-on from this order was that of course we were never allowed to question him either.

That first season we were coming to terms with a man, the like of whose methods and personality we had never seen before. Even John Robbo started to take notice. I gradually saw a difference when we came in for training. More often than not, the manager wasn't there, he left things to his assistant, Jimmy Gordon. We didn't know where he was but the idea of his all-knowing presence somehow caused us to sharpen up. He would suddenly turn up, claim to have been playing squash, make a few observations, then disappear again. Sometimes Peter Taylor would be there, sometimes he wouldn't. Bit by bit, Clough's way of doing things paid dividends and we began buying into his dream and our own future.

At the beginning of Clough's second full season, the boss made it clear he expected nothing less than promotion. It was a kind of ultimatum. We either got promotion or he'd get players in who would. So it was with relief as much as anything else when we managed to achieve his command by scraping into third place. No-one gave us much chance of surviving in the top flight that first season, let alone win anything. No-one, that is, except the manager. Clough had no interest in the way many teams played in those days. He particularly didn't like long balls lumped to a big man up front. Speculative balls into the channels were for teams with no talent as far as he was concerned. We would live or die playing his way: keeping possession; getting the ball out to the wide players; lots of crosses; midfielders who didn't lose the ball. No matter how other sides played, we were to play Clough's way. For us there was no other.

The manager took us all to Mallorca towards the end of that first season in the top division, as he often did at moments of pressure. Sometimes he went himself and left us to get on with things back home. Clough was one of those managers who believed that football at the highest level, like in all sport, is won and lost by the small things, the one or two percent that makes the difference between victory and defeat. Part of this is the way players deal with the relentless pressure that accompanies the striving always to improve. There is no standing still in football. If you don't keep improving you are going backwards. Some players take to this reality better than others. The best managers develop strategies to enable their players to cope and even use the pressure as a means of improvement. There is no one way of doing it, all great managers are different. Brian Clough used it by pretending it didn't exist. To him, football was a simple game played by idiots. The idiots couldn't fail to be successful provided they did what they were told by someone who was a genius, that is, Clough himself. Pressure, what pressure? "Pressure," he would say, "is going down a pit everyday to dig coal."

Clough's eccentric approach can be seen in the build up to our first European Cup Final. We flew to Munich for the game against Malmo on the Monday, with the match due to take place in Bayern Munich's fantastic Olympic Stadium on Wednesday. We arrived in the evening. We stayed at a nice but hardly great hotel in the Bavarian mountains outside the city. It was in the middle of nowhere really. The first thing we noticed as we drew up outside was that the hotel had no training pitches or anything much in the way of outdoor facilities. Once we were installed in our rooms, Clough called us together. "Right, you lot," he said. "This is what you're going to do. Tomorrow morning I want you in the lobby at nine o'clock in your tracksuits. I've organised training." This was unusual. At other clubs it might be normal but with Clough it was highly abnormal. What kind of training could he mean?

So there we were the next day, all bright-eyed and expecting at most a light training session. We should have known better. There was nothing planned at all that related to football as far as any of us could see. Then he gave us our orders. He began pointing at various indoor facilities: "There's a dart board, there's a pool table, there's the bar but there's no drinks in it. Just relax. I'll see you at six o'clock." And with that he was gone. It turned out that Clough, who often encouraged a bit of social drinking, had decided that because we had all been drinking the week before, when we were on one of our Spanish getaways, there would be no alcohol in Germany.

Not only that, he wouldn't let us train the whole time we were in Munich. The one player this affected more than any other was goalkeeper, Peter Shilton. Shilts had a pathological aversion to not training. He simply had to train every day, otherwise he became unbearable. He'd been doing his routine for years and needed to keep it going. He begged Clough to organise something for him. In Shilton's case, Clough relented, perhaps because he knew and understood Peter's needs and he respected him as the best goalkeeper in the world. Or he may have been making a point to the rest of us. If that was the case, none of us knew what the point might be. Anyway, he got Jimmy Gordon to find Shilts a 'suitable' place to train on his own. Whether the venue was chosen by Clough or Gordon I don't know. It turned out to be on a traffic island at the junction of two busy roads. It was almost bare of grass with just a smattering of rough shrub in the middle. On driving by, local motorists were surprised to see the world's number one goalkeeper going through his training routines on the patchy grass which made up the island. The rest of us were banished to the bar with no drinks. That was pure Clough and of course we won the European Cup. Malmo never stood a chance.

Perhaps here I can explode a myth that has grown up about the manager and his relationship with Peter Taylor. Clough and Taylor were a team. A brilliant team! But there was no doubt who was boss, never ever! However, Clough's relationship with Taylor was hugely important to the success that both of them achieved. Look at each one's performance when the other was not at their side. It was never that good. Taylor at Brighton and later at Derby – and Clough at Leeds – had all been failed experiments in one way or another. Together, they were an irresistible force. When Taylor finally left Forest, his reasons for breaking up the partnership – so he told Clough – were that he wanted to retire and live with less stress (Taylor suffered from heart problems). Clough understood and was sympathetic. Then suddenly, out of nowhere, Taylor took the manager's job at Derby, of all places. Since that moment it has become an established 'fact' that Taylor's actions destroyed the relationship between the two men. It is said that the mutual antagonism was so great they never spoke to each other again. Now there was bad feeling, sure. Clough saw Taylor's actions as a terrible betrayal, no question. But it was far more complex than that.

Towards the end of my time at Forest, and after Taylor had become Derby's manager, I began to suffer a few niggling injuries, which was unusual for me. I also got that bad injury on England duty. So concerned did Clough become at the length of my absences that he bought a replacement right-back, Kenny Swain, from Aston Villa. Gradually, however, I began to return to fitness and was ready to reclaim my place. Then one day the boss called me and another player, Mark Proctor, into his office.

"Will you two go out on loan?" Clough began.

This was a shock but we had no choice but to listen to what the boss had to say.

"Where to?" I asked.

The gaffer shuffled a little and didn't answer straight away, which was unusual for him. He was seldom lost for words. He looked a bit shifty, to be honest. Then he blurted it out. "I've been talking to Peter and he needs a couple of players of your calibre."

"You mean Derby?"

"Yes."

Now as a Nottingham boy there was no way I was going to Derby. Mark wasn't too keen on the move either.

Anyway, no disrespect to Derby, but I saw it as a step down, which I could not accept. I told Clough this. A pained expression came over his face. "Look," he said. "Let me drive you over to Pete's house, have a word with him, then make up your mind. If you're not interested in going there you can tell him yourself." I didn't want to do it but agreed only because it was Brian Clough doing the asking. So Clough drove Mark and me to Taylor's house, way out in the middle of the Nottinghamshire countryside, not even near a village. When we arrived, Clough went into the kitchen for a cup of tea with Peter's wife, Lillian, while Peter made his pitch. The talks went on for a couple of hours before both of us told him we were going to stay at Forest. Neither Clough nor Taylor was too pleased at this turn of events.

"Well you can find your own way home then," Clough said. Then he softened. "Could you give us a couple of minutes? I want a quick word with Pete. Go and have a cup of tea in the kitchen." We duly went to the kitchen where Taylor's wife made us a lovely cup of tea. While we were doing this, Clough and Taylor secretly left the house. Like two naughty boys, they scuttled off to do who knows what and left us out in the sticks with no transport.

We went to speak to Taylor's wife. "What's the matter, love?" she asked me. We told her what had happened and could see a grin begin to form on her face. "Never mind," she continued. "Have another cup of tea and call a cab." Well, two hours later, the cab had still not arrived. We didn't know if Clough and Taylor had instructed the cab company not to pick us up or what had happened. It was now past eight in the evening and we decided to leg it. Over styles and fields we went, cutting ourselves on the undergrowth and tearing our clothes. Eventually we reached a village pub where we had a couple of drinks to calm us down. From there, we managed to get a taxi home to Nottingham, arriving about midnight, exhausted and bemused. If Clough and Taylor had really fallen out to the extent that everyone now believes, no-one had told them on that day. We never did find out what they got up to but I'm sure they must have been having a right laugh.

There are so many stories about Brian Clough. To me, he was a complicated man who gave the impression that everything was simple. He often had a bit of a cheeky smile but that was an expression of his satisfaction at his own genius rather than an encouragement to a player. Nonetheless, he was central to my whole career. I respected him but I'm not sure to this day if I liked him. I still haven't worked him out and I was at his side for ten years. Since then I've played under other great managers. I've been a manager myself. Still, Brian Clough looms the largest of all. He wasn't like Bobby Robson, who treated you like a son. He wasn't like Sir Alex Ferguson, an equally huge personality of whom you'll hear a lot more later. He wasn't like George Graham, the great disciplinarian or Ron Atkinson, the great comedian of football managers. He was Clough.

For all of us footballers who came under Clough's influence, he took us on a mind-boggling journey, one that will probably never be repeated. I can only liken him to the Pied Piper. To lead a team out of the second tier and win the League at the first attempt would today be the stuff of childish fantasy. As for back-to-back European Cups – forget it. But Clough did it. With us! The more peaks we conquered, the more we wanted to please him. We ran through stinging nettles for him. We would have run through a wall into a nuclear reactor if he asked us to. I think it is true to say we will never see his like again.

Chapter Seven

THE ROAD TO LONDON

Somehow – and I can't say how – the start of the 1980–81 season just didn't feel the same as before. That may seem a strange thing to say given that we had won the European Cup for the second time just a few short months before. But the feeling became more certain as the great Forest team began to break up over the course of the next eighteen months. What had started with Woody the previous year proved not to be a one-off but a trend. The season saw the departure of quite a number of other players as the boss tried to construct a new side to take the club forward.

The highest profile transfer out was Garry Birtles, who went to Manchester United for £1.25 million. Garry was never the same player again. Having played with him and seen him at close quarters turn some of the best defenders in the business I can tell you he was an absolutely top-draw striker. Quite why he failed at Old Trafford is a mystery, except to say that Brian Clough knew how to play to Garry's strengths and I don't think the same can be said of United. Also, as I found out some years later, Manchester United is a massive step up, no matter what clubs you've played for in the past. It's not easy for some players to manage. The only thing I can put it down to is that Garry – as I've said previously – was continuously homesick for Nottingham and his old mates. He would return whenever he could, which couldn't have been good for his form. Maybe this homesickness meant he was unable to really embrace his new status as number one striker at one of the world's biggest clubs. He just preferred to be in the town of his youth rather than in one of the big cities of Europe.

For me, the saddest departure was that of Martin O'Neill, who left for Norwich. Not only had we played together down the right side for so long with such incredible success, I regarded Martin and his wife, Geraldine, as close friends. The team would definitely lack something big without him in it. Our talisman, Kenny Burns, and his partner at the centre of defence, Larry Lloyd, both moved on, as did the midfielder, Archie Gemmill. Kenny had become one of the most consistent defenders in the country. With him, the Clough method paid massive dividends. In the strikers' department, John O'Hare, whose opportunities to play were becoming less and less as age crept up on him, called time on his period at the City Ground. It wasn't that long before Trevor Francis joined the exodus. Just as Trevor's arrival for a million pounds sent out a message to the world, so his departure said something about where we were heading. There would still be some marquee signings but, as I said, it just wasn't the same.

In their places came good players but the question was: could we all gel to produce another great team? One of those marquee signings was Justin Fashanu. His transfer from Norwich was very high-profile. Poor Justin would later be the first footballer to come out as gay and there is no question he suffered for it. Such was the pressure on him he eventually committed suicide. When he arrived at Forest, I was at first detailed to room with him on away trips. At the time, I didn't know he was gay, none of us did. Sometimes the manager called him a "poof" in training but we thought that was an example of Clough's use of insult rather than the reality. After all, Clough insulted everyone in one way or another. Looking back, I can see the lengths Justin must have gone to in order to disguise his sexuality – and what it cost him.

On the first occasion we shared a room, during a pre-season tour of Spain, I was blissfully asleep. I awoke to the sound of a very loud banging on the walls or something. It was a huge commotion. Then I saw the door. It was a thick, strong door but it had a huge hole in it. I jumped out of bed, now fully awake and rushed to open the door. It looked like the room was under attack. There was no sign of Justin. I flung the door open to see doors opening all down the corridor and half-asleep players putting their heads out demanding to know what was going on. I went back into the room and heard the sound of sobbing coming from the bathroom. I went in. Justin was bathing his hands – covered in blood – in the sink, and was moaning. He had smashed through the door with his fists. They were bruised and bloodied. I thought it was someone with an axe trying to get in, not someone trying to get out. He didn't appear to be fully awake, almost like he was in a really bad dream. I got the impression he was reliving some dark incident from his boyhood but I have no idea what it was. A doctor was summoned and Justin was helped back into bed. Needless to say I didn't get another wink of sleep for the rest of the night.

Such was football culture in those days that I never discussed the night's events with Justin. You didn't talk about those sorts of things back then. It felt awkward and unmanly. Of, course everyone knew what had happened. And being footballers, some of the comments were a bit close to the edge. Perhaps I should have been more sympathetic but as a professional athlete I could not afford to have my sleep disturbed like that. I didn't dislike Justin, we always got on OK. But what if it was the night before a big match and he did that again? I refused to spend another night in the same room as him. Incidents like this soured relations between Justin and the manager. Clough realised his methods just didn't work with Justin. That's not surprising given that Justin was a disturbed individual in many ways, as his door-smashing showed. Instead of his football improving, his form dipped, which in turn led to even fiercer criticism from the press and the manager. He eventually left Forest for Notts County, but not before being forcibly escorted from the training ground by burly policemen following yet another altercation with the manager.

At first, the season looked to be going well. We went on an unbeaten run – which included a 5-0 demolition of Stoke – and felt good. It seemed our whole season caved in, though, when we crashed out of the European Cup in the first round. For two years, the greatest of all club prizes had been ours. It had made us famous wherever football was played. We expected to do better than this. We were confident enough going into the first match, the away leg, against CSKA Sofia of Bulgaria. The truth is we were very poor on the night, while the Bulgarians surprised us with the strength of their display. We lost 1–0.

Like a wounded tiger, we roared straight back, beating Leicester 5–0 in the League and Bury 7–0 in the League Cup. But then we lost to Arsenal. Consistency, which had been one of our hallmarks in the previous three years (we established a record for going the most games undefeated), was beginning to desert us. Nothing could be a better example of this than the return leg against CSKA. It was a disaster. We just couldn't get going, they scored on the break and we again lost 1–0.

The Bulgarians went absolutely wild. No-one blamed them. We were back-to-back European Champions, after all. It felt terrible. We were out. Forest under Brian Clough were a team I loved playing in. I loved the type of attacking football Clough encouraged. I loved the way we played. I loved the belief we had. After the defeat by CSKA, I asked myself whether we could salvage our season. As a team, I don't know if we believed we could. It was a massive blow.

As if to rub salt in our wounds, we were out of the League Cup before Christmas. Like the European Cup, we had made the League Cup our own. Three years in the final, two of them won. In our worst performance in the competition since our days in the second division, we were dumped out by the emerging Watford side put together by Graham Taylor. I was out injured but I felt the defeat as much as anyone. Watford's style of play was all direct football, getting the ball up front as early as possible with long, hopeful punts. It was the opposite of what Clough – and therefore the rest of us – believed was the right way to play the game. That made it all the worse when they beat us 4–1. This was ominous.

For once, the FA Cup provided our best performances of the season. We knocked out Bolton, Manchester United and Bristol City in a run to the sixth round. However, at that stage we went out in a replay, beaten by Ipswich. We also relinquished the European Super Cup, to Valencia on away goals. In December, we travelled to Tokyo for the World Club Championship against Nacional Montevideo of Uruguay. Once again, we were beaten. In a bad-tempered game, full of niggling fouls and off-the-ball incidents, the Latin Americans edged it 1–0.

Aston Villa came from nowhere to win the League. They went all the way in the European Cup the next season and won it with one of Forest's old boys, Peter Withe, getting their winner in the final. At least it wasn't Liverpool. We finished seventh that season, nowhere near good enough considering what we had achieved. But I remembered where we were three years earlier. Expectations in Nottingham were probably unrealistically high. But you couldn't get away from the fact that we won nothing that season and worse, would not have a

European campaign to look forward to. We didn't finish high enough in the League to qualify. At the end of the season another bond with the past was broken when Jimmy Gordon retired. He was replaced by the veteran, Ron Fenton.

Throughout their time at Forest, Clough and Taylor were not content just to bring in players on big transfers. They enjoyed plucking footballers from non-league clubs, such as Garry Birtles or, later, Stuart Pearce. They also liked bringing youngsters through the ranks, like myself and Woody. We were followed by the likes of Peter Davenport, Colin Walsh and Steve Hodge. One of the youngsters who stepped up during this time was Danny Wilson, who would remain a friend of mine. Danny and I often discussed the idea of coaching when we left the game, which was unusual for a young player. Many years later, I installed him as my assistant when I became manager of Barnsley. Some of the fees Forest received when many of the young players who came through the system were transferred were huge. However, we needed immediate results, not future profits.

We didn't get them. The season 1981–82 saw a further decline. It wasn't by much. But at the very top there is only a small gap between success and failure. We did quite well in the first half of the season. Our League form was good and we started making inroads into the League Cup once again. We cruised through the first three rounds against Birmingham, Blackburn and Tranmere. After Christmas it all started to go wrong. It wasn't that we or the management were doing anything different. Success just wasn't happening for us and for once Clough couldn't do anything about it. I was now a senior player and took it upon myself to help youngsters and newcomers whenever I could. I noticed that they looked to me for inspiration more and more. I was always happy in the dressing room, I loved the banter and I knew I could help gee-up the next generation of players. So that is what I did and the manager seemed to appreciate it, although he never said as much.

My efforts didn't help at first. In the New Year we lined up to face Wrexham in the third round of the FA Cup. It was at the City Ground. It should have been a home banker. But that FA Cup hoodoo struck again and Wrexham knocked us out 3–1. We had always been able to recover quickly from defeats in the past but this time we took a knock to our confidence and we went ten League games without a win. Spurs knocked us out of the League Cup and we finished eleventh in the First Division. Once again we couldn't qualify for Europe. The manager was not pleased.

Peter Shilton left in the summer, to be replaced by Hans van Breukelen. It was another piece of the old team to disappear. Perhaps the departure that had the biggest effect, though, was Peter Taylor, who retired to many tears then promptly took the job as Derby manager. I continued talking to many of the players who had moved on. I met up with a few of them on England duty. Woody often told me how great his life had become since his move to Germany. For the first time I started having the odd thought about leaving myself. Also, my contract was up soon.

In early 1980 I embarked on a relationship with Debra, a Nottingham girl who came from the same area of the city – Clifton – as me. We had been virtually inseparable since we first met. She was the reason I wanted to slip out of our mountain hotel after the European Cup Final in Madrid. Two years later we were thinking more seriously about our future. The prospect of marriage was in the air and we both wanted children. It was time to take stock and do what was best for both of us. Before, it had always been what suited me. Now there was more to consider.

In the end, I decided to sign a two-year extension to my contract. Two more years to see if I could help raise the club back up to the very top. Half-way through what was until then another mediocre campaign, Clough seemed to get the old magic working again and we got better and better as 1983 went on. We finished fifth, only two points behind Watford, who themselves were second. Needless to say, Liverpool won the title – for the second year running. While we did poorly in both cup competitions, our disappointments were more than made up for by our League position, which meant we qualified for the UEFA Cup. That was a real achievement for a side with more than its fair share of young players. This was the season I was injured and Kenny Swain came in. After I turned down the loan move to Peter Taylor's Derby I won back my place. My reappearance coincided with the team's revival. I was back.

My final year at Forest was fantastic. I played in virtually every game. Yes, we made early exits from both cup competitions but our form in the League was back to near its very best. We were top goalscorers in the division, with Peter Davenport getting seventeen. We hit five goals on four separate occasions. Our attacking style won over a whole new set of fans. We finished third, which was pretty astounding. Who finished first? Who else? Liverpool, again!

It was in the UEFA Cup, though, that we really shone. We had been out of Europe for two years. I was so proud to be back playing at that level. I was really pleased I had stayed for the extra two years. If I had left when we were at a low, I always would have wondered what might have been. This way, I was again fighting at the top. We put a huge effort into our European campaign. It ended in massive controversy, with Clough stalking the training ground muttering about "conspiracies" and "fucking cheating – again".

There were enough of us remaining from the games against CSKA who felt we still had something to prove in Europe. For our season in the UEFA Cup, the manager was really up for it. During the two years of drought, Clough had often seemed more detached than I had ever seen him in the past. Whether his drinking was getting the better of him I don't know. The prospect of the break-up with Peter Taylor must have also affected him. But when Taylor actually left, after a short period, for whatever reason, Clough was rejuvenated. He promoted people from within to his coaching staff and ruled the roost even more. For the first time, he was succeeding without Peter Taylor by his side.

Routine victories against Vorwaerts of Hamburg and PSV Eindhoven of Holland got us back in the European groove. Then came the dream draw. Forest versus Celtic! First leg at the City Ground! Yes!

At first, things didn't go to plan. Celtic did a job on us and got out of Nottingham with a 0-0 draw. That made them firm favourites to go through. But that was only if you forgot our European pedigree. We were never more dangerous than in situations like this. Having to go away in Europe and get a result. Clough was flying. It could have been Cologne all over again. As we went up to Glasgow, the manager was more relaxed than I had seen him in years. We were back in the old routine, going for walks, not doing much training, drinking at the manager's command. I had been through it all before. Along with a few other senior players, I continued to help the young players understand the ways of the manager and what they had to do to please him.

Before the away leg against Celtic, Clough told anyone who would listen that his new Forest team were as good as before. We were, he said, the "new, improved version." Walking out at Parkhead was the most deafening experience I had known since Barcelona. The atmosphere was absolutely unbelievable. If ever we needed to produce a disciplined performance, this was it. And produce it we did. It was a big effort. We gave a great account of ourselves. I don't think it's an exaggeration to say we played them off the park. In the process we broke their supporters' hearts. Goals from Colin Walsh and Steve Hodge gave us a 2–1 win. Both players had come through the ranks like me. It was a special moment.

Brian Clough once again held court for the world's media. He was the hero. He could do no wrong. He confidently predicted we would win the UEFA Cup.

There is no doubt that Clough had a talent for getting up the noses of the powerful. That was why he had been kept out of the England job when he was clearly the most qualified candidate. He was the kind of character who the men in suits wanted to 'take down a peg or two.' Part of what irked his critics was that the press lapped him up. He was a natural performer and always controversial. His predictions of triumph could not fail to be heard in Switzerland, the headquarters of UEFA.

Clough's pronouncements looked to be coming true as we eased past Sturm Graz in the next round. We were then drawn against the Belgians of Anderlecht in the semi-final. They were a reasonable enough side but we didn't see anything to frighten us. Everything looked to be going according to plan when we brushed them aside 2-0 in the first leg. We were more than confident of getting through to the final. However, in the return leg, everything went wrong for us and matters got so bad that the integrity of UEFA itself was called into question.

First of all let me say that we did not play well in the game in Brussels. Sometimes this happens. Sometimes opponents do better than you on the day. But still, our 2-0 lead from the first leg should have been enough to see us through. In the game, however, the referee – one

Mr. Guruceta – seemed to be making a few strange deci-sions as the match progressed, all of them in favour of our opponents. We were 3-0 down and in danger of crashing out of the competition when Paul Hart scored a late goal which would have won us the tie on away goals. Everyone could see it was a perfectly good goal. Everyone, that is, except Mr Guruceta. We were convinced we had done it. Our celebrations, however, were cut short when, to our horror, the ref ruled out Paul's goal. He disallowed it for no reason whatever that anyone has ever been able to see, either at the time or since. It was perhaps the only occasion when the Forest players questioned a referee's decision. We were, to be honest, outraged.

As a senior player, I thought it right to approach the official. But as he waved me away I gave him a mouthful. I can't remember exactly what I said but it probably shouldn't be repeated here anyway. Of course my inter-vention had no effect on the decision and we were denied our rightful victory. None of us thought it was an honest mistake. Taken alongside other decisions the referee had made, we were sure we had been cheated.

The fall-out from that match is still going on to the present day. At the time, Forest complained to UEFA and they were forced to investigate, although we got the distinct impression they didn't want to. After months, it was admitted by the directors of Anderlecht that they had paid money to bribe the referee. I think it was about £20,000. The appeals lasted years. The directors of Anderlecht changed. Eventually, no punishment of any consequence was handed down. In recent times Forest have been going through the relevant tribunals and courts to try to win compensation for the loss we suffered through that bit of corruption. So far, the club have not received a penny although they continue to press their case. At this rate, Forest may receive something in about fifty years time.

Of course, the biggest way Anderlecht profited from their crime was that they reached the final of the UEFA Cup. It wasn't the first time something like this had happened and it won't be the last. But as the main victims on this occasion, the ejection from Europe probably affected Forest badly for years afterwards.

For me, that season was the end of the line at Forest. It felt so good that I could leave the club on a high. After discussing my future with Debra and a few close friends and family, I decided to pursue new pastures. At about the same time Don Howe got in touch. He was manager at Arsenal, where he had helped win the double as assistant to Bertie Mee back in 1971. He was now back and this time in the manager's chair. Howe let me know he was interested in signing me for the Gunners.

This was a turn up for the book. Arsenal! Wow! The idea of playing for them was fantastic. And I knew the Don from my time with England. What a challenge. The money was good, too, much better than I was getting at Forest. Arsenal were a club for whom I had the greatest respect. They did things the right way. The Arsenal players I met on England duty were always full of praise for the club. Better still, Howe had brought Woody back from Germany and the prospect of renewing our friendship and playing with him again was another reason for considering Howe's offer extremely seriously.

I talked to Debra. We were from Clifton. We were born and brought up in Nottingham. Did we want to go to London? All those people? All those bright lights? Yes we did.

Before that, though, there was the little matter of getting married.

Chapter Eight

LONDON

Debra and I had been together for over four years by the time my transfer to Arsenal went through in the summer of 1984. We were living happily in Nottingham and had built ourselves a good life. But when we talked about moving south, one of the things we both wanted to do was get married. We spoke about it and decided to tie the knot before we departed for London. Unfortunately, we left the details to the point where there wasn't much time to organise the nuptials. I began to panic as the arrangements became more and more complicated and the date for our move to London got closer. And we hadn't told anyone yet.

In the end we threw all the plans out, just went to the registry office in Nottingham and got hitched. Only a photographer was invited to attend. The photographer was the Forest club cameraman, John Sumpter. I told him to bring a friend to be our witness. He brought his brother. Although he acted as a witness to our wedding, I've not seen John's brother from that day to this. I'm ashamed to say that Debra and I didn't tell our parents we were about to be wed, mainly at my urging. For some reason I just couldn't cope with it. Afterwards, we drove first to Debra's parents' house and told them what we had done. They were really great about it and gave us their blessing and their congratulations. When we arrived at my folks' house my Dad was there but Mam was at work. This wasn't how it was supposed to be. Dad seemed genuinely pleased although somewhat taken aback by the news. He too gave us his congratulations, which was lovely. The trouble was I was getting more and more worried when I couldn't get my mother on the phone. At that precise moment she was somewhere in the hospital but no-one knew where. I tried again and again, to no avail. Mam discovered the wedding had taken place when a patient told her he had heard it on the news. It wasn't how I wanted her to find out. In fact I was mortified that it was even on the news. It wouldn't be the last time the press would get to my family with a personal story before I did, as you'll see later. Anyway, as far as the wedding was concerned, you can imagine the stick I got, all of it deserved. I can't totally account for our behaviour, even at this distance in time, but the formalities all seemed to get on top of us, especially me.

My journey to Arsenal began when Don Howe phoned me during the long summer of 1984 when there was no England team in the European Championships. If I remember it right, it was July and we were due to report to Forest for the pre-season any day. "I'd like to talk to you, can we meet?" Howe said, in a cloak-and-dagger sort of way. I pressed him for more information but he didn't want to talk too much on the phone. For some reason or other, I wondered whether it was anything to do with England. After all, it was with England that I had worked with Howe in the past. I found out what was on his mind when he drove up to Nottingham and we met in semi-secrecy at my house. Don looked this way and that, making sure no-one was observing him. When we got into the house he sat down, had a cup of tea as we exchanged hellos and began his pitch. "I want you with me at Arsenal," he said, "and I'm ready to talk terms." He looked this way and that again as though he half-expected someone to be listening at the window or the door. I was flattered. And the thought of working with the Don excited me. I enjoyed training sessions with him when I was on England duty – as much as I enjoyed any training at all, which I didn't. Don was steeped in football, he could remember everything, lots of it from before the war, or that's how it seemed. He was a fountain of knowledge.

The Don told me he had big plans for Arsenal. He was going to make the team an attacking force in the First Division once again. He also made an attempt to sell the club to me, but Arsenal needed no selling. They were a great club. Always have been, always will be. We quickly moved on to other matters like my wages. The contract details were thrashed out there and then and that was it. The days of agents and long, drawn-out negotiations had not arrived in football back then. It was generally just you and the manager. My thoughts went back to the club I was leaving. I had to talk to Clough. So I arranged to meet him just before the lads were due off on a pre-season trip. I told him I wanted to go. Although he at first said I would be a fool to leave, he soon realised I was serious. He was ready to offer me a new contract to stay at Forest but my mind was made up. Eventually, Clough was fantastic about it and allowed me to leave for a reasonable fee – £250,000. Forest were the club that had nurtured me, had taken me on a journey of success and which I had come to love. But I was no longer responding to the ways of Brian Clough. I was also pretty much the last player from the glory days still remaining at Forest and I really needed this new challenge.

Moving to London was fantastic. Yes, I had travelled the world with Forest but it was now time to see whether I could cut it living and working in the capital. It wasn't so much the football, I was pretty sure I could cope with that. No, it was the fact that there are many distractions in a city like London. There is so much to do, and the bright lights had turned the heads of so many people who thought they could handle it. I wasn't going to be one of them. I was happy in myself and my relationship and plunged into my new life with gusto. One thing that really pleased me was the article Brian Clough wrote about me in his column in Nottingham's local newspaper when I departed. "As I see it," he said, "Viv left the club simply because he wanted a change after ten years at the City Ground. And who can blame him? He gave Forest magnificent service." It was also great to know that I would be linking up with Woody once more. Don Howe had brought him brought him back from Germany and intended him to be one of Arsenal's main strikers.

The first thing I noticed that was different at Arsenal

Mam and Dad.

Me and my brother Donald.

Winning my first football award.

The Legendary duo of Peter Taylor and Brian Clough.

Cloughie, not known for pulling his punches, presents me with the player of the year trophy.

Forest team, bikes and all, outside City Ground.

Training with Trevor Francis before Munich final 1979.

Winners of The European Cup, Munich 30th May 1979.

Champions of Europe.

Lining up with the Nottingham Forest Team and European Cup.

The European Cup.

Celebrating at the Player of the Year Awards' Gala with a few mates including
Tony Currie, Peter Shilton, Garry Birtles, John Robertson, Derek Statham,
Cyrille Regis, Laurie Cunningham.

Best ever Forest team voted by the fans: Back row left to right: Ian Storey-Moore,
Kenny Burns, Stan Collymore, Peter Shilts, John Robbo, Viv Anderson, Big Larry
Front row left to right: Martin O'Neill, Tony Woodcock, Archie Gem, Steve Stone,
Des Walker, Trevor Francis. (Stuart Pearce was also voted in, but couldn't attend.)

"Hot shot" defender signs for the Gunners!

Tackling Clive Allen in a heated Arsenal v Spurs North London Derby.

With Pat "God" Jennings and former Forest team mate Tony Woodcock.

Sharing a joke with the great Don Howe.

Shoulder to shoulder with Tony Adams,
one of the greatest defenders I had the honour to
play alongside.

Receiving the player of the month award from
Arsenal manager George Graham.

The Arsenal *Football Club*
Season **1984-1985**

STANDING (left to right), Terry BURTON (Coach), David CORK, Brian TALBOT, Viv ANDERSON, John LUKIC, Pat JENNINGS, Stewart ROBSON, Ian ALLINSON, Colin HILL, Roy JOHNSON (Physio)
SEATED (left to right), Paul DAVIS, Charlie NICHOLAS, Tommy CATON, Raphael MEADE, Don HOWE (Manager), Kenny SANSOM, David O'LEARY, Graham RIX, Paul MARINER, Tony WOODCOCK

Arsenal team 84–85.

was the feel of Highbury when you walked through the doors. It wasn't just the famous 'marble halls'. You could taste the atmosphere of tradition and success in every corner. As I came to understand, this could sometimes weigh heavily on the players. In Arsenal's case, whatever you did tended to be compared to the exploits of the double-winning team of 1971 (before that, I'm told, it was the team of the 1930s but only Don Howe could remember that far back). Now admittedly, the double-winning team were brilliant but it seemed to me that many at the club just couldn't let it go. To them, nothing could ever be as good as that. I think this negative attitude finally began to change after George Graham's championship-winning campaigns in 1989 and 1991 but was only finally laid to rest in the Arsene Wenger era.

If Highbury, with its unique atmosphere, was the first difference I noticed, the main change from what I had been used to was Don Howe's training methods. Under Clough, training, especially during the season, was minimal, with lots of walks and a few five-a-sides. Don Howe was more mainstream. We went for hard runs, trained with weights and were strictly monitored all the time. Luckily for me, I had been exposed to some of this way of doing things with England. Howe was the number two to both Ron Greenwood and Bobby Robson, so I thought I had a good idea of what to expect. Believe me, it was hard. For someone like me who was not the greatest trainer unless it was ball-work, training under the Don was especially difficult.

On my first day at Arsenal for pre-season training, Howe

sent us on a five mile run. What an introduction! All of us started together bar the manager. After four miles I was way, way behind everyone else. I hated long-distance running, especially the cross-country. I was slogging away and doing my best but it was a real effort. Suddenly I heard footsteps and regular puffs of breath coming up behind me. I turned round. It was Don Howe, who had started running forty-five minutes after the rest of us. Now here he was about to overtake me. I had to sprint flat-out over the last hundred metres in order not to be beaten in a cross-country by a sixty-five year-old man who remembered the thirties. I have to say that as prepared as I thought I was, that run was a rude awakening.

The manager told me Arsenal had needed a replacement for Pat Rice at right-back for at least a couple of years. Since he had retired it was something of a problem position. This was what I wanted to hear. I knew I could fill Pat's shoes, and he was good, very good. It all meant my position in the team was secure, at least if I performed as I knew I could. Don Howe had been Bertie Mee's assistant during the double-winning season and he was very ambitious to take Arsenal back to the top. He had got the job after Terry Neill's unsuccessful spell in charge and he seemed determined to bring back the good times. We had some very good players, notably the great Pat Jennings in goal. Pat was as calm, cool and collected as anyone could possibly be. For a goalkeeper, he was like Buddha. In fact we called him 'God'. Not for him the shouting and finger-pointing at defenders when an opponent shoots from 45 yards. Although he was nearing the end of his career when I arrived (he was replaced by John Lukic) some of the saves I saw him make were simply out of this world. One-on-one with a forward he was the best. He could be looking one way, stick a foot out the other way, and save a shot he had no right to get anywhere near. No problem!

Kenny Samson was a left-back of total class. His natural ability never ceased to amaze me and he worked hard on his game so he could make those surging runs up the left flank that were his trademark. He held off a strong challenge for his England place by another very good English full-back, Derek Statham of West Brom, and ended up with over eighty England caps. We had Brian Talbot running the midfield, with Tommy Caton (who sadly died young) and the incomparable David O'Leary at the heart of the defence. Up front with Woody was Paul Mariner, another top striker who had played for England. In addition, the talented Charlie Nicholas was brought down from Scotland to add some flair to the team going forward. On the face of it, we looked like we had a solid enough side to push for honours.

Charlie had been a sensation at Celtic. As a Glasgow boy himself he was revered on the terraces at Parkhead. He was so, so gifted and the fans loved him for that as much as his goalscoring feats. The year before he came to Arsenal he had scored forty-odd goals for Celtic, which cemented his already huge reputation and brought the club the Scottish League title. As a reward, Charlie told me, the always stingy Celtic board had offered him an increase in wages – of eight pounds a week. We all couldn't believe it. It was such an insult. He would have loved to have continued playing for his boyhood club, but they did absolutely nothing to entice him to stay there. So off he went, into the waiting arms of Don Howe and the five mile runs. Charlie was a catalyst for us. He was the one we looked to, the one who could turn it on, who could produce something a bit special and win us games.

Charlie and Paul Mariner had the two loudest voices I have ever heard. When either of them spoke they could break glass a hundred yards away. It wasn't that they shouted as such, they just had extremely loud voices. They were so loud you couldn't tell what they were saying half the time. If you watch Charlie on TV these days, you'll see that although he's managed to tone it down a bit, that voice still goes some when he gets excited. Whenever Charlie and Paul were together, it was best to stay well clear. One day, for some reason I can't remember, we were training on the Highbury pitch. At Highbury, the dressing room had a window that looked out onto the street. After training Charlie and Paul struck up a conversation by the open window. As one of them bellowed something, so the other bellowed even louder. I can't remember what the conversation was about. It could have been the weather. So loud did their dialogue get we all had to leave the room. We heard later that a neighbour across the street had heard them and thought there was some kind of riot going on. They complained about the noise to the club, who had to explain that no-one was hurt or killed. Either one of the two players could have found a job as a fairground barker if they hadn't been so good at football.

As often happens in football, as soon as I joined Arsenal, we had to play my old club at the City Ground. It was only the second game of the season. I wondered what kind of reception I'd get from the fans. I asked myself if I'd be able to concentrate on the game. I wished I'd had a few more matches for the Gunners under my belt before this fixture came round. In the event, the crowd was fantastic and gave me a great reception. It was an emotional return. Perhaps too much so! We didn't perform too well on the day and Forest beat us 2–0.

That first season was in and out. On our day we could beat anyone but we could also lose to anyone on another day. Inconsistency was our defining characteristic, to the frustration of our supporters, who turned up in fantastic numbers week after week. I remember one Saturday we were away at Villa, who by then had won the European Cup. We hammered them 6–0. The week after that we meekly succumbed to West Brom at home. Don Howe began tinkering, always looking for what he called the "right blend". The Don, a brilliant coach, could often be uncertain when it came to picking his best team, particularly after a couple of bad results. Some of that was because he loved talking football and swapping opinions, some of which became his own. As a manager he didn't always know when to give a player a bollocking and when to put his arm round him. Motivation of players was a bit of a mystery to him. The uncertainty was felt in other ways too. When we got a good result playing poorly, Don was never sure whether to praise the result or get on our backs for the performance. Everything had to be black or white. When there were shades of grey, which was a lot of the time, the Don was lost. In the end it did for him. If there was one thing George Graham brought to Arsenal it was the certainty that he, George Graham, and he alone, knew who the best eleven were and how they should be treated.

I was pleased with my own performances under Howe and I was generally left out of much of the criticism the team took from the papers, which, when you are a huge club like Arsenal, dissect every error, every point dropped. I knuckled down to the harsher training methods and made sure I never slacked, even for a moment. My attitude began to pay off as I put in some of the best displays of my career. I settled into the Arsenal way of doing things easily and soon felt I had been there all my life. I only missed three games in three years.

I got my first goal for my new club at the end of September, in a League Cup game against Bristol Rovers, which we won 4-0. Somehow, I found myself bounding forward as the great Graham Rix put in a perfect cross from the left. I continued into the six yard box and I nodded it in. Simple!

Debra and I also settled well into life in the capital. There were dinners at the best restaurants and hours spent at the most famous night clubs in the world. I was never a playboy or anything like that – and more often than not when I went out I would be accompanied by my wife – but I think it's fair to say that both of us loved the London life. We took to it like ducks to water.

Clubbing would sometimes prove to contain more drama than football. One Friday night (we had no game that Saturday) Debra and I were at Tramps, partying with Simon Le Bon (the singer of Duran Duran) and George Best. Now wherever you went with Bestie, you could be sure the drink would be flowing. This particular night was no exception, in fact George seemed to be drinking more than ever – if that was possible. By about 5am he was paralytic. Then he let us know he wanted our attention and tried to make what turned out to be a slurred announcement. "I'm supposed to be getting married today," he said. At first we didn't believe him but it soon became clear he was serious. He was actually due to marry his fiancé, Angie, later that morning. "What are we going to do with him?" Simon asked. Debra said we had to get him into some kind of better shape. So Simon Le Bon, Debra and I tried to get him sobered up, at least to the extent that he would be able to make it to his wedding. This was easier said than done with George, who had more ways of finding an alcoholic beverage than anyone I've known. We tried coffee, we tried walking him about. In the end, the task proved impossible. George passed out and that was it. He failed to show up for his own wedding. Thankfully, he did manage to make it for the rearranged ceremony, which took place a few weeks later.

Back on the pitch, the season was turning into one of missed opportunities. We just couldn't put together any kind of decent run to challenge for the title. It was all the more annoying because we had good players who were playing reasonably well. Don Howe was providing dossiers on the opposition, not that it did much good. We went over every little detail again and again. By the end of these talks we knew what our opponents had for breakfast. I suppose at Arsenal, the pressure was far greater on the manager than it had been at Forest. There, Clough was king. At Highbury, you always felt the manager's job was only lent out for a limited time. A few bad results and the boss would be out. It wasn't as cut-throat as today, when a manager can be sacked only a few matches into a season, but at the big clubs in those days there was always speculation concerning the manager's position if the team was faltering. And always there was pressure to win.

The effect of the detailed attention on the opposition was that we became a bit more defensive than necessary at times. This was not what Howe wanted. His instinct was to encourage us to attack at every opportunity. But we became known as a team that first of all looked to stop our opponents from playing. It was around that time that the 'boring Arsenal' tag became commonplace. I didn't think we were boring – how could we be with Charlie Nicholas in the team – but we certainly did not find it easy to play the expansive football that Don Howe craved. More often than not, we were praised for keeping clean sheets far more than we ever were for producing a great piece of skill or scoring a wonderful goal. The Don had wanted his Arsenal to play flowing, attacking football. But instead our reputation was for organisation and a good defence.

It's funny but my own performances were top-notch all season, in a team that was stuttering at best. The problem was that, despite the dossiers and the hard training, the manager chopped and changed our team and our system depending on what his thoughts were that week or how the opposition was set up. Often, we would have no idea of our likely formation week to week. At a club like Arsenal, the team was expected to challenge for League titles and lift at least a cup every season. So our League finish of seventh (Everton won it, thirteen points clear of Liverpool) and our poor showing in the cups – which might not have been a bad return at some clubs – was not good enough for Arsenal. There would have to be a big improvement.

Chapter 9

COMETH THE HOUR

At the beginning of my second season at Arsenal, Don Howe's assistant, John Cartwright, decided to alter our style of play completely. It was a most un-Arsenal type of change and it didn't bring the required improvement. For a few seasons, the English football world had marvelled at the way Graham Taylor had lifted Watford from the depths of the old fourth division to the heights of the first, where they finished second and secured a place in the UEFA Cup. They had also reached the FA Cup Final in 1984 although they were beaten by Everton. All in all, Taylor had performed wonders at Watford. There were arguments, though, over the way that success had been achieved.

The problem was, football purists – and I would include myself in their number – thought that Watford's system was old-fashioned, not to say Neanderthal. That is, they played long balls up to the front players – particularly Luther Blissett – in what was termed the direct style. In this method, the midfield was often bypassed as defenders hoofed the ball upfield. Even with two wingers of pace and skill, one of them John Barnes, Watford more often than not continued to overuse the long ball. It was, at best, a percentage game. At its worst, it was ugly anti-football. The problem was that in England, it was proving to be very successful and it provoked huge debate within the game and in the media. At Watford, although Taylor played with wingers, it is for the long ball that he is most remembered.

John Cartwright and Don Howe became convinced that this was the way Arsenal should play. Now while it is acceptable for teams who cannot afford to buy the best players to adopt this sort of tactic, for Arsenal and the club's fans it was beyond the pale. Arsenal supporters were used to seeing midfield players of the calibre of Liam Brady pulling the strings. Neither our midfielders nor our forwards, both of whom had to change their game, were best pleased. Charlie Nicholas suffered most. His whole game was based on his skill when the ball was played to his feet. He was no good when he had to run down the channels all day. Brian Talbot, who had learned his football under Bobby Robson at Ipswich, and Steve Williams, who had been bought to bring his midfield skills to the team, both expressed their strong disapproval, as did Graham Rix, our wide player on the left. Indeed, Williams voiced his discontent at every opportunity and was dropped from the side.

I didn't like these tactics, I was used to playing in tandem with right-sided wide players and had become adept at using the space they provided. I also liked looking for a pass, short or long, playing out from the back. Now when I got the ball I was expected to bang it up into the channel or onto the heads of the forwards. That left little opportunity for crafting attacks through the opposition's midfield. It wasn't as bad for us full-backs, though, as it was for the likes of Steve Williams, who found his particular talents were almost worthless in such a style. Although I told the Don I didn't like it, I felt it was my job to play in whatever style the manager dictated and I was, after all, paid to get on with it and give it my best shot, which I did.

That season, 1985–86, was again one of treading water for Arsenal. The fans weren't too pleased and attendances at Highbury started to dip. In fairness, this wasn't just a problem in North London. Throughout the 1980s, terrace hooliganism had been getting worse. The terrible events at the Heysel stadium in Brussels, when a clash between Liverpool and Juventus supporters at the European Cup Final resulted in many deaths, sent a signal to the decent fan that football stadiums were dangerous places to be. English clubs were banned from playing in Europe. It was a bad time. For a while, football lost its place in the hearts of those who made up its huge mass of support. There was even the prospect that the game would wither on the vine and die. It is difficult to imagine now, but during that season, football was no longer shown on television as the two big companies, BBC and ITV, refused to screen it.

At Arsenal, the malaise was felt hard. We were a club in the best traditions of English football. We had players who would draw big crowds anywhere. But during this period, it seemed like our performances on the pitch mirrored the disillusion of our fans.

Liverpool lifted the title (again), by two points from Everton, who had won it the previous season with a great side put together by Howard Kendall. They were denied their opportunity to test themselves in Europe because of the ban. I know it always rankled with Peter Reid, because he told me. I don't know how I'd have felt if I had won the League then been unable to go into the European Cup and have those fantastic experiences. Through no fault of your own! I sympathised with Peter and the rest of his team.

Whether or not there was a ban on English clubs in Europe, Arsenal wouldn't have made it into continental competition anyway. We finished seventh. Again! Even West Ham were above us. That meant there had been no improvement on the previous season. That is simply not good enough at a club like Arsenal. We had a tilt at both the FA Cup and the League Cup, but after starting well we were knocked out of both competitions at the quarter final stage. In the FA Cup we went out to Luton after a second replay, while in the League Cup Aston Villa beat us 2–1 in a replay at Highbury after we had gained a hard-fought 1–1 draw at Villa Park. It wasn't why I had come to the club.

Don Howe was a good coach, there is no doubt about that. I experienced his methods with England and Arsenal and I think I can say he was second to nobody in his coaching skills. As a manager, I don't think he developed the necessary feel for the top job. Perhaps also his best days were behind him. Put it this way: at the end of the 1985–86 season change was in the air. The Arsenal board needed a new man to take them back to the level they expected of their team. They also needed someone who could galvanise the club's fan-base.

George Graham had played in the double-winning team. He was, by all accounts, an extremely cultured and mild-mannered midfield player, one of only a few to have played for both Arsenal and Manchester United (I would become a member of this select club soon enough). He also played for Chelsea. When he was nearing the end of his career at Crystal Palace, Terry Venables convinced him to become a coach. His first managerial job had been at Millwall, where he excelled. He arrived at Highbury with the coaching reputation of a defensive-minded disciplinarian. I don't know how or when the transformation from stylish football player to tough, no-nonsense manager occurred, but I will say this: it was always hard to swallow the line that Graham was as nice a player as he would have us believe.

When he arrived, Graham showed great skill in dealing with the departure of Don Howe. He called us together as a group and looked at us for a few moment with that square jaw of his. "I know some of you will be upset that Don has gone," he said. "But all of you now have to look to the future. You have to look forward. I'm here. That's that. Work hard and you'll be OK with me." He said it in that gentle, rolling Scottish tone. It was perfect. It said everything that needed to be said.

He used to tie us defenders up. Literally! The back-four were often roped together in training so that we couldn't be pulled apart from each other beyond a certain distance. So when one moved to the left, we all moved to the left. If you didn't go when the rope was on you would soon be made to look a fool as you slithered around on the ground. Does that make sense? Me neither! However, as time went by, the back four started to develop an uncanny collective move-ment. We became a unit, always sure of where each other was and what we had to do. Unlike at Forest, the full-backs played out wide but just in front of the centre-backs, with the job of stifling anything the oppo-sition tried to do in our area of the pitch. We were supposed to usher our wingers inside so they never got the chance to cross. At Forest it didn't matter if the winger went outside as long as you prevented him from getting a cross in. At Arsenal, George Graham wanted the winger inside before he could go on a run. He didn't want even the smallest percentage that gave the winger a chance to cross. I felt confident enough to challenge him on this philosophy from time to time but, as I said before, it is the boss who dictates the system of play. At least George was prepared to debate the matter with me but I wasn't able to change his mind. We had our ups and downs but I have to say that George was proved right. With the squad he had it was an effective way of playing. At least he knew what he wanted, which was a refreshing difference from the Don Howe period.

Another change Graham made to the defence was to get us to play higher up the pitch. If an opposing midfield player had the ball, our midfield was expected to pressure him. The full-backs would advance up the pitch to stop the ball played out wide. If he tried to knock it over the top we would more often than not catch one of their forwards offside. The only option left would be a pass to another midfield player, where the move could be strangled, or back, where it posed no problem.

Around that time, some very good young players were beginning to emerge from the youth system, including Paul Davis, David Rocastle and Michael Thomas, players who would take the club to new heights. Graham always encouraged the youngsters. He recognised that Arsenal's youth set-up was one of the club's greatest strengths. He gave the rest of the players the respect he felt was due to senior professionals – as long as we were prepared – after discussions if need be – to accept his way of doing things.

The one player Graham didn't seem to rate was his fellow Scot, Charlie Nicholas. It was because of Graham's unwillingness to put his trust in Charlie that the manager became known as someone who had no faith in flair. That wasn't the whole story though. Graham was always obsessed with his team controlling the midfield and having an organised defence. But once that was achieved, he liked to attack with panache. He brought plenty of flair players up front in his time at the club, whether in the transfer market (Ian Wright) or from the youth team (Paul Merson). But, for some reason, he just didn't get Charlie. Now Charlie is the first to admit that when he originally came to London from Scotland he made some bad decisions which gave him what was an undeserved reputation as 'Champagne Charlie'. He never took to staying in a hotel. We both stayed in the same place for a time while we were looking for houses and I always got the impression that Charlie didn't really like it. On the pitch he rarely produced the consistency he should have. It had also been difficult for him when John Cartwright brought in the direct style of play. At the time George Graham came, Charlie's confidence was low. But trust me, Charlie was a special talent, as even Graham would have to admit before the season was out.

One of the youngsters Graham brought through was Tony Adams. When Tony was added to the defence it was obvious from the word go that he would have a great career. It wasn't simply his physical strength that imposed itself on you but his attitude. He displayed an absolute determination to succeed in every tackle. He also possessed another rare quality: leadership.

1986–87 was due to be the last season of my three year contract with the Gunners. It was George Graham's first campaign in charge. I felt I had unfinished business with Arsenal. I had come to Highbury for a number of reasons: the challenge; the money, to play for one of England's great clubs. All played a part. But most of all I came to win trophies and medals. As the new season got underway I really did think we could achieve success with Graham. He had something of the Clough about him. However, I thought it would take at least a couple of years to get into a position to win something – especially since the manager was beginning to put his faith in the production line of young players. I began to think about renewing my contract. I was entering my thirties and knew that my next deal needed to be a good one. Graham indicated that a new offer would be made to me at the end of the season. That could never happen today, where new contracts are sewn up (or not) well before the expiry date of the old one. In those days, even when a player decided to leave at the end of his contract, a transfer fee was payable. That has now changed completely.

We started the season quite well, but it was the period between November and the end of January that really announced the club's revival. During that time we went seventeen League games unbeaten, with thirteen wins. It was incredible. The fans loved it. George Graham loved the fact that we were hardly conceding any goals even more. Arsenal were back. As February dawned we were top of the table. For the first time since I arrived, there was a real buzz around the place.

As the senior player, when I looked around the team, I wasn't sure it was ready to win the League. It was talented, yes, and strong. But it generally takes a bit of time for youngsters to come good. Even when we were top of the table, I felt this. I was as excited as everyone else that we had got this far but I could see the younger players were getting tired at times. That made me redouble my efforts. I was the one who had won the medals. I was the one who had won the title and European Cups. I had to lead by example. The way that young team managed to find the strength to carry on, in that and the following seasons, amazes me to this day.

Our form in the League dipped towards the end of the season. We were soundly beaten at Manchester United, when David Rocastle got sent off following a clash with Norman Whiteside. Somehow, that adversity affected the players more than it should have and we lost five of the next eight games. The other three were drawn. We also went on a goal drought, scoring one in nine. We fell to fourth, which is where we remained until the end of the season. Despite the end-of-season downturn, it was Arsenal's best finish for years. Everton lifted the title once more for the second time in three seasons. What was worse, much worse, for our north London fans, however, was the fact that Spurs had stolen a march under the management of David Pleat and had finished ahead of us in third. This wasn't in the script at all.

Again, our performances in the FA Cup flattered to deceive. I can hardly even remember the games now. I do know that Watford defeated us 3–1 at Highbury in the sixth round and we were out. To this day, the FA Cup is the one medal missing from my collection.

It was in the League Cup that we showed exactly what we were capable of and I can certainly remember that. All of us at the club were aware that we needed to give our long-suffering fans something to cheer. We did that by letting them get their first sniff of a trophy for seven years. It was the League Cup that gave the team the platform to go on and perform great deeds.

Of all our matches on the way to Wembley that year, the one that is most fondly remembered by Arsenal fans is the semi-final victory over Spurs. And remember, this was the Spurs team of David Pleat which reached - but lost - the FA Cup Final that year. They had the country's leading goalscorer of the day, Clive Allen, who hit 49 goals that season. They also possessed two absolutely brilliant talents, Chris Waddle and Glenn Hoddle. They were hot favourites. We were a young side. Also, some of our best players, including Charlie Nick and Graham Rix, had suffered injuries throughout the season. But this was Spurs. It meant an awful lot.

We lost the first leg at home by a slender margin, 1-0, with Clive Allen scoring their goal. That was a deflating result. Spurs fans were cock-a-hoop, ours dejected. If Spurs were favourites before the game they were now odds-on. The manager didn't panic though. He told us we could still win, that we hadn't played too badly. Somehow, his belief transferred to us.

As the second leg unfolded at White Hart Lane, Allen again scored and Spurs were in control. To all intents and purposes, we were out. It was simply a matter of playing out time, surely. We would have to pull something big out of the hat if we were going to turn this round. That night, though, that steely determination that George Graham had begun to instil was running through the side.

I played a massive part in our revival in the tie. It was probably the best thing I ever did for Arsenal. I went up for a long throw from David Rocastle, hoping to steal in unnoticed. The ball eluded everybody except big Niall Quinn who got a head on it. The ball landed at my feet. I forced it into the net. That lifted the whole team. We were on top and Spurs began to look jittery. In the blink of an eye, Quinny got his toe to a ball, and he swept it into the net. Cue pandemonium. The crowd went berserk. The players went wild. We were 2–1 up at their place and the tie was all-square.

That goal broke Spurs and energised us. It meant the game would go to extra time. We pressed and pressed during the extra thirty minutes but could not make another breakthrough. Spurs also had a couple of chances. I think both sets of players were drained at the end. I described my goal again and again to everyone after the game. The forwards got fed up with me telling them they couldn't hit a barn door. I was in heaven.

In those days there was no away goals rule in the League Cup so we had to go to another replay. The venue was chosen by the toss of a coin and Spurs won it. So it was back to White Hart Lane for the decider. The atmosphere across North London was electric. Everywhere I went – shopping, in petrol stations, at restaurants, in the streets – members of the public would either be congratulating me and urging me on (if they were Arsenal fans) or telling me we would lose big-time (if they were Spurs).

Yet again, Clive Allen was the danger man. Rarely can someone have scored three goals in a cup tie and ended up on the losing side. He put Spurs in front. First blood to them. Their fans seemed to settle back, ready for the win. But we conjured an equaliser from Ian Allinson and it was game on. The tension inside White Hart Lane was incredible as the match approached its climax. Inside the last ten minutes, we went forward and the young David Rocastle put us ahead for the first time in the tie. We had been playing for 250 minutes and now, at last, we were in the lead with just a few minutes to hang on. Gone was the recent downturn, we were now on a roll. Spurs gave it a go and we had one or two scares but we powered into the final. For our fans, it was a double celebration. Not only had we reached a major final for the first time in some years, we had beaten their greatest enemy to get there.

As I mentioned earlier in this book, games between Forest and County were never what you would call proper derbies. Arsenal and Spurs, however, is the real thing, one of the best. I loved playing in games against them. When I scored that goal – one of seven I managed that term – I fully realised what it meant to the fans. I was the toast of our half of north London for weeks. What's not to love about that?

Having said that, for me personally there was another game on the road to Wembley that meant an awful lot. It was the fifth round tie in January 1987 against Nottingham Forest. It was one game, winner take all, at Highbury. In the three years I spent at Arsenal I was never on the winning side against Forest in the League. I didn't like that. I wanted my new team to beat them. Any professional feels the same, that's why you often get great performances out of players when they line up against their old clubs. But for Arsenal, I either lost or drew every game against Forest. Except for that League Cup tie. We were superb that night, it came in the middle of our unbeaten run and we walloped them 2–0 in front of a capacity crowd. Stuart Pearce missed a penalty. Our goals were scored by Charlie Nick and Martin Hayes. The fans were back now as well. They were buying into George Graham and the team in a big way. It was a fantastic turnaround from the nowhere days of Don Howe.

And so to the showpiece at Wembley. Against Liverpool (aaaargh)! I was in my element, letting the youngsters know exactly how I'd knocked the Scousers out of the European Cup single-handed, as well as seeing them off in the League Cup Final. Liverpool – to echo Brian Clough – so what!

Ian Rush put them in front and the crowd waited for the inevitable victory that would follow. After all, it was oft repeated in those days that Liverpool never lost when Rush scored. And until that match it was true. But no-one had told Charlie Nicholas. He at last showed his class. On the biggest occasion since his move to London from Celtic in 1983, Charlie bagged the two goals that won us the Cup. For perhaps the only time, Champagne Charlie had come up trumps when it mattered. It couldn't have happened to a nicer bloke, even if he is Mr. Motormouth at times.

This was what I had come to Arsenal for. To feel once again the thrill of winning. It was obvious to me that this team could really achieve something big in the next few years. I wanted to be part of it. Then I got a phone call from Bryan Robson.

Chapter Ten

FIRST FOR FERGIE

It was the most I could do to keep looking at the floor. There we were on the training ground ready for our normal workout. But Fergie was having none of it. He was not a happy bunny. Sir Alex Ferguson is one of those managers who make it their business to know every little thing that goes on in their club. He does it better than anybody. You can't hide anything from his gaze. When you know him, you understand this way of operating. And there is no escape. So why would you want to hide anything from him? That's how he maintains such a high level of performance in his players. They come to realise there is nothing that he doesn't know.

Fergie felt the need to be aware of what his players were up to when they were on their own time as well as when they were on club business. He had spies and informers all over Manchester who kept him up to speed. If he hadn't been a football man he would have made a great head of MI5. This was the opposite of what I was used to under Cloughie, who seemed to know everything anyway without anyone having to tell him, or George Graham, who simply expected you to follow his commands. For Ferguson, there was no 'own time'. And when anyone transgressed in a way he didn't like he came down on you like a ton of bricks. It was the whole building. His rage was like a hurricane not a hair-dryer.

The problem really was that we were all frustrated. When I was transferred to United, it soon became clear that Ferguson was fed up with the behaviour of some of those he considered over-paid players who were failing to perform. He wanted to infuse his team with youngsters, trained from an early age in the United cause. The trouble with the first crop in the late eighties was that there were some talented individuals but collectively they were not really good enough. Not like the Aberdeen players he had brought through in his previous job, who had conquered Scotland and Europe. Don't get me wrong, there was a sprinkling of excellent players but the team just wasn't producing on the pitch. It would take a couple more years yet before the FA Cup came back to Old Trafford, followed by the Cup Winners' Cup and the incredible success that came in its wake.

Anyway, on this occasion on the training ground, it seemed the young Lee Sharpe came in for the most criticism, although I think it fair to say that Lee was a bit of a pussycat compared to Norman Whiteside, Bryan Robson and me. Now Robbo could (and did) put his drink away, mostly with Norman Whiteside and yours truly. Lee wasn't in the same class. But we all felt the vicious side of Fergie's tongue at one time or another. We often got grassed up for drinking and staying out late. This time, having heard about a drunken binge the day before, Fergie had obviously had enough.

If I remember it correctly, Fergie started by berating all of us as time-wasters. Moreover, he bawled: "You are time-wasters who can't hold your drink. You wouldn't last five minutes in Glasgow." Looking at Sharpey, the manager's eyes narrowed. Then he exploded. The rant lasted a good five minutes. All I can remember of it were the last few words. "As good as you are I've got someone better in your position. And he doesn't drink. If you're not careful, next week he'll be in and you'll be out." None of us, least of all Sharpey, thought he was serious. Then we saw Ryan Giggs ....

I was Alex Ferguson's first signing for Manchester United. I was also the last player to be transferred from Arsenal to Old Trafford, the previous one being George Graham. The move came out of the blue. I had been all set to negotiate a new contract at Arsenal when I got the call from Bryan.

"Your contract's up isn't it?" Robbo enquired.

I had roomed with Robbo on a number of England away games and he and I discovered we had similar ideas on the way football should be played and the way players should be motivated. Robbo was dubbed 'Captain Marvel' by the media for his no-holds-barred style. But he was also an extremely gifted footballer. Sometimes this got overlooked because of his all-action approach to the game. I identified straight away with his views: they were the same as mine. Robbo was never content simply to be a player; even for England he made sure he always had his say. At United, he was extremely proactive. When Ferguson arrived from Scotland, he was shrewd enough to recognise that Robbo could be an asset over and above what he contributed on the pitch.

"Yeah, but the boss said I'd be offered a new one," I replied.

"Look," Robbo continued, "The manager said he needs a right-back. He also said he wants some proper experience. I told him you were the man. He agreed. I said I'd phone you to see what your situation was."

Was this real? I thought. "Come on Robbo, you're having a laugh," was the best I could manage. I was thirty-one years old. Now here was the greatest club in the land courting my services, through my mate, Bryan Robson.

"If you're up for it, the boss wants to meet you."

"I'm there."

Ferguson had not long been put in charge of United after the departure of Ron Atkinson. He was in no mood to let Manchester United's years of underachievement continue. He bristled with intent. "We need a right-back and you're the one I want," was all he said when I spoke to him on the phone.

I was surprised to say the least. And flattered! In a nanosecond hundreds of thoughts flashed through my mind. I was a United supporter, man and boy; the club had rejected me as a youngster, surely this was vindication, the most fantastic turn of events; if

Arsenal were big, United were massive. I had come to love Arsenal, the way they did things was superb and the intensity of the supporters was never anything less than impressive. And I like to think I gave them three good seasons which helped them to the success they have maintained to the present day. The only club that could have tempted me away was Manchester United. It was personal.

Fergie, would you believe, wanted to meet me at a motorway service station. I was immediately impressed with the way he conducted himself. On top of that he made me a fantastic financial offer. It was far in excess of what I was being paid by Arsenal, and my wages there weren't bad. But more than that, I wanted to play for him.

George Graham was a bit put out when I told him. But there was nothing he could do. My contract was up, I could sign for whomever I liked. If I had been offered a new contract at any time before Robbo's approach I probably would have accepted it. I would have been more than happy to stay at Arsenal. But it never occurred to me that a club of United's stature would want to sign me. After all, I was 31. Maybe it never occurred to George Graham either because he didn't really enter into serious contract talks with me. Perhaps he took it for granted that no club bigger than Arsenal would come in for me so he thought he could bide his time.

George got his own back when it came to the transfer fee United would have to pay. He demanded £450,000, which was ridiculous for a defender of my age. I'm afraid I went public and criticised him in the press. "I accuse George Graham today of sheer greed in attempting to screw a £450,000 transfer fee out of my move to Manchester United," I told the Daily Mirror. "Nearly £500,000 for a full-back who will be 31 next month? Come on, George, you've got to be kidding. Arsenal's demand is extortionate," I continued.

Back then, when a player came to the end of his contract, he was free to move. But a transfer fee was payable. If the two clubs in question couldn't agree the fee it went to a tribunal which tended to split the difference. In the end, the tribunal decreed that United pay Arsenal £250,000 for my services. This meant that the Gunners recouped their outlay on me when I left. Despite the arguments over my departure, I still retain a great affection for the club and its fans. Overall, I really enjoyed my time at Highbury and I definitely helped in the club's revival after years without success.

My manager was now Alex Ferguson. The knighthood came later. I had played under Clough, Howe and Graham. I thought I had seen it all. I had seen nothing.

In the years since he arrived at Old Trafford, enough has been written about Sir Alex Ferguson to fill a large library. His deeds are legendary and his character and motivation have been analysed to death. Just about everyone on the planet has an opinion about him. Scores of players who played under him have had their say, as has the man himself. Let me make this clear. Sir Alex has always treated me – both as a football player and a man – with the utmost kindness and courtesy, sometimes beyond the call of duty.

Let me give you an example. At one point in the middle of my career with United I was becoming more and more frustrated. Injuries had plagued me. I'd be out, get back in for a few games then get injured again. It was something I wasn't used to. And when I did play I didn't do myself justice. The trouble was, the team had not been progressing as everyone had hoped and my poor performances were not helping. I had been picked for a televised game. It was against Liverpool. I don't remember too much about the match, except that I played so badly I was substituted early doors. I was furious, as much with myself as with the decision to take me off in such a way in front of the TV cameras. Without really thinking, I committed one of football's cardinal sins: I ran straight to the dressing room, collected my things and went home, without saying a word to anyone. This you don't do. No-one did it to Ferguson and got away with it. Players were transferred out for less.

My wife Debra almost had a heart attack when she heard the keys opening the front door to our house. She was watching the game on television and naturally thought I was still at the ground. When she saw it was me she was flabbergasted. I couldn't remember driving home, I was in that much of a state. I knew I had done wrong but I was too angry to know how to put it right. It was Debra who convinced me to apologise to the manager. I went in on the Monday and rather sheepishly asked to see him. I was regretting what I had done big-time as I waited for Fergie's reaction. There would surely be fireworks and some severe disciplinary penalty. It might be the end of me at United.

Instead, Ferguson was sympathetic. "I understand your state of mind," he said. "I know you want to do well and you've had some bad injuries." He went on to say there would be no action taken against me. He put his arm round my shoulder. But he let me know in no uncertain terms that if anything like that happened again, "that will be it for you here". Needless to say, nothing like that ever happened again.

At all times he was a gentleman in his dealings with me. Even in the incident with Sharpey I described earlier, Fergie did not turn his wrath on me too much.

Our first meeting after Robbo's call was one of those motorway service stations, Watford Gap or Leicester Forest East or somewhere. Agents were not a force in the game back then. As I have said previously, transfer matters were generally conducted between manager and player. Unfortunately, Fergie had not bought wads of cash but did offer me a lucrative deal, including a substantial increase in the salary I was getting at Arsenal. This was confirmed some time later when I met Fergie and the United Chairman, Martin Edwards, in a hotel in Nottingham. Edwards seemed in awe of Fergie, which was unusual in a Chairman. In my experience, most Chairmen hate their manager. The feeling is generally mutual.

Even if the Gunners had offered me a new contract, it was extremely doubtful they could match the amounts on offer from United. Fergie had been lured from Aberdeen, where he was extremely successful, partly because he was promised the funds to buy the players of his choice by Martin Edwards. I was his first choice. Maybe that's why we have such a good relationship. Anyway, it wasn't just the money. Ferguson let me know forcefully his vision for the club. He pointed to the success in Europe he had brought to Aberdeen. He dismissed United's recent performances as "rubbish" and told me how he was going to make the club great again. There was no doubting him. Where George Graham cajoled you into believing he could bring back the good times, Fergie was just adamant. It would happen. No question. United were not then in the position that they are now. They had not won a League title for over twenty years and had got nowhere in Europe in about as long. Yet I could do nothing but believe him. It was an incredibly passionate sell. I was hooked. I agreed there and then.

At first, Debra wasn't too keen on moving north. She loved it in London, as did I. She even made a good case for staying at Arsenal for football reasons. Arsenal under George Graham, she said, were the team to watch, Fergie had a mountain to climb. No-one had done it at United since Matt Busby. I had to agree. But in the end I couldn't turn Fergie down. To be fair, Debra knew that and supported me. Now, even though we have been divorced for some years, Debra has not taken the opportunity to move back to London and has stayed in the north-west, which she now loves.

It was pleasing to me that much later George Graham said that he wished he could have kept me at Arsenal. He tried lots of players in my position after I departed, including the left-footed Nigel Winterburn, but never found a proper replacement until he signed Lee Dixon. It is comments like that one that become part of a footballer's most treasured memories. After all, George had every reason to resent me after my outburst in the Daily Mirror, even if what I said was true. But he was big enough to give me credit. I was sorry he left Arsenal under a cloud following the 'bung' he received from a transfer fee. In my dealings with him there was never any question of dishonesty. I have witnessed far worse in my many years in the game than anything George Graham ever did. None of their crimes, though, were ever investigated, let alone punished.

Obviously, the team I went into at Old Trafford was not Fergie's side. It was, in the main, Ron Atkinson's construction. Of the players Fergie inherited, one stood out like a colossus. The rock, the player on which the side was based, was the incomparable Bryan Robson. For me, Robbo was the complete midfield player. He could do everything: tackle; track back; pass short or long and he scored goals. His will to win was extraordinary and if a few more of United's players had shown his determination, success would have been guaranteed. The only player who could come anywhere near him at the modern Manchester United is Roy Keane. Keano was lucky in the sense that he had a great team around him and so achieved the kind of success at Old Trafford that eluded Robbo.

Robbo always thought about the game and liked to swap opinions with all the other players all the time. Robbo and I became the greatest of friends. We spent lots of time together discussing tactics: how the team was performing, what we could do to improve, things like that. We also spoke about how we might make a great management team one day. We agreed that once our playing careers were over, if one of us was ever offered a management role, the other would come along as well. Some years later, as most football followers will know, I answered the call to be Robbo's number two at Middlesbrough.

There were some good young players coming through at United. Norman Whiteside was the first and the most notable. Unfortunately for him, his knees could not take the pressure put on them and continually gave him problems. It was because of this that he never really fulfilled his undoubted potential. He was a superb player when he was fit, so powerful and full of menace for opposing defenders. There were others too, like Mark Robins, who scored a memorable goal in the FA Cup against Forest in 1989–90, which, many say, kept Fergie in his job when things were looking bleak.

Debra and I had not long moved into a new house in Hertfordshire when the call came from United.

It took some time to organise a move north. In the meantime, I commuted up the motorway or stayed in hotels. That is not the best way for a footballer to live but sometimes it is a necessary evil. I was never fazed by that kind of situation. It wasn't what I would have liked in a perfect world but I made the most of it. Some players completely lose their form after a few weeks in a hotel. The best managers try to take this into account, even though it's not always easy. All the time I was living in the hotel, Fergie did his best to make me feel at home. Once again, he was proving as good as his word.

The one thing Fergie always seemed to want to achieve was good, attacking football in the Manchester United tradition. He was proud of the way his Aberdeen side not only won, but won with real style. This is one of the reasons the crowd took to him. It was never enough at United merely to win. Like a handful of clubs around the world – Real Madrid for instance – the United fans demanded their team play with flair and entertain them. I could understand this; they had, after all, been brought up on the Busby Babes, then the great team of Best, Law and Charlton. I would have been the same as a supporter. But I had been schooled in the ways of Clough and Graham and I saw winning as the only thing. Of course I would prefer to win with style – who wouldn't – but winning was the primary aim, never mind anything else. It was so long since United had occupied the highest levels of English football that a whole generation of supporters had grown up since they last won the League. To me that had to change. It wasn't as if they had played brilliantly either. For little spells they looked good but it always ended in tears.

Fergie understood all of this. It was his genius that he saw no contradiction in creating a team which could both entertain and win. It took him some years and I was gone by the time his plans came to full fruition. But I believed in his vision. Only Fergie could have seen the value of Eric Cantona and had the nerve to put his faith in him. Only Fergie would have gone into a season with a team brimming with talented kids, as he did with the Beckham generation. Look at the way Fergie supported Bryan Robson's input. His masterstroke with Cantona was to make the Frenchman a kind of father-figure to that young generation, all of whom worshipped him. For my part, I like to think that in my time there I contributed something important to the culture of success on which the modern Manchester United is built.

Fergie's approach can be seen in the difference between defending for United and defending for Arsenal. There was no rigid plan like there had been under George Graham. We worked on defending, yes, but we weren't expected to play the other side in one fixed way. We had to improvise a bit and we were expected to get forward at every opportunity. Attack was as important as defence, not merely a bonus. And we didn't look to play the offside game which was such a feature at Highbury. It was also a more open approach than had been the case at Forest. There, I would know where everyone was on the pitch at any given time. Under Fergie, for instance, my wide player, who should have been in front of me when I got the ball, was often somewhere else entirely. It took me a while to adjust. But it was exciting. To play this way, though, good players were required in every position.

This won't surprise you. In Alex Ferguson's first seasons at United (mine as well), Liverpool, with John Barnes recruited from Watford, won just about everything. The only relief came in the FA Cup when they were the hottest favourites for years but got beaten by the other long-ball gurus of English football, Wimbledon. Liverpool's persistent success niggled with Fergie even more than it did with me. Finishing second to them in my first season at United should have been a source of pride but I'm sure Ferguson seethed. Second. Not bad to most. To Fergie, nowhere!

It was no surprise to me that some years later he ditched his plans to retire. When anyone asks what could possibly continue to motivate him, now he has won two Champions League trophies and any number of domestic honours, you could do worse than tell them that more than anything he wants to beat those eighteen Liverpool titles. He has a burning desire to vanquish the Anfield dragon once and for all, like Forest did in the European Cup. In his darkest days when he faced the sack he was continually confronted with Liverpool's success, not just on the pitch but as a club. Liverpool always gave the impression of being morally superior to everyone else. I don't know how they managed it but they did. What better climax to a career could there be than doing what for years was believed could never be done and overthrowing the Scousers' record. This, I believe, is what drives him on. He is already immortal.

Fergie allowed a culture of alcohol at United. Where Clough had encouraged social drinking and Graham had simply expected his players to regulate their intake, Fergie's Glaswegian roots and old-school career made him tolerant to the point where it sometimes got out of hand. That was when he would come down like a ton of bricks as in the story at the beginning of this chapter. I'm not sure whether this did any of us any favours in the long run, but then Fergie's record speaks for itself.

I don't think Fergie actually approved of his players' drinking habits. In his autobiography he said that when he first arrived at United he was shocked to discover the extent of the drinking. However, he also admits that he didn't want to impose a complete ban and let players – Paul McGrath was one – promise to give up the booze without actually doing it. It was the one area where he sent out mixed messages. He didn't like it but he never stopped it. Maybe that's why he needed his spies.

As I went into my first season at United, all those type of thoughts could not have been further from my mind.

What I wanted was to show what I could do on one of the greatest stages in the world of football. I could not have imagined some of the dramas that were about to occur at the club.

Chapter Eleven

UNITED

The team I joined at Old Trafford was a work in progress. Alex Ferguson had arrived the previous season after the reign of Ron Atkinson failed to reach the goal set out for him – winning the League title. It probably wasn't Big Ron's fault: the trophy had eluded United since 1967. During the initial half-season Fergie spent at Old Trafford, the team were down to 21st place and were staring relegation in the face. By the end of the season, though, Fergie managed to lift the side to mid-table respectability. That was quite an achievement considering how bad things had got but it was nowhere near good enough for United. The mini-revival towards the end of the campaign, however, ensured that expectations remained high. Most people thought the improvement Ferguson had brought during the second half of the season would be continued and taken forward.

I felt extremely proud that such a high-profile manager had made me his first signing. I also knew I would be the first of many. Sure enough Ferguson soon brought in a number of new recruits, the most noteworthy being Brian McClair from north of the border. Already at United was a player Fergie had discovered, Gordon Strachan. Gordon had been central to Fergie's all-conquering Aberdeen side. He was a busy and skilful midfield player, something United had been missing for a while. For some reason, the manager and Gordon seemed to suffer from some sort of mutual resentment. You could feel it when they spoke to each other but neither of them let on what exactly the cause was.

During the course of the season, Fergie also bought the sixteen year-old Lee Sharpe from Torquay. His transfer fee, said to be £200,000, was the highest ever paid for a player on the Youth Training Scheme. This programme, part-funded by the government to help reduce unemployment among youngsters, was the main route into professional football for the majority of young players in those days. Sharpey was the highest-profile product of the system. He was always likely to come to a big club like United, after getting rave reviews for his performances in the West Country. In December, Steve Bruce arrived from Norwich after some protracted negotiations over his transfer fee, which in the end reached over £900,000.

The players I teamed up with who were already at United were a great bunch of individuals but had not been moulded into a team. Some were outstanding, like Bryan Robson. Others had shown enormous promise, like Norman Whiteside, who was still only 21, although he had been playing in the first team for five years. There was also the old-stager, Paul McGrath, and my team-mate from Forest, Peter Davenport. Jesper Olsen, one of the players Ron Atkinson thought would transform United, was also still around. Jesper captivated the Old Trafford crowd when he was on his game but I don't think he was really a Fergie type of player for whatever reason. It wasn't too long before he was on his bike.

Before I settled in there was a bit of a problem to overcome. When I was at Arsenal, we played a really bad-tempered game against United at Old Trafford. United won it 1–0 but that in itself wasn't really the trouble. It was the sending off of David Rocastle that really rankled. I felt Norman Whiteside had provoked him beyond what was acceptable. David was a teenager and although he was only a couple of years older, Norman was far more street-wise, having been in the first team since he was a sixteen year-old. He had also played in a World Cup. When Norman slyly trampled on David for about the third time, David reacted, kicked out at Norman and was dismissed by the referee. I was incensed, as were the rest of the Arsenal team. As the game progressed, the two sides went at each other even more ferociously. At one point, while the ball was at the other end of the pitch, I squared up to Norman and, believe, me, I was ready to have him. Norman wound me up even more when he laughed and said: "Hit me, go on hit me, I'd love you to hit me." He knew that if I did, I too would be sent off and Arsenal would be down to nine men.

Something inside stopped me from laying him out. But I was still fuming. It kicked off again in the tunnel at the end of the match, with more players joining in and Norman again coming on strong. It was an unsavoury encounter. And I felt Norman was the main contributor to the mayhem.

When I was next on England duty and met up with Robbo again, I took him aside and gave him a mouthful. "That Whiteside," I said to him, "he's a fucking wanker." Robbo laughed until he saw I was deadly serious. "Norm didn't mean anything by it," he said, "I bet we've both done worse in our time." I wasn't too sure.

Fast-forward to my first appearance at the United training ground. Robbo, the captain of the side, was the undisputed leader of the players at United off the pitch as well as on. He was involved in many behind-the-scenes activities, as I think you will know from his part in my transfer. Anyway, on that first day he took the trouble to introduce me to each member of the squad individually. When we got to Norman, Bryan suddenly turned to me and said: "Tell him what you said to me about him, tell him what you think of him." I was a bit embarrassed but I had to repeat my insults and why I made them. In response, Norman stood his ground. We indulged in a bit of banter and left it at that. However, the atmosphere between us remained strained.

A couple of weeks later Norman approached me after training. "Listen," he said, "let's try and sort this out. Let me take you out for a drink. I know a great pub down the road where they serve the best bitter in Manchester." I was impressed that the youngster had made the first move. So off we went for a drink.

I think it's fair to say that the modernisation of pub interiors that had been taking place across the country for a few years had passed the Pamona Palace on the Chester Road by. It had sawdust on the floor and you could imagine the spittoons hadn't long been removed. Its customers fitted the place perfectly. They looked like they'd kill you as soon as look at you. There were more tattoos than in a Hannibal Lector film. Norman seemed quite at home.

"Two pints of bitter please," he said.

"Can I have some lime in mine?" I asked.

Uproar!

Having lime in your beer not only insulted the so-called 'best bitter in Manchester' but was also badly received by the other customers in the bar. To them, no man had lime in his beer. Ever! They started making noises. Norman saved the day by telling them I had been ordered to dilute any alcohol I drank by the manager. He said it was to get me fit enough to play for Manchester United. They appeared to accept his explanation. Norman and I had a right laugh when we left the pub. The ice was broken.

From that day to this, Norman and I have been the best of friends. I have spent some great times with him and I've been skiing with his son. After we both retired I helped with a golf tournament that bears his name.

There were never any problems between us again. Fair play to him for taking the bull by the horns and trying to sort out the bad feeling between us.

It was still the old days. I had seen – and been part of – drinking sessions at Forest and Arsenal, but they were nothing compared to what went on in Manchester. On a given day, often the Monday following a Saturday match, Robbo would declare that after training he wanted all the players to come along to what he called a 'team meeting'. Everyone had to attend, even the overseas players who weren't used to it. These 'team meetings' would take place at various bars and drinking clubs in the centre of Manchester. We didn't favour one place over any other. We tried them all. We would be there all day and sometimes into the evening and beyond.

Now, when footballers get together they tend to talk about – football. Even when they are pissed. Robbo would instigate discussions on what we were doing wrong on the pitch, what we were doing right and what we could do to improve. Everyone was expected to have their say. Sometimes the chat centred on one person's perform-ance. Other times we were fixated on the team and our roles in it. The more we drank, the more we knew how to win the League.

These sessions may seem crazy now. But back then society was different, not just football. Then, more or less everyone drank and there was something suspi-cious about you if you didn't. There is no way that could happen today. The drinking culture is not what it was in football, what with the introduction of scientific measures to test fitness and the modern emphasis on things like nutrition and fluid intake. I don't even drink much myself anymore. Not only that, everybody has camera phones today. If such gatherings as those at Manchester United were going on it would not take long before the press got hold of pictures. They would then be plastered all over the papers, accompanied by unfavourable and lurid headlines. Back then, few knew about our 'team meetings'. One of those who did, of course, was the manager and to him, they must have been useful. He never took measures to ban them. He only didn't like it if he thought we couldn't hold our drink or if we were partying rather than talking football. With his spies all over the place he generally knew what was going on. Although he didn't like it, he tolerated drinking provided it didn't affect performances or bring the club into disrepute in some way.

As I've mentioned before, Robbo was right up there as a drinker. A number of us weren't far behind. Poor Paul McGrath suffered from terrible problems with alcohol. He loved his drink. The trouble was, he only had to have a couple of pints and he was tipsy. After four he was blind drunk. He passed out more times than he passed the ball. It was an accepted part of the day-to-day routine in those days that we would get regularly merry. But the truth is we were always ready for training and always sober on the days leading up to a game and on match day itself. Fergie himself was not a huge drinker, preferring his Bordeaux Clarets to anything stronger. But his background meant he was well up to speed with how footballers behaved and he made it his business to know as many of the details as he needed.

Another thing about the old days: as I wrote previously, crowds had gone down with the rise in hooliganism and the ban on English clubs playing in Europe. Our gates averaged around 38,000 in the League, which was well down on what United had been used to over the years. Our biggest League attendance that season was 48,000 for the game against Spurs. That brought our average up a bit but there was no question the game was suffering. It was big games in the FA Cup that brought out mass support. Today, the opposite is the case, which I think is a shame. It was fantastic to see the crowds flock back in the 1990s but no-one could have predicted that the League would end up as so much more important than the FA Cup. In my first season at United our largest crowd was the fifty-odd thousand that turned up for the FA Cup fifth-round game against Chelsea, which we won. Other clubs were suffering from the downturn too. They also relied on the FA Cup for the really big gates. For instance, the competition provided Arsenal with their largest number of spectators that season, 54,000 for our visit in the sixth round.

We started the 1987–88 season with two draws, 2–2 away to Southampton, when Norman Whiteside bagged both our goals, followed by a 0–0 at home to my old club, Arsenal. It wasn't a great beginning but as soon as we recorded our first win, a 2-0 defeat of Watford, with goals from McClair and McGrath, we picked up big-time.

That season was the best of my three-and-a-half years at Old Trafford. We finished second in the League, with Brian McClair scoring twenty-four League goals, the highest total for the club since George Best over twenty years before. Unfortunately, that would not mean we could play in the UEFA Cup because of the European ban. The worst thing was – you've guessed it – Liverpool secured another title, nine points ahead of us. We drew both games with them that year, with the match at Anfield being remarkable because we came back from 3-1 down at half-time to level the score at 3-3. We were never really in with a realistic shout of finishing first, though. Liverpool were just too good, although it hurts me to say it. Forest took third spot, eight points adrift of us.

Although everyone knew Liverpool were on a different plane to the rest of us – they had the team of John Barnes and Peter Beardsley – finishing second led the supporters to think we would be in a position to mount a serious challenge to the Scousers the following season. However, the good times had to be postponed for a while as we went backwards in the next campaign. Still, the feeling among the players and the management was that it was only a matter of time.

Norman Whiteside was suffering a bit that year, although he weighed in with his fair share of goals.

His build meant that his body was under too much stress and his form and fitness began to suffer. The Old Trafford pitch was a quagmire back then. You couldn't play football on it. It was that bad. So Norman had to chase long balls, win headers and scrap. He was always willing but it did his body no favours. It got so bad that half-way through the season he opened a rift with the manager by asking for a transfer, which the rest of us didn't know about at the time. It was not granted by the board but the writing was on the wall for Norman. He was a likeable guy and a very good player. Had it not been for his physical frailties he would have been a great. As it was, it would not be too long before he was shipped out to Everton and was never the same force again.

As I said, the FA Cup provided the huge crowds. They were games which produced the most fantastic atmosphere. Having beaten Chelsea, we were confident of getting a result at Highbury. I once again looked forward to visiting one of my old stamping grounds. This was especially true with Arsenal as I looked on the club as the place where my career had taken off for the second time. I think I had exorcised any Forest ghosts by then. We didn't do ourselves justice on the day, though, and we lost 2–1. There was to be no FA Cup run that season. As for the League Cup, we made it to round six before going out to an Oxford side who were then in the top flight. It is hard to imagine today since Oxford are no longer even in the Football League, let alone the First Division. In those days they were riding high and actually won the League Cup in 1986.

I made thirty appearances in the League that term. My personal highlight was when I scored my first United goal, the opener in a 3-1 victory over West Ham at Old Trafford in March. I also got on the scoresheet in the away League game at Oxford, which we won 2-0.

But it was the twelve games in which I didn't play that proved to be an omen. It was the beginning of a period for me the like of which I had not experienced before in my career: a prolonged spell of being plagued by injury and out of the team.

Alex Ferguson took many things into account when he signed a player. Would the player fit into the team well? Could he make the step up to the plate and perform for a big club like United? What was his character like? That type of thing. One of the manager's most important considerations was how many games you had missed through injury. He believed that some players, no matter how good, were injury prone and he would never get the best out of them. I had missed only three games in three years for Arsenal. I had sustained only one major injury in my career – the dislocated knee which I got on England duty while I was at Forest – so I was a very good bet indeed.

Halfway through my first season I got kicked on the heel during a game. I can't remember the exact circumstances. What I do remember is that the pain was terrible and would not go away. More often than

not I couldn't train and could only play with corti-
sone injections. Sometimes it was so bad I couldn't
put my foot down. When I failed to respond to the
attentions of the club's medical team, I went to a
series of doctors and hospitals to find a cure. Lots
of different treatments were tried, including radio-
therapy. Nothing worked. At one consultation I was
told that bone fragments had become detached and I
needed an operation. Then a doctor informed me that
scar tissue resulting from the operation could make
matters worse. I didn't know what to do. The injury
just wouldn't heal. I was on the verge of having the
operation. Just before I was due to go under the knife
I was referred to Dr. Basil Hallal, who was doctor
to the British Olympic team. He said he thought it
might be a simple problem and prescribed a course
of anti-inflammatory tablets. Within forty-eight hours
the pain had reduced by so much I could jog for the
first time in months. It was remarkable. But it made
me wonder why none of the other medics who had
examined me could find out what the real cause of
the injury was. I was very grateful to Dr. Hallal. I was
still not a hundred percent pain-free but I made it to
the end of the season and hoped that by the next pre-
season, I would be over it. It didn't quite work out
that way.

After reporting back for pre-season in July, everything
seemed to be OK. I had no pain in my heel and felt good
about going into the new season. Then one day, after
training, I was doing some ball-work by myself. I think I

was tired and shouldn't have been doing it. I heard my knee go. I knew what it was. I had done it before and that time I was out for months. I had dislocated my knee. Again!

The following season, 1988-89, I managed only five starts in the League. It turned into the worst season of my career. I was continually on the treatment table and putting in rehabilitation work. I know it all helped in my eventual recovery but at the time it seemed to be making no difference at all. I think I became a bit depressed. I saw the guys most days and, even if I couldn't participate, they always made me welcome. That was important as it kept me feeling included and stopped any depression in its tracks. Fergie encouraged me to remain part of the squad and go to all the games. He always made time to ask me how I was coming along. I appreciated the manager's way of dealing with it, I can tell you. It was still, by a long way, the most frustrating part of my career.

In the time I was out of the side, United's performances on the pitch became erratic. The outlook was so promising at the start. The great Mark Hughes came back from Barcelona, via a stint at Bayern Munich. His return was welcomed by players and fans alike. He was a legend at United and everyone fully expected him to pick up where he had left off: scoring goals and making a nuisance of himself to opposing defences. We heard rumours – which found their way into the press – that the young Newcastle prodigy, Paul Gascoigne, was coming to United. Fergie told us that Gazza was "99% sure" he would be joining us at Old Trafford. Then suddenly, out of the blue as far as we were concerned, he decided to join Spurs. There's been a lot of comment over the years as to whether Gazza – given his problems – would have been better served coming to Old Trafford. Who can say, but I do think he was one of those individuals who succumbed to the distractions London has to offer to a well-paid young man.

The team did manage a couple of good spells that season. They got themselves up to third in February. Fergie was determined to try the crop of youngsters he had at his disposal alongside the more experienced players like Sparky Hughes and Robbo. During the campaign, the manager gave the seventeen-year-old Lee Sharpe his debut, alongside Mark Robins, who I think was only a couple of years older than Sharpey. The one who made the biggest impact, however, was Russell Beardsmore, who stole the show in a game against Liverpool and scored a great goal. He was the toast of Manchester for a time but – skilful though he was – he could never replicate his early great perform-ances. Although these young players paved the way for the great team of the 1990s, it's strange, but all of them faded from the game before their time, for one reason or another.

From third place in February, United's season crashed. Our wins dried up and we dropped like a stone to elev-enth, which is where we finished. That was appalling for a club like United and doubts about Fergie started creeping into the press and onto phone-in shows on the radio. These doubts would turn into a full-blown campaign for his head before too long. I was frustrated that I wasn't fit enough to help out the team, which I'm sure my experience would have done. The players had no doubts about the manager, we believed in his dream. Never once during this dark period did his confidence waver. He was working to a plan, which may have taken longer than outsiders thought it should to work, but Fergie always gave the impression that he knew exactly what he was doing.

Once again, our two biggest crowds of the season were in the FA Cup. First up was a fifth round home tie, not against one of our big rivals, but lower-division Bournemouth. Bournemouth had knocked United out of the competition not many years before so interest in the match was intense. Over 52,000 came to Old Trafford to watch Brian McClair score the winner in a tight match. The game I really wanted to play in but couldn't because of my damn injury was the sixth round tie at home to Forest. This drew a massive 54,000. The noise was deafening from the Stretford End that day. I listened from the stands, tingling. But Forest nicked it 1–0. Our FA Cup dream was over yet again. But not for long!

There was one consolation in what had been an extremely disappointing season for me. My old mates at Arsenal pipped Liverpool to the title in that famous game at Anfield, which they won with a goal from Alan Smith and that late, late strike from Michael Thomas. I could have hugged them. It did make me think, though, if I had stayed at Highbury, whether I would have avoided those injuries and been part of a title-winning team again. Those thoughts did not last too long. As I've said before, football is about the next game, not the last. I had no idea when my next game would be. What I had to do was get fit and hope matters would improve the following season. They did for United, after a few scares. They definitely didn't for me at all.

Chapter Twelve

TRIUMPH AND TRAGEDY

During the summer of 1989 my injury problems seemed to ease a bit. It's one thing to feel OK out of season, though, and quite another to be match-fit for football. The question in my mind was: could I get myself really fit for the new campaign? Having missed so much of the previous season I was desperate to get over my injuries and back in the team. I had been at United for two years and while the first of them had gone well, the second was an injury-plagued disaster for me. As I think you will be aware by now I was never a great one for training. I did what was necessary and I always tried to be enthusiastic but I didn't enjoy it like some players. The worst thing for me was cross-country running, as you'll know from my Arsenal experience. When I ran, I liked to have a football at my feet. At Forest, I was always last when we did a cross-country during pre-season. Larry Lloyd, who was not the quickest I've ever seen, would beat me. At Arsenal on that first day, even Don Howe almost beat me. But this particular summer was different. I had been out for virtually the entire season and I felt I had to do something extra to make sure I gave myself every chance of a successful return. So I decided that I would not use pre-season training to get fit, I would be super-fit by the time pre-season started.

To achieve full fitness I went on cross-country runs by myself. Lots of them! Believe me, they took some doing. I didn't like them but I knew I had to work super-hard to achieve what I wanted – a full come-back. It worked. By the time the players met up I had been training on my own for over a month. The rest of the squad couldn't believe the condition I was in. They had to play catch-up through the whole of July. I breezed through the pre-season and thought I had done enough to impress the manager. I was pretty pleased with myself.

I had also drawn quite a bit of controversy because of a quote I gave to the author, Andrew Longmuir, who had written a book about me published the previous season. In it I said – and I later repeated it to the press – that "If a forward is going through, I'll try to get the ball first, obviously. But if I have to I would upend him. In that case I would expect punishment from the referee." The statement didn't seem to me to be anything particularly out of the ordinary but the authorities didn't like it at all and I had the prospect of FA charges hanging over me for months. In the end, no action was taken. Somehow, the fact that I had been out injured for such lengthy periods made the story more newsworthy. I don't know why. It was really a storm in a tea-cup. It came around the same time as I was embroiled in another massive showdown, this time with John Fashanu of Wimbledon. I'll tell you all about that later. What I do know is that it took me some time to put the matter of the quote behind me.

I was sad when Norman Whiteside was allowed to go to Everton. Norman and I may have got off on the wrong foot but I had come to enjoy his company and appreciate his talent. I liked the way he played the game. He was like an early version of Wayne Rooney when he was on form and firing on all cylinders. But Fergie wasn't satisfied. Not so much with Norman's playing contribution as the state of his fitness, particularly his knees. When he sold Norman it was an example of the manager's methods and the standards he expected. I also wonder if Norman asking for a transfer had anything to do with it. I don't think there was ever any question of Norman's ability but his tendency to suffer from continuing physical niggles meant he was not a Ferguson-type player. He did well enough for Everton but he never recaptured the form he had shown in his early days at United.

Paul McGrath left too, going to Aston Villa, at the time managed by Graham Taylor. He was another player whose injury record was suspect. Everyone thought Paul's combination of bad knees – which left him unable to train on a regular basis – and his fondness for Pernod would signal the end of his time in the game. But Paul proved everyone wrong. At Villa Park he extended his career beyond what any of us thought was possible. Graham Taylor made special arrangements for Paul and let him miss training on a regular basis so he could play in games. I think he also got him a minder to ensure Paul's drinking didn't get out of hand. That would never have happened at United. No-one was more pleased than me that Paul had a great time at Villa and enhanced his reputation as a top-quality defender. He even won more caps for the Republic of Ireland. I knew the examples of Norman and Paul could happen to me if I didn't remain fit. Their experience was a lesson for me. If you were constantly out of the team, it wouldn't be too long before you were out of the club as well. I had become more prone to injury than at any time in my career. Fergie just didn't fancy players who were continually out injured and he moved to replace them as quickly as possible. I was pleased I had put in all that extra training by myself in the summer. But I still feared my time would be called if my physical condition wasn't one hundred percent.

Perhaps the most surprising departure was that of Gordon Strachan, who went to Leeds. He first helped them to promotion then won a League title with them two seasons later in 1991–92. Strachan was an extremely creative midfielder and was one of United's few real successes at the time. He was a busy player with lovely ball-skills and he had been the most important part of Ferguson's side at Aberdeen. We became aware, however, that some problem had developed between Strachan and the manager but we never actually knew what it was. Even if Gordon had told us, we probably wouldn't have understood a word he was saying. Gordon goes into the broadest of Scots accents when he doesn't want to engage. What made this endearing rather than annoying was that he could be extremely funny as well as enig-matic. So we assumed there was some sort of contrac-tual dispute but we never found out what really went on. Both Fergie and Gordon blamed each other for the falling-out, as you can see by reading both of their auto-biographies. Fergie felt Gordon had misled him over a new contract, Gordon denied he had ever agreed to one. It turned out that Fergie believed and supported Martin Edwards, who claimed Strachan agreed to stay at United. He disbelieved Strachan's word – that he had not agreed to anything. Martin Edwards would later repay Fergie for his loyalty with interest. All we knew was that Gordon was gone. His success at Leeds led to comparisons with Johnny Giles, a similar player to Strachan who had left United for Leeds in the early sixties and had become the final piece in the jigsaw of Don Revie's well-oiled machine of a side.

As usual, there were a number of signings both in the summer and during the season. Neil Webb, an elegant midfielder, arrived from Forest and Paul Ince, all combat-iveness and 'up-and-at-em' mentality, came from West Ham. Incey suffered a lot of criticism over his move to United because he foolishly let himself be photographed in a United shirt while he was still technically a Hammers player. Participating in the photo-shoot might have been a bit immature of him but as a player, Incey was second to none. He had a bit of the Bryan Robson about him. He was full of menace. The forward, Danny Wallace, and the ace defender, Gary Pallister, were also added to the squad. But for me, it was the fact that Fergie brought in a midfielder who could also play right-back, Mike Phelan, that began to be a bit of a worry. It occurred to me again that the manager didn't think my fitness and form could be relied upon. I really shouldn't have been surprised. I was thirty-three years old. Maybe my age told against me. I thought I could overcome any physical problems because I had looked after myself as well as anyone during my time in football. Also, earlier on in my career, I had seen off Kenny Swain when Brian Clough thought I couldn't do it anymore. I believed I was good for another couple of seasons at the top at the very least.

The bitter truth is I was never first-choice right-back for Manchester United again. That season I played in only fourteen League games, an improvement on the season before but not what I wanted at that stage of my career. However, I recognised that I had decided to play for one of the biggest clubs in the world and competition for places was bound to be intense. If you were out for a long period injured, then it was just tough. Get over it! It went with the territory. I was one of the senior players and I commanded some respect for that and for my achievements in the game. For my part, I did everything I could to contribute to the team through the encouragement of other players and expressing my opinions. It seemed to be appreciated and I was often sought out by younger players for advice, which I was always happy to give. However, what I really wanted was to play.

Since I went to every game while I was injured, I was in a good position to gauge how the side was performing. I had many talks with Robbo about this. Once again, in my absence, the team was not looking as if it could get anywhere near winning the title. In fact the opposite was the case. One day, Robbo called a 'team meeting'. He was not pleased with some of Gary Pallister's defending and asked me for my opinion. I agreed with him. Poor Pally! As the drink flowed we pulled his game apart, told him he shouldn't be doing this, should be doing that, and generally gave him a hard time. We pointed out the defects we thought he had in his positional play and what he should do to put them right. To be fair to him, he took everything we said on board and went on to become one of the best defenders in the game. Pally wasn't the only one who suffered this treatment. We all went through it at one time or another. It was a way we could get things off our chests and try to take responsibility for our performances. Yes, those meetings were fuelled by alcohol, but we all reckoned we gained a lot from them, as well as a hangover.

The 1989–90 season began with a bang, in more ways than one. Our first match was at home to the Champions, Arsenal. It was good to see players who were so recently my team-mates again, although I was a bit embarrassed by events that day. As for the match, we brushed them aside and won comfortably 4–1. It was a great start against the team who had foiled Liverpool so brilliantly just a few short months earlier. There was talk afterwards that with performances like that we could win the League ourselves this time. But it was what occurred before the match kicked off that preoccupied the nation rather than our magnificent performance. What happened was bizarre. I've never seen anything like it before or since. And, through no fault of our own, it made us something of a laughing stock across the whole country. Some – although not me – said the incident blighted our whole campaign.

I had met our Chairman, Martin Edwards, on a number of occasions. He had been part of my discussions with Alex Ferguson when I first came to the club. He came across as a decent, if somewhat distant man. You could never be sure what he really wanted from his term as owner of the club. His attitude to both the players and the manager, however, was impeccable. He was a real, old-school gentleman. There were those around Old Trafford who remembered his father, Louis, who sounded to me like a completely different type of character – ruthless and uncompromising as opposed to Martin's more reserved way of conducting himself. Along with Matt Busby, Louis created the modern Manchester United. Busby gave the fans the team, Edwards gave Busby the money to pay for them. The two of them oversaw the progress of the club to the position where it was one of the top three football clubs in the world and perhaps the most famous. It was a hard act to follow for any son. Edwards senior died suddenly after a TV programme, *World in Action*, questioned his business methods in gaining control of United in the first place. Upon his father's death, Martin, instead of selling his interests, decided to take up the reins himself.

By the end of the eighties, though, we were told that Martin Edwards had grown disillusioned with his ownership of United and wanted to sell. We didn't pay much attention to the rumours, footballers don't really concern themselves with such things as ownership – unless their wages aren't paid or the best players are sold. None of this was likely to happen at United. And no matter what

Patron:
HER MAJESTY THE QUEEN
President:
H.R.H. THE DUKE OF KENT
Chairman:
SIR HAROLD THOMPSON, C.B.E., F.R.S.
Secretary:
E.A. CROKER

INTERNATIONAL COMMITTEE

R. Wragg (Chairman)	L.T. Shipman, C.B.E.
Sir Matt Busby, C.B.E.	L. Smart
N.W. Hillier	P.J. Swales
E. Kangley	J.C. Thomas
J.B. Mears	J.F. Wiseman
F.A. Millichip	

* * * * * * * *

TEAM MANAGER . . . . R. Greenwood
COACH . . . . W. Taylor (Manchester City)
ASSISTANT COACH . . . . G. Hurst (Telford United)
PHYSIOTHERAPISTS . . . . F. Street (Arsenal)
N. Medhurst (Chelsea)
TEAM PHYSICIAN . . . . . . Dr. P.J. Burrows (Luton Town)
ADMINISTRATION OFFICER . . . . A. Odell

INTERNATIONAL MATCH

ENGLAND

v.

CZECHOSLOVAKIA

To be played at the
Empire Stadium, Wembley
on
Wednesday, 29th November, 1978
Kick-off 7.45 p.m.

ENGLAND SQUAD

1.	R. Clemence	–	Liverpool
2.	P. Shilton	–	Nottingham Forest
3.	V. Anderson	–	Nottingham Forest
4.	P. Neal	–	Liverpool
5.	E. Hughes	–	Liverpool
6.	D. Watson	–	Manchester City
7.	M. Mills	–	Ipswich Town
8.	P. Thompson	–	Liverpool
9.	T. Cherry	–	Leeds United
10.	R. Wilkins	–	Chelsea
11.	T. Brooking	–	West Ham United
12.	R. Kennedy	–	Liverpool
13.	A. Currie	–	Leeds United
14.	S. Coppell	–	Manchester United
15.	K. Keegan	–	S.V. Hamburg
16.	R. Latchford	–	Everton
17.	P. Barnes	–	Manchester City
18.	A. Woodock	–	Nottingham Forest

HEADQUARTERS

West Lodge Park Hotel

Cockfosters Road

Hadley Wood

Hertfordshire

(Tel: 01-440 8311)

ARRANGEMENTS FOR TRAVEL AND ACCOMMODATION

SUNDAY, 26TH NOVEMBER, 1978
ASSEMBLY. All players should make their own arrangements in order to arrive at West Lodge Park Hotel by 6.00 p.m.

7.00 p.m.   Dinner at West Lodge Park.

MONDAY, 27TH NOVEMBER, 1978
10.30 a.m.   Training session at Dame Alice Owen School Playing Fields, Whetstone.

N.B. THIS TRAINING SESSION WILL BE OPEN TO PRESS AND PHOTOGRAPHERS.

1.00 p.m.   Lunch at West Lodge Park.

Arrangements for the remainder of the day will be announced at Headquarters.

TUESDAY, 28TH NOVEMBER, 1978
9.30 a.m.   Depart from West Lodge Park Hotel by motor coach for Bisham Abbey National Recreation Centre, nr. Marlow, Bucks.

11.00 a.m.   Training session at Bisham Abbey.

1.00 p.m.   Lunch at Bisham Abbey.

2.30 p.m.   Training session at Bisham Abbey.

N.B. THESE TRAINING SESSIONS WILL BE PRIVATE.

4.00 p.m.   Depart from Bisham Abbey by motor coach for West Lodge Park.

7.00 p.m.   Dinner at West Lodge Park.

WEDNESDAY, 29TH NOVEMBER, 1978
Arrangements for the morning and afternoon will be announced at Headquarters.

6.00 p.m.   Depart from West Lodge Park by motor coach with police escort for Wembley Stadium.

7.45 p.m.   ENGLAND v. CZECHOSLOVAKIA

Players will be free to disperse after the match if they wish, but accommodation will be reserved at the London Euro-Crest Hotel, Wembley, for any players who wish to stay over the Wednesday night.

SPECIAL NOTES FOR PLAYERS

1. Fitness to play. All players must acknowledge receipt of these arrangements, and signify their fitness to play. In the event of a player being subsequently unfit to play, he must telegraph or telephone immediately to The Football Association.

2. Fees and Expenses. In addition to travelling expenses all players in the squad will receive the match fee of £100.

3. Equipment. Shirts, shorts and stockings will be provided by The Football Association. Players are requested to bring with them athletic slips, shin guards and football boots, which must be properly studded. All players are advised to take with them soap and towels for personal use.

4. Exchange of Shirts. Please note that any players wishing to exchange shirts with opponents after the match should do so after both teams have returned to their dressing rooms and in no circumstances should this exchange of shirts take place on the field of play.

5. Press Reports. Players are forbidden to comment upon the match in television or radio programmes or in Press Reports before or after the game. The Football Association regulations are that players selected to play in International and other Representative matches under the jurisdiction of The Football Association must neither write nor allow to be written under their signature articles in which criticism of match officials or players is expressed, or the result of any match forecast.

16 Lancaster Gate,
London, W2 3LW.
Telephone: 01-262 4542

Ted Croker

Secretary

My debut game for England: England v Czechoslovakia Players FA Match Itinerary Booklet (note the mis-spelling of "A Woodock").

On the training ground with Dave Sexton, the former Chelsea, Q.P.R., Man Utd, Coventry City and England Under 21 manager.

Fred Street examines my damaged knee.

Wearing my first of 30
England caps.

England Senior Squad 1979.

Me, Tony Woodcock and Les (F.A.Security man) look on at Egyptian defender Rabei Yassin and team mate in prayer after the match.

Bobby Robson tests the "pyramid formation", without much success!

Tension brews as we line up before kick off for England. England Tour of
USA/Mexico 1985.

Istanbul 14.11.84 Scoring for England v Turkey.

On the ball for England.

Training session for England.

England team fly out to the World Cup Finals. Luton Airport 1982.

Beating Roy Aitken to the ball. England v Scotland.

Splashing about with John Barnes, Mexico.

Ambassadorial, for England World Cup Bid 2018.

club you are at and whoever is in control you still have to perform the same on the pitch. This time, though, we had no choice but to take notice.

A couple of days before the opening game it was announced to the public that the Chairman had indeed concluded a deal to sell his shares to some bloke we'd never heard of called Michael Knighton. We found out at the same time as the rest of the world, through the media. Knighton, we read in the press, was a businessman who was ready to pay ten or twenty million pounds, or some such figure, to become owner of United. He was also quoted as saying he wanted to invest in the team. United fans were a bit fed up with the Edwards dynasty by then. They felt the Chairman wasn't spending enough on players. So they were ready to take this new owner to their hearts. It was only when we arrived at Old Trafford for the first game of the season though, that we realised exactly what this meant for us.

Knighton came into the dressing room before the match and was introduced to each of us as the new owner. We were all polite as we exchanged pleasantries. Knighton acted like he was one of the players, all enthusiasm and banter. We thought that was a bit strange to start with. Then, out of nowhere, the podgy Knighton produced a bag in which he had an extra-large United kit. "I want to run out with you when you go onto the pitch," he said. Fergie didn't look too pleased and the players were a bit bemused. We glanced at each other trying to suppress our amusement. But he was the new owner. And if the new owner wanted to make a prat of himself then so be it.

As everyone saw on that night's *Match of the Day*, we took to the pitch with the deafening roar of the Old Trafford faithful ringing in our ears. Only this time, we were led out by a tubby, middle-aged guy in full kit and boots, who ran into the penalty area, did some keepy-uppy in front of the Stretford End and fired a couple of shots into the net. He milked the applause but looked knackered. To be honest, us players took the piss out of him. None of us had ever experienced anything remotely like it before. Robbo was particularly scornful. "What was that fucking idiot doing?" he said as we lined up to kick off. None of us could answer his question, partly because we were still laughing. Thank God we won. I don't want to think what the crowd might have chanted if we'd gone a goal down.

Fergie didn't like it at all. To him it was a "tawdry side-show" that interfered with his preparations. He didn't think Knighton had any class doing something like that. I could see his face turning purple. I don't think he thought much of Knighton as a person, either. He certainly never had a good word to say about him. Knighton showed up at the training ground a couple of times but the manager made it clear that in his realm, even owners were unwelcome if he said so. It was a bit of a gamble on Fergie's part and I wonder if he would have stayed had the Knighton deal gone through.

As it happened, the Knighton deal did not go through.

He had difficulty coming up with the promised finance and the whole agreement to buy the club disintegrated. The revelation that Knighton didn't have the money, along with his preposterous appearance at Old Trafford before the Arsenal game, made us the butt of every comedian's jokes. However, Knighton's inability to seal the deal was probably the luckiest thing to have happened to Martin Edwards. He made tens of millions of pounds more than he ever would have done in the Knighton deal when he floated the club on the Stock Exchange and later sold out completely to the Glazer family. At the time, when we saw Edwards around Old Trafford, he often looked pained, as if he was aware that his error of judgment over Knighton had made United a laughing stock and sullied his own name. To be honest, it was a bit sad.

After the Arsenal win, our League campaign turned into United's worst since the relegation season back in the seventies. It was capped by a dreadful performance at Maine Road in September, when City beat us 5-1. At one point we were again down to twenty-first in the division and relegation was a real possibility. Our finishing position of thirteenth was not what had been expected and it brought increasing calls for the manager's head. Despite the four we managed in the first game, we continually struggled to score enough goals. Sparky was our top scorer with thirteen in the League – not a great return really! I hate to have to write this but who do you think were Champions yet again. I'm not even going to say their name.

Fergie's position looked very insecure, with a raging clamour building for him to be given the sack. Having got nowhere in the League, gone out of League Cup early on in a terrible 3–0 defeat at home by Spurs, attention turned to the FA Cup, our last possibility to salvage something from the season. The shrewd bets were on the manager departing sooner rather than later.

Incredibly – and this is one of the reasons he is a great – Fergie took it all in his stride. If the speculation was affecting him he never let it show to the players. I was sure there would be no change of manager, despite what the press whipped up. Martin Edwards continued to treat everyone, including Fergie, with great respect and made it clear that the manager had his full backing. When he said it, it didn't sound like one of those 'votes of confidence' which often precede the sack. We never believed Fergie would be fired, even though the press were convinced he was only days away from picking up his P45.

I still continued to feel niggles during the season and I didn't make too many League appearances. Fergie did include me in the team for four of our FA Cup ties, though, all of which we won. Whether that was because I happened to be fit when the Cup came around or Fergie now saw me as a fringe player no longer up to playing in a large number of games I don't really know. Whatever, the first game in the Cup that season was a third round tie against Forest. This match is widely credited with saving the manager's job. In the days leading up to the game at the City Ground, the press was full of stories that if United failed to win, Fergie would be out. There was a feeling among a section of the fans that employing the Scotsman had just not worked and a change was needed. There were even predictions that Howard Kendall, who had left Everton, was being lined up to take over. Whether any of this was true or not, I cannot say. I can only repeat that none of us thought he was on his way out. But there was no question the pressure was on to save our season.

It was a game we could easily have lost. Instead, a Mark Robins goal took us through to the next round, after the game had swung this way and that. Mark's strike has been referred to ever since as the goal that saved Ferguson. I'm not so sure that this was the case but it did make a great talking point. I'm convinced the Michael Knighton episode scarred Martin Edwards. The last thing he wanted was more upheavals and his judgment questioned again. On top of that, I think he genuinely respected Fergie and thought he was still the only man for the job. Then there was the store Martin Edwards put on Fergie's backing for him in the Strachan affair. I don't believe the board would have sacked the manager even if we had lost the Cup tie at Forest.

After playing a full part in wins against Hereford and Newcastle in the fourth and fifth rounds, we went to Bramall Lane for the quarter-final against Sheffield United. Although we won the tie 1–0, for me it was to be the end of the line that season. Both my injury plague and my FA Cup hoodoo struck at the same time like a perfect storm. I landed awkwardly after a tackle and something went in my knee. It didn't feel like it had when I dislocated it but there was definitely something seriously wrong. I limped out of the game. It turned out I had tweaked a ligament. This injury was not one of those career-threatening knee ligament problems. And it wasn't bad enough to warrant an operation. But any ligament injury is serious and in my case the only cure was rest and rehabilitation. I would be out for a while. So I missed the semi-final against Oldham. We won that in a replay. I was back in contention for the final against Crystal Palace. But Fergie not only didn't pick me, I wasn't even on the bench. We won the final in a replay. I wasn't picked for either game. In the team's moment of triumph I was left dejected. Worse, the boss decided to play midfielder Paul Ince at right-back. Now Incey was a very good player but to me he was no kind of full-back. He basically had no idea of how to play in the position and was badly exposed in the first game.

I watched the two games with mixed emotions. The first match, a 3–3 draw after extra time was a magnificent spectacle. Ian Wright, just coming back from a broken leg, got two for them and Sparky Hughes scored two for us, his first FA Cup goals of the season. Fergie showed how ruthless he could be once again when he dropped goalkeeper Jim Leighton for the replay. Jim, who was Scotland's first-choice keeper, had made some bad mistakes in the match. So Fergie left him out. The press said it was the most monumental gamble of Fergie's career but the manager knew what he was doing. After the first match he realised he couldn't rely on Jim any more. So in came the veteran Les Sealey, who had come to United on loan from Luton as cover. Les pulled off at least three great saves in the second game, vindicating Fergie's decision. The replay didn't live up to the excitement of the first game and we shaded it 1–0, courtesy of a goal from another of Fergie's youngsters, Lee Martin. It was as bad-tempered as the first match was free-flowing. Amazingly, the eccentric Les Sealey gave his Cup-Winners medal to Jim Leighton. Of course I was pleased that United won the Cup but I was frustrated that I wasn't a part of it. I celebrated with the rest of the lads and don't get me wrong, I enjoyed it. But I had been at United for three years, I had only one year left on my contract and deep down I was wondering what my future now held.

Chapter Thirteen

REAL LIFE

A funny thing happened at the start of the 1990–91 season. England had done really well in that summer's World Cup in Italy, reaching the semi-finals for the first time since the triumph of 1966. I had been involved in all international tournaments since 1980 but this time I was watching like everyone else. I knew how much it took to get within a penalty kick of a World Cup Final and I felt for the English lads, most of whom were friends. Amazingly, England's performances had a huge affect on the country and its football supporters. Following years of decline, suddenly the crowds were back and there was a new optimism in the air. United's average gate topped 40,000 for the first time in years. After hooliganism, Heysel, Hillsborough, the European ban and the appalling fire at Bradford, all of which occurred in the 1980s, football had reached its lowest point anyone could remember. Now, with Gazza's tears and Lineker's goals, the whole atmosphere lifted.

More good news came before the start of the season. UEFA, at its annual meeting in Switzerland, relaxed its ban on English clubs. This meant that Manchester

United were back playing in Europe in the Cup Winners' Cup following the replay victory over Crystal Palace. It made all the difference to players to know the country was back in the mainstream, not shunned, as it had been for those past few years. The ban had a terrible effect on the English game. It set us back years and cut us off from the rest of the world of football. With UEFA's decision and the World Cup semi-final, we could all look forward to better times at last.

Amid the upturn in the country's fortunes I was presented with a new problem. Despite the fact that I felt fit again, Fergie paid over £600,000 to bring Denis Irwin to the club from Oldham. Irwin could play either side of the defence but it was obvious to me that he was first in the pecking order for the right-back spot. My position in the team was under its greatest threat since I had arrived. The feeling grew that I was on borrowed time at Old Trafford.

Despite the arrival of Denis, the manager went to great pains to keep me feeling included. He never made me false promises about my position in the side. Nevertheless, he encouraged me to play the role of senior professional, which helped keep my enthusiasm intact. For my part I was always a bit of a bubbly character around the dressing room and I made it my business to keep smiling and contribute in any way I could. This wasn't a forced attitude; it is just the way I am. I would rather think about the positives. After all, there might be suspensions, transfers, injuries ... ... then who knows? I might get back.

It wasn't to be. I played in only four matches up to Christmas and one of those was a pre-season friendly against Waterford in the Irish Republic. I scored a goal in that one. But when the proper action started I was again out in the cold. I managed one game in each of three competitions, the League, the Cup Winners' Cup and the League Cup. But Denis Irwin was installed as the number one right-back and he occupied that position in most games, with Clayton Blackmore on the left. If there was an injury to Irwin, Mike Phelan came in. Phelan was often on the substitutes' bench, which meant there was no room for me. The one good thing was that my injuries seemed to be over. I was now fit and would stay that way for quite a while. At the time, it wasn't much of a consolation.

I didn't sulk: that is just not my style and it rarely gets you anywhere. I threw myself into training, turning out for the reserves and helping the team in my role as senior pro. Although I didn't know it at the time, I scored my final goal for United on 10 October in a 2–1 home win against Halifax in the second leg of a second round League Cup tie. It was an emotional goal for me for more reasons than the obvious. A week before the Halifax match, the great Peter Taylor died. He was a huge influence on my life and career. He was also much undervalued for his contribution to the game. I felt the loss. My mind went back to the day Taylor and Cloughie ran away and left me and Mark Proctor at Taylor's house. I smiled to myself.

It was typical of Fergie that he brought me into the team

for the next match. I think he knew I would want to play well for Peter. I was pleased to be in the team at last and very pleased indeed to have scored. I even thought there might be a way back into the side after what I thought was a good performance. That one game, however, came back to haunt me as the season progressed, as you'll see later.

My problem was that the team was doing much better in the League than we had managed in the previous two seasons, when we finished eleventh and thirteenth. My first season, where we ended up second, now seemed like a long time ago. In 1990–91 the club came in sixth, which wasn't fantastic but a massive improvement on what had gone before. Arsenal won the League again under George Graham. By then I had flown the Old Trafford nest.

I could see that Fergie was now determined to push on. Never mind that I had been injured for much of the last two years and wasn't part of the team which had displayed such poor form. I suppose I was tarred with the same brush. With me, the manager was never less than supportive, even when he was letting me know that if the right offer came along, I should consider it seriously. He told me I still had a future in the game. I suppose that what he meant – but was too kind to say – was that I had no future at Manchester United. This was typical of his dealings with me. He had decided I was now a fringe player and there is no way he would ever compromise on what he thought was best for the team. That is one of his greatest strengths as a manager. He is unafraid to ring the changes when he thinks it necessary. Remember the Jim Leighton-Les Sealey saga in the Cup Final. But he never put any pressure on me to leave and, it was reported in the press, actually tried to get me back on loan after I had moved on to Sheffield Wednesday.

Fergie really doesn't care if his decisions raise eyebrows elsewhere! Neither does he flinch at going out on a limb in public. He will berate officials and defend his players if he thinks it is to the team's advantage. He is a warrior-manager who loves "feisty encounters" with big-name opponents. He loved the battles, the mind games, the feeling he got when his decisions proved to be correct in the face of criticism. He was never afraid to ship a player out, no matter how big they were. In later years he saw off David Beckham when he let him go to Real Madrid. That was a time when David was one of the most famous people – let alone sportsmen – in the world. It was a massive call but Fergie came out of it so well, United went from strength to strength. Ruud van Nistelrooy seemed to be at the top of his game when he was transferred out but Fergie had spotted a player becoming more injury-prone. And when he was displeased, as with Gordon Strachan or later Jaap Stam, the player was on his way, no matter how good he was. With me, he let me know he still valued my input to the squad and wanted the best for me. Looking back, I think Fergie and I had a special bond. He also went out of his way to let Debra know he had my best interests at heart.

When I consider that period now, I think the fact

that Fergie let Mike Duxbury go to Blackburn before the season started was, in its own way, a vote of confidence in me. Or perhaps it was a sentimental act on Fergie's part. If it was, it would probably be the only one he ever made in his football career. Duxbury had been my only rival for the right-back position before Mike Phelan and Denis Irwin came in. That he sold Duxbury and kept me showed, I think, that he still retained some faith in my abilities. The point was, I could no longer compare myself in skill and talent to other full-backs and find them wanting. There were any number of youngsters coming through in the game. But they were rookies, even Denis Irwin (although I have to admit that Denis became one of the great full-backs after he took over from me). It was now simply a question of fitness for me. I knew my position inside out and I had played for enough different managers to realise I could change my game according to the way a manager wanted to play. If anyone thought it was my age rather than my injuries which blunted my opportunities, they were mistaken. I wasn't prepared – yet – to entertain any thought of ending my career. I was still, I believed, one of the best right-backs in the game and had plenty left to offer.

As Christmas drew closer, I got the nod that something was in the wind. Over the holiday, an approach was made by Ron Atkinson, who was then managing Sheffield Wednesday. In another act of friendship and kindness, Fergie said that I could have a free transfer, which meant I could negotiate a good signing-on fee if I took up the offer.

I still had six months to run on my contract. Fergie recommended to the board that they let me leave for nothing. They agreed, and the decision on whether to go or stay was passed to me for consideration.

I think Fergie's empathy with me went beyond his admiration for my football skills. His boyhood in the toughest of neighbourhoods of Glasgow, his time in the industrial grime of the Clyde in the steel industry, both made him a natural socialist. Even today, when he is rich beyond belief, he has hung on to the philosophy that he took in with his mother's milk back then. That, I think, is what enabled him to identify with the son of a Jamaican immigrant. He knew how difficult it was for me to forge a career in the days when there were hardly any black footballers or role models. In his own way, he too had developed the strength of mind to overcome humble beginnings. We had that in common and I think he recognised it long before I did.

There was another side to Fergie's concern for my wellbeing, which extended into my my time with my next club, Sheffield Wednesday. Debra and I had been together since 1980. We were married just before my move to Arsenal in 1984. We enjoyed a great lifestyle and we were happy together. We went to the best restaurants and hotels, were driven about in limousines and travelled all over the world on holidays. You could say we had all the trappings of luxury. The one thing that we didn't have, and both of us wanted – desperately – was children. Unfortunately, however hard we tried – and believe me we did try – it just wasn't happening. Bit by bit, this began putting a strain on our marriage. I think my injuries also had an effect. I must have been difficult to live with as I sustained knock after knock in my time at United and put so much of my focus into getting fit. Anyway, after various tests we were told that the only option open to us was *in vitro* fertilisation, or IVF. It was a big step but we decided to give it a go. We were upset when at first it didn't work. But we were told this was not unusual so we persisted and eventually were thrilled when Debra became pregnant – with twins.

I have rarely spoken of the heartache that followed. Even now, it is difficult to put into words the pain we lived through in the following nine months. We were absolutely ecstatic that twins were on the way. Scans showed they were a boy and a girl. I was walking on air. For me, it was the icing on the cake, the one thing in my life that was missing would now be filled. The same was true, I think, for Debra. We had success, a fabulous lifestyle and public recognition. Now we would have children. It was the only thing we wanted. It was perfect.

Debra's pregnancy went well for the first few months. Then, one day in March 1991, it's all a bit hazy now, but I think we were due to play a big match. Debra was told by doctors that something was wrong. Our beautiful daughter was not developing properly. Tests showed her lungs were not working as they should. She was, the doctors said, unlikely to survive outside the womb. This was the most devastating thing I had ever heard.

Missing Cup Finals and being out of the team, things which seemed so important before, meant nothing. Debra tried to protect me. She didn't know how or when to tell me the terrible news. She understood that I had to be focused to play professional football. But after she let me know what the doctors had said how could I focus on anything other than this tragedy? I don't even remember how we got through those times. We decided to name the two children there and then. We called our son Charlie and our daughter Gabrielle. The name Gabrielle came from the archangel Gabriel in the bible. On reflection, I don't think I gave Debra the support she needed at that time. However bad it was for me, what must it be like for a woman to hear that? And if anything could be worse this was: Debra had to carry both babies to full term in order for our boy, Charlie, to have a chance to survive.

In virtually her last act on this earth, when the time came, Gabrielle rolled over to allow Charlie to be born normally. I can't account for that. Nor, I think, can anyone else. Gabrielle hung on for an hour then passed away. We didn't know what to feel. We were so happy to have Charlie yet were destroyed at the death of Gabrielle. Nothing prepares you for the loss of a child. And you never get over it.

My manager at Wednesday, Ron Atkinson, along with Alex Ferguson and his wife, were absolutely incredible to us at this awful time. Fergie and his wife had twins. Maybe they also experienced problems, I don't know. Maybe they realised the risks being pregnant with twins can pose. Either way, they understood somehow the trauma we suffered better than anyone else. To this day, when Fergie sees Debra, he asks after Charlie.

Perhaps I should have been left out of the team in the wake of these events. At the time I thought I was fine to play. Maybe I was. I believed I was. You learn to hide your vulnerabilities when you are a professional footballer. But I could not possibly have been in the right frame of mind, even if I didn't know it myself at the time.

Looking back, perhaps that Christmas was the right moment to leave United. A new start, that's what we needed. The chance came when Ron Atkinson came calling that December. Wednesday, suffering from an injury crisis, needed short term help in defence. Big Ron was convinced I could do a job. "You can do great here," he said. "This club can revive your career." I was interested, not least because my old team-mate from the European Cup win with Forest, Trevor Francis, was the team's senior player. Danny Wilson was there too. I would be going back among friends.

Wednesday had been relegated the previous season and were in Division Two. But they looked as if they could get back up to the top flight at the first attempt if they had a good second half to the season. This was where I came in. I was wanted to bring some much-needed know-how to their quest for promotion. Dropping down a division? Suddenly, that didn't seem important in the scheme of things. I was promised first-team football, which, I think, was what I needed at that point. Over Christmas, after talking it over with Debra, I decided to leave the club of my dreams for a new challenge across the Pennines. I signed for Wednesday in the first week of January 1991, two months before the bombshell of Gabrielle's situation hit us.

Fergie was still looking out for me. I was owed some money in bonus and loyalty payments. It could have dragged on and on with United wanting Wednesday to pay and vice-versa. Fergie stepped in and not only organised the payment, he convinced the board to pay me more than I was actually due.

It was a wrench to leave United. They were my boyhood club. I always wanted to play for them. But in the end, the life of a professional footballer is not governed by such things. The days of the one-club footballer were being left behind. And, as I had discovered so painfully, there were things in life that were far more important than football.

I still kept in touch with the players at Old Trafford, particularly Robbo. Debra and I continued to live in the Manchester area and I commuted to Sheffield. I watched as United made it all the way to the Cup Winners' Cup Final. I felt sure they could beat the mighty Barcelona. I was as pleased as they were when two goals from Sparky – the second was one of the great goals of all time – won the trophy for my old mates. Having appeared in one match during the European campaign, I felt I had made at least some contribution to the triumph in Europe. That success was as important for England as it was for United. For England, it showed we could still compete on the European stage after being isolated during the time of the ban. For

United, winning their first European trophy since the European Cup in 1968 paved the way for the even greater victories to come. Much as I could share the feelings of achievement over United's accomplishment, though, I was now playing for the team of a potential rival. Only I wasn't allowed to be there when the two clubs clashed for one of the country's big prizes, all because of that game at Halifax.

Chapter Fourteen

BAD TACKLES IN THE TUNNEL OF HATE

Bryan Robson was a hard bastard, no question. I mean no disrespect to those other Manchester United enforcers, Nobby Stiles and Roy Keane. Both of them could put themselves about. They could look after themselves too. Roy even had the audacity to tell the world about how he deliberately went after Alf-Inge Haaland in retaliation for some supposed offence against him. I'm sorry, Keano, but Bryan was way ahead of you. He didn't just crock any old midfielder who couldn't fight back. He went after players with big reputations who were renowned for mixing it.

We were playing Wimbledon in their heyday during the eighties. The game was held at their old Plough Lane ground, where the stands were so close to the pitch you felt you could reach out and shake hands with their supporters. Not that you'd want to, mind you. Their fans were definitely not the type you got at the tennis, that's for sure. In the match, Wimbledon, as was their way, kicked us all over the park. Robbo was not best pleased. He was in an even worse mood when Terry Gibson, an ex-United forward, put the Dons ahead. He said he was going to do something "special". He snarled instructions to Mark Hughes and Norman Whiteside, telling them exactly what he wanted them to do when they kicked off. This is how it went: Hughes to Whiteside, Whiteside back to Robson, standing on the edge of the centre circle, directly opposite Vinnie Jones.

Now I don't think it's an exaggeration to say that Vincent Jones was one of the most brutal tacklers the game has ever seen. Throughout the circle of ex-players, stories are rife of Vinnie's tackles, none of which involve any finesse on his part. Broken bones and torn ligaments were the order of the day when you faced Vinnie. And that was when he was on his best behaviour. Paul Gascoigne can testify to his dark side, having been on the receiving end of Jones's testicle squeezing act, carried out on the blind side of the referee but caught by an alert photographer from the tabloid press. Contrary to popular opinion, Vinnie could play a bit too. I think he just preferred not to most of the time. I'll tell you what, though: none of us ever thought for a moment that Vinnie would end up conquering the movie world, appearing in major films in both London and Hollywood and becoming an international star. He's even been on Celebrity Big Brother for God's sake. He's brilliant at it isn't he? Fair play to him for all of that.

Anyway, on this occasion the ball was rolled back to Robbo, who deliberately miscontrolled it, allowing it to drop about a yard in front of him. He knew Vinnie would be unable to resist giving him the charge on the pretext that the ball was there to be won. Sure enough, Vinnie careered towards the ball. Just as he reached it, however, Robbo's boot came over the top and his studs crashed into Vinnie's leg, almost snapping it in two. Vinnie was carried off. Robbo not only put Vinnie out of the game, he had done it such a way that the referee couldn't get a good view. He pleaded innocence and wasn't even booked. To Vinnie's credit, he could take it as well as dish it out, unlike some players I could name. Whenever he saw Bryan after that he'd say, "That was a great tackle, Robbo, the best anyone has ever managed on me.".Then he would smile ...

Bad tackles are a fact of life in football. I've put in a few myself. As I mentioned in a previous chapter, I got into trouble with the FA for saying that I'd foul an opponent rather than let them get past me. I didn't mean it literally. Or maybe I did. Well, it had a degree of truth. Very occasionally, though, bad blood goes further. Think Zidane's head-but in the 2006 World Cup Final. Sometimes it gets personal. Apart from the incident with Norman Whiteside, which was soon resolved after I went to United, there was one other incident in my career that falls into this category. It created untold column inches in the press, arguments at FA headquarters in Lancaster Gate and a law suit at the High Court in the Strand.

Again, it was United versus Wimbledon. Now, Wimbledon played in a certain way: the Wimbledon way. Under the stewardship of first Bobby Gould then Dave Bassett and Joe Kinnear, they played aggressive, in-your-face football. They had nurtured Vinnie Jones, remember. The Wimbledon side took up the long ball game that had brought success to Watford and they perfected it. On top of that they were very physical and tried everything they could to intimidate opponents. We all like a good physical battle with no quarter given or expected. But Wimbledon played right on the edge. It was often ugly. The club had come from non-league nowhere to the top flight, where they did well year after year. They definitely punched way above their weight. This didn't mean that they attracted too many supporters to their games – on the contrary, their crowds were the lowest in the division – but they seemed to revel in their outsider status. In 1988 they gave me a right laugh when they won the FA Cup, beating what was supposedly an unbeatable Liverpool side containing John Barnes and Peter Beardsley. They had a few tasty players on the pitch and some you wouldn't want to spend much time with off it. For such underdogs, they were strangely unloved in the world at large. Supporters of football respected their achievements but hated their methods. And they always seemed to up the aggression factor when they played one of the big teams. And they came no bigger than Manchester United.

The big one occurred after a Wednesday night League Cup third round match at Plough Lane in November 1988, during my second season at United. Despite all our run-ins, I was genuinely sorry when Wimbledon later had to leave Plough Lane to lead a nomadic life around the grounds of the other clubs of South London.

The game was a bad-tempered affair from start to finish. The most bad-tempered player of all on the pitch that night was John Fashanu, Wimbledon's centre-forward and the brother of Justin. For the record, we lost the game 2–1. I had been suffering from the heel injury that was such a blight on my time at United. I wasn't really fit enough to start but Fergie gave me a seat on the bench. In the second half he brought me on as a substitute to help shore up the defence. From the moment I hit the field Fashanu started giving me the verbals. I don't know why he singled me out. He appeared totally out of control. He called me a 'big-time Charlie' among other things and kept urging his team-mates to put me out of the game. He complained to the referee whenever I went near him, saying I was 'fouling bastard'. Now I may have many faults but I don't think anyone who knows me thinks I'm a 'big-time Charlie' or a 'fouling bastard'. From some of his comments, I got the impression Fashanu resented the fact that I was a regular England player, something I thought he wanted to be more than anything. He won three caps or so in his career, I believe. "Think you're an international eh?" he said at one stage. "We'll see about that. You won't be an international for long when I've finished with you."

There had been running feuds going on the whole game. It was an unsavoury performance by both sides to be honest. I mean, we were prepared to mix it ourselves when necessary but this time it went further than that. For some reason – and I don't know what it was – matches between us had simmered with trouble for some time. Two weeks before the Plough Lane encounter in the Cup we met in a League game at Old Trafford. Among other assaults that took place that day, our goalkeeper Jim Leighton was roughed up and lost one of his teeth. Before that, in the League game at their place, Robbo had his nose broken. Then there was the incident between Robbo and Vinnie Jones. Normally, you just accept these things, as Vinnie did when Bryan crocked him, but we got the distinct feeling that Wimbledon were deliberately setting out to bend the rules as far as they could in their matches against us. We responded in kind and I think it's safe to say that by the time we met in the League Cup tie both teams were a car crash waiting to happen.

The arguments continued after the final whistle. As we went towards the tunnel there was all manner of shouting, pushing and shoving. I tried to confront Fashanu.

"What's your fucking problem, John," I asked.

"Fuck off," was Fashanu's reply and he tried to push me away.

I stood my ground and we eye-balled each other for a moment or two. Then Fashanu exploded. Without any warning his arms came up like a boxer and he punched me twice in the face – hard. I went backwards and down and all hell broke loose. I kind of came to and saw Fashanu running away down the tunnel. God knows how, but I got to my feet and chased him. I tried to kick the door open but by then I was feeling the effects of Fashanu's assault. Someone fell over me as I was half lying on the floor. The next thing I remember is staggering into the dressing room with the help of the United players. It was pandemonium. When I came to my senses, I saw everyone fussing around me but it was hard to take it all in. A policeman came into the dressing room and started asking me questions. Apparently, Fergie had witnessed the fracas and had summoned the law. At the time I just wanted to get out of there. I put it down to a momentary rush of blood on Fashanu's part and when I was asked if I wanted to press charges, I said no.

If I thought that would be the end of the matter I was sadly mistaken. First, the story was all over the next day's papers. "The Tunnel of Hate", they dubbed it. At that point it was only known that some kind of fight had broken out but no-one knew who the participants were. When fights occur on the pitch, everyone can see what has happened but in the tunnel after a match there are no members of the public or the media present to witness anything going off. The press filled this gap in their knowledge with speculation. It soon came out that I was the victim of a punch but Fashanu failed to own up to his part in it. In fact he denied it was anything to do with him, saying: "Don't point the guilty finger at me." All those at Wimbledon closed ranks and for a while refused to reveal who was involved or what had occurred. At first suspicion fell on the Wimbledon centre-back, Eric Young, but that was because he was the player who had tripped over my body while I was half on the floor. Eric, an honest pro, hadn't done anything.

Although the Wimbledon people knew what had happened, they continued to refuse to identify Fashanu. Their manager at the time, Bobby Gould, was particularly cagey and everyone took their lead from him. This didn't surprise me as Gould's first instinct would have been to protect his own player. What shocked and saddened me was that Don Howe, one of my mentors in football and Wimbledon's coach at the time, didn't speak up. I suppose he was under orders.

It was United's manager who broke the silence and put the press straight. The police confirmed that Fergie himself had made a complaint to them, hence the constable's appearance in the dressing room. Our manager issued a statement, saying: "I saw exactly what happened and John Fashanu hit Viv with two punches that knocked him back yards. If that had been a Manchester United player he would have been on the first train home and finished with this club." That brought the FA into the picture. The Chief Executive, Graham Kelly, insisted that Fergie tell the governing body what had happened. "Alex Ferguson is an official of a club and as such he has a duty to report misconduct to the FA. It's his obligation under FA rules," Kelly said.

The FA's stance forced Fergie to prepare a witness statement in writing and send it to them. After they received his evidence they asked Wimbledon to respond. Once they considered both submissions they charged both Fashanu and me with bringing the game into disrepute. I couldn't believe it. Nothing I had said during the match or after it was any worse than the banter you would hear on the pitch every week but Fashanu claimed he had been "provoked". The truth was he assaulted me. If players hit out after the kind of clash that took place between Fash and me, there would be punch-ups after every game. Nevertheless, a hearing was arranged at which we would all have to give our side of the story. I was the victim. Now I too would have to defend myself. It was a disgrace.

In the wake of the FA's decision, Fashanu started giving interviews to the press. He continued to protest his innocence of throwing a punch but when that was exposed as a sham he shifted his position, saying "Viv started it." Then he did something unforgiveable. In a press interview he said that we had been feuding for a long time and I was jealous of him. He implied, although he didn't say it directly, that I was envious because he had, in the past, embarked on an affair with my wife, Debra. This was a totally untrue comment and, quite naturally, infuriated both Debra and I. He also told The Daily Star that I had lied in my version of what had happened in the tunnel. The paper printed Fashanu's remarks it as if they were true. We sued the newspapers who carried these stories, eventually won the case in the libel court and were awarded £35,000 in damages, which was a lot of money in those days. It didn't get that far with The Daily

Star. The paper admitted it had been duped by Fashanu and, to be fair, printed a fulsome apology.

In the middle of all this, Fashanu did the most unbelievable thing. He rang my house. Debra took the call. Fashanu told her that "if we play our cards right" we could keep the story going and make a fortune from the press. He actually wanted to turn the whole thing into a money-making opportunity by conspiring together with us to invent further stories which we would sell to the newspapers. Debra gave him short shrift. She was furious and so was I but we decided not to report Fashanu's approach. With the FA hearing due, we didn't want to escalate the dispute.

Before the hearing at FA headquarters took place, Manchester United announced that they would be taking ten witnesses to Lancaster Gate to speak on my behalf. The party included a United board member, Maurice Watkins, who is also a lawyer. Watkins gave both Debra and I incredible support during this period, especially in the libel case. He explained procedures to us, told us what we should focus on and generally helped in every way he could. I was pleased he was coming to the FA.

When it became known that one of United's team was a solicitor, Fashanu asked the FA if he could be legally represented as well. The FA turned him down. At first, he denied that he had made any such request. But it was confirmed by the FA themselves, who explained to the press that Fashanu had indeed asked them if he could bring his solicitor to speak for him. But, the FA explained, legal representation was not allowed. They went on to say that their rules stated that if a witness or club director also happened to be a solicitor, they could attend, but only in a non-legal capacity. Otherwise, Fashanu was not entitled to have his solicitor in attendance. Today, there would be no question that all parties involved would have their own legal representatives in any disciplinary proceedings. In the nineties, when I was at Middlesbrough, we had the celebrated advocate, George Carman, speaking for us in front of the FA when we were deducted three points for not fulfilling a fixture. But back in the eighties, the FA operated by rules which had been in force for decades, a time when the notion of the parties having any legal rights would have appeared absurd.

The hearing was a farce. The panel listened to the evidence, found Fashanu guilty, and gave him what was effectively a slap on the wrist. He got a three match ban and a £2,000 fine. They also found me guilty of "provocation". I received a one match ban and a fine of £750. I was at first surprised and then angry that this was happening. The verdicts and punishments bore no relation to what had occurred. It was a complete fudge on the part of the disciplinary panel and, to me, the FA didn't come out of the case very well.

The outcome was particularly infuriating for the Arsenal midfielder, Paul Davis. He had been banned for nine matches – including two England games – after he had been caught on camera punching Southampton's Glenn Cockerill and breaking his jaw. He had also pleaded provocation but in his case the FA wasn't interested. He couldn't understand how Fashanu got off so lightly. He never really recovered from the incident. Fashanu was lucky by comparison. It was a distasteful end to a very distasteful business.

Chapter Fifteen

FLYING HIGH WITH OWLS

Sheffield Wednesday was just what I needed. After all that had happened in my time at United, both personal and professional, going to Hillsborough was a breath of fresh air. First of all, Ron Atkinson had assembled a very talented group of players. They were far better than I realised. In my time at Wednesday, in addition to Trevor Francis and Danny Wilson, there was Nigel Pearson, who was a leader if ever I saw one, Nigel Worthington, Carlton Palmer, David Hirst, Peter Shirtliff, the American John Harkes, and the superb Chris Waddle, among a number of other quality performers. Second, I had been so happy to go to Manchester but it never occurred to me that most of my time at Old Trafford would be spent fighting injuries. Perhaps a change of scene would help.

Wednesday's regular right-back, Roland Nilsson, had suffered a long-term injury and it looked fairly serious at the time. That's why Ron Atkinson wanted to sign a replacement for the rest of the season at least. I spoke to both him and Fergie before I made up my mind. I also talked to Debra, who was enthusiastic and thought it could be a good move at that stage of my career. Atkinson offered me an eighteen month contract, promised me regular first-team football and told me: "We can definitely get promotion if you come here." That was music to my ears. Only an hour's drive from my home, Sheffield Wednesday – traditionally one of the big clubs of England – looked to be the ideal place for me to relocate to. It was a great opportunity.

Another reason for having a good feeling about Wednesday was Atkinson himself. Larger than life, Big Ron's personality ruled supreme over the playing side of the club. The board were anonymous: Ron happily fronted everything. The team had been relegated on goal difference the previous season but that had not dented the manager's confidence or vitality. He was convinced we would get back into the First Division straight away and when we got there, he told us, we'd do well. That season there would be automatic promotion for the top four clubs, which reduced the odds on us a bit. The First Division was being increased in numbers from twenty to twenty-two, so two teams went down and four went up. That situation was tailor-made for someone like Atkinson, who had the ability to motivate his players when push came to shove. Just like those days when I started at Forest, the second tier of English football was competitive and you needed to scrap to get out of it. Big Ron revelled in it.

Atkinson's teams also played the kind of football I liked. It was similar to the way we operated under Clough at

Forest and Ferguson at Manchester United. We got the ball on the floor and played a passing game. We were encouraged to attack, and that included the defenders. The full-backs were told to overlap as much as possible. It was perfect for my game and I knew straight away I would enjoy it.

Big Ron Atkinson was a massive student of the game. If you asked him any football question, no matter how obscure, he knew the answer ninety-nine percent of the time. On the rare occasions he didn't know he would be so annoyed with himself he would make a point of finding out. He was a wannabe player and loved to participate in the five-a-sides. To be absolutely honest, he wasn't very good and always ended up the last pick. His football career had been as a central defender in the lower leagues so his skills left something to be desired. He took the jokes we made about his playing ability in good heart, though, and they didn't do anything to curb his enthusiasm. He was an open person who spoke his mind and was very good with words. His appearances in the media, where he was continually in demand as a television pundit, added to his aura. As a manager, he was one of the best. It was easy to see why he had been poached by Manchester United.

I was both shocked and surprised when, some years later, he made a racially-charged comment on TV about Marcel Desailly when he thought the microphone was switched off. To me, Ron Atkinson is not a racist. He always treated me with complete respect. He was known throughout the game as the manager who had done more than any other to bring the first generation of black players into the English game when he was manager of West Brom. He took the down-at-heel midlands club and made it into one of the most exciting outfits in the English game by selecting the first clutch of British black players and building his team around them. No-one had the nerve to do this before Atkinson. I don't know what he was thinking of when he made the comment about Marcel but it is something for which he paid a heavy price. He was public enemy number one for a while and the controversy killed his career in the media stone dead.

Amazingly, as soon as I left Manchester for Sheffield, my injury problems ceased. I felt better, physically, than at any time since my days at Arsenal. And the more I played for Wednesday, the greater the improvement in my performances. Within a couple of months I was playing as well as I had ever done. It was around that time that it was reported that Fergie wanted me back at United on loan to help them in the final stages of their Cup Winners' Cup campaign. I couldn't go in the end because Wednesday needed my services. It was an unbelievable transformation. I don't know what to put it down to: maybe the injuries had run their course anyway; maybe the change of scene helped me to recover; or maybe I was getting over the trials and tribulations of my personal life. I don't know. But whatever was happening I felt as if I had been given a new lease of life.

I played in most of Wednesday's League games from the moment I arrived in January 1991 to the end of the season. We finished in third place and were promoted back to the First Division, just as Big Ron had predicted. However, the game I played for Manchester United against Halifax in the League Cup meant I couldn't appear in the competition that season for Wednesday. I was cup-tied. Such was our form, though, that in my absence the team ploughed through the rounds, beating Chelsea in the two-legged semi-final, and made it all the way to the final. At Wembley they were to face who else but Manchester United. And I couldn't play.

United were massive favourites, obviously. They were First Division; they were on their way in the Cup Winners' Cup; they were Manchester United. How could they fail to win?

But against the odds, Big Ron got the drop on Fergie in that final. I think it started before the game. We had a coach trip from our hotel to the stadium which was due to take around forty-five minutes. Big Ron organised entertainment for the journey. He arranged for a popular comedian of the day, Stan Boardman, to join us on the coach. Boardman didn't stop cracking jokes for the whole of the time we were on the road. We were in stitches at Stan's antics from start to finish. We were still laughing when we got off the coach and walked into the stadium. It really set us up for the game and was a ploy worthy of Brian Clough at his best. Big Ron was showbiz, there is no question about that.

As I think back to the match at Wembley – and remember, my powers of recall are not the best – it was a fantastic game settled by one outstanding goal from John Sheridan. For United, Robbo and Paul Ince were magnificent but Nigel Pearson, especially, and the rest of our team, were better. Sheridan was a skilful player who never really got the credit I think he merited. He was bought by Brian Clough for Forest but Clough decided early on he didn't fancy him and left him in the reserves for months on end before selling him to Wednesday. Clough also publicly questioned John's ability. His goal that day at Wembley was a beauty, one that was fit to win any match and a great answer to Clough's criticism of his game. It came after a free kick from Nigel Worthington was headed out by Gary Pallister. Sheridan, just outside the box, caught it on the volley perfectly and it screamed into the net. I think Les Sealey got a hand on it but couldn't keep it out. We could have had more but the one goal proved to be enough. Wednesday had beaten the mighty United. I was as enthusiastic as the most diehard Wednesday fan as I watched Nigel Pearson lift the trophy, the club's first for over fifty years. The city of Sheffield was buzzing.

After the game at Wembley, I took a six-pack of beer to share with Steve Bruce and Bryan Robson, partly in commiseration, partly to enforce my bragging rights. Brucie and his wife had been very supportive of Debra and me in our troubles and it was good to spend some time with him that day. As you will have gathered, Robbo and I were friends from day one. Neither Robbo nor me is surprised Steve has turned into a top manager. He just knew what was right and what was wrong and although he could be uncompromising he always played it straight. That's something Robbo and I have always loved about Brucie. He was also the most dependable centre-back you could wish for. How he never played for England is a complete mystery to me.

At the end of the season we had hardly finished our celebrations over promotion and our cup win when we began to hear a disturbing rumour on the grapevine. Big Ron was wanted by Doug Ellis to be his manager at Aston Villa following the departure of Graham Taylor. We didn't want to believe it. Atkinson was the club at that time. But it was true. I don't know what went on between Ron and the Wednesday board but he left for Villa Park that summer. As we contemplated the upcoming season with the big boys, our manager upped and left. For a while we were in a bit of turmoil, so much did we believe in Big Ron's influence over our success. But being footballers, before long the players turned their attention to who might be recruited to take on Atkinson's job as manager.

Danny Wilson got it spot on, I don't know how. "I phoned Trevor (Francis)," he told me. "I said to him, you know who's gonna get the job don't you? He said he had no idea. I said .... it's you, Trevor, it's you." Danny was sure Trevor would be the board's choice, even though he was still a top player and had no experience of management. I don't know how he worked it out but Trevor was indeed appointed player-manager a few days later. We all wondered what Danny knew that we didn't. In fact, he's like that. He just knew.

As it turned out, the departure of Big Ron didn't have a negative effect on the team. We raised our game and went from strength to strength. The players took responsibility and Trevor grew into the managerial job overnight. He began to limit his own appearances as a player as he assumed the mantle of manager and boss. He was also shrewd enough to realise that he had inherited a good team from Ron Atkinson. He had trained, played and relaxed with the group of players at his disposal and he understood our strengths and weaknesses from that experience, a knowledge he used extremely well. Of course, I had known him since our glory days at Forest. I can still see that header in the European Cup Final. Trevor and I always got on well and we knew where each other was coming from. One of the first things he said to me after becoming player-manager was that he didn't intend to make any major changes. He'd carry on playing in the same way as Atkinson, with essentially the same players. It was an intelligent way to begin his career as a manager. If I remember right, he was true to his word and the only significant new player he added to the squad in my time was Paul Warhurst from Blackburn.

Although the ban on English clubs playing in Europe had been partly lifted, the new policy did not yet extend to the UEFA Cup. So our League Cup win did not automatically bring European football to Hillsborough.

Under different circumstances we might have been frustrated at missing out on Europe but this particular season was dominated by thoughts of being back in the top flight. In the event, our first season after promotion to Division One, 1991–92, was absolutely fantastic, better than anyone associated with the club could have imagined. For me, it felt great. I was back in the groove. Being free from injury was fantastic and I was enjoying my football again. Roland Nilsson returned from his injury earlier than expected but he couldn't dislodge me from my position. Then, Trevor Francis went one step further than any manager I had played under. He made me captain when Nigel Pearson wasn't playing. I loved the role. I had become something of a leader at Manchester United but this was just brilliant. I liked it. A lot!

We started with a bang and won four in a row during September. One of those wins was against Forest at the City Ground, which we won 2–1. It was one of the few times I finished on the winning side in the League against them. Cloughie said hello but I don't think he was too pleased at the end. Clough was coming to the end of his illustrious career and would suffer relegation before too long in his final season at Forest. He never did anything by halves.

When we played Manchester United at Hillsborough that season, I was captain of Wednesday and Robbo was captain of United. It was a wonderful occasion for both of us. The game was a close-fought encounter which ended in a 1–1 draw. As fate would have it, both

United and Wednesday were right up there with the leading pack for most of the season. For United, it was nothing less than expected and they had high hopes of lifting the title. We were the surprise package, having our best season since 1961. In the end we were both beaten to the crown by Leeds, who won the League under the management of Howard Wilkinson. United finished second and we were third. It was my best season in years.

By this time, the European ban was totally ended. It was the final recognition that English football was back, free now from the problems of violence and ready to embrace all-seater stadiums. It was only three years since the dreadful events at Hillsborough when over ninety Liverpool fans were killed at the FA Cup semi-final against Forest. In those three years, we had entered a new era, where such tragedies would hopefully be in the past. It was fitting that one of the first English clubs back was Sheffield Wednesday. Our League position ensured that we were in the UEFA Cup. I even chipped in with a fair quota of goals in our League campaign to help us get into Europe.

I also played some games as a centre-back. It started when we had injuries in defence. I think the first time was the away game at Forest. At the age I was then, it proved to be quite easy for me in that position and I took to it like a natural. Playing at full-back demands more running, you have to get forward and back, forward and back. You have to make crosses on the overlap and be able to put in crunching tackles to stop your opposing winger.

As a central defender I concentrated on defending and reading the game, which I always loved and tried to perfect. I only tended to get forward at set pieces when I was playing centre-back, which saved my legs. It was all the better because we were winning and the crowds at Hillsborough were fantastic. I was loving it. And playing in a new position ... amazing!

While I was enjoying life again following our tragedy, Debra was left to look after Charlie most of the time, which was a full-time job. I did my share when I was home – I loved being with Charlie – but Debra bore the brunt of the work. He, poor thing, suffered quite a lot in his childhood, particularly with a sleep disorder which left him awake and active for much longer periods than is usually the case. He had so much energy it was incredible. A footballer's life, though, entails regular trips away from home and at the times when I was wasn't there, Debra had to cope alone. She did a magnificent job but a rift in our relationship was appearing, I think, due to these new circumstances and the trauma of our experiences. We tried to keep our marriage working but I suppose the truth is that, little by little, we were growing further apart. Eventually there would be huge consequences.

My contract with Wednesday ran out at the end of the 1991–92 season. At the grand old age of thirty-five I thought I was playing better than ever. So did Trevor Francis, who offered me a one year deal and told everyone that I was central to his plans. He said I would be "invaluable" in the European campaign. He was so enthusiastic about my contribution, I couldn't say no. Not that I wanted to. It wasn't nostalgia for Forest, he told me, it was because I still had what was required. I took the offer, looking forward to at least another year at the top and maybe more. All the woes of my footballing life at United were well and truly behind me. I had come back, good as new. And I had joined a club which was geared for life at the top after a period in the doldrums. It was a fabulous two and-a-half year swansong.

There had been enormous debates in English football around that period about the best way to move the game forward and take advantage of the upsurge in interest following Italia 90. There was talk of a European Super League with the big clubs of each nation breaking away from their national leagues. Vast amounts of money were said to be on offer from the new satellite television service, BSkyB. In response to these developments, the football authorities formed the Premier League, to be introduced for the 1992–93 season. It was the decision that transformed the game in this country and the lives of the top players. From that moment on, the money pouring into football increased in a way I had never seen in all my years as a professional and it changed the game forever. Bit by bit, players had moved from being like serfs, totally at the mercy of unscrupulous chairmen, to being in the box seat when it came to their careers. It wouldn't be long before agents ruled the roost. I had seen the old world. Now I could see the new world. I straddled both eras. Believe me, for the top players, the new one was better.

In the first season of the new Premier League, we again did well at Sheffield, though not quite as well as the previous year. We finished seventh. At last, Manchester United fulfilled Fergie's quest and won the title for the first time in a quarter of a century. I was pleased for them and took some pride in my contribution to the club's resurgence.

Wednesday's UEFA Cup run was not what we would have wanted, however. In the first round we easily beat the part-timers, Spora Luxembourg 10-2 on aggregate. In the next round we drew a very good team, Kaiserslauten. The first leg in Germany sealed our fate. Despite a good goal from David Hirst, we lost 3-1. In the return, we got a creditable 2-2 draw with goals from John Sheridan and Danny Wilson. It wasn't what we had hoped for when the season started. However, I was pleased for Danny that he got a European goal. While we were together at Hillsborough, we renewed the friendship that we had begun all those years before at Forest. Danny, also coming towards the end of his career, loved to talk about the game, just like Robbo and me. Our friendship would be cemented in an unforeseen way at the end of the season.

The lack of a good European run, however, was completely overshadowed by a unique set of circum-stances that unfolded as the season progressed. The domestic campaign that year will be remembered for the way Sheffield Wednesday and Arsenal, locked together in mortal combat, dominated both Cup competitions.

Wednesday began to progress in the FA Cup. So much so, we made it all the way to Wembley. It was fantastic to play in an FA Cup Final at last. Even better, was that I led the team out as captain. After all my years of suffering that old FA Cup hoodoo, this was a turn up. Who would have thought I would get there with Sheffield Wednesday, a team that, when I joined, had not appeared in an FA Cup Final since 1966? Promotion, third in the League and an FA Cup Final, all in three years! It was like Forest in the old days. As fate would have it yet again, we were facing one of my old teams: this time it was Arsenal.

Ian Wright gave the Gunners the lead in the first half but David Hirst grabbed a great equaliser after an hour. If I thought my FA Cup hoodoo was laid to rest, what about this: I was injured and had to come off. After playing for over two years without a serious injury I had to limp off in the showpiece game of the season. Can you imagine? The match ended 1–1 so a replay was required. Of course, my injury had not healed so I was still out when it took place. I missed the game, which Arsenal won 2–1. I was gutted. What made the defeat so much worse was that Arsenal had beaten us by the same score in the League Cup Final earlier in the season. That was another choker. That year remains the only time both finals have been contested by the same two teams. Fair play to Arsenal, they probably just about deserved their wins. We felt we could do it. We had got so near but just couldn't get across the line in either final.

By the summer of 1993, my contract had again run out. Trevor was keen to keep me and I was keen to stay. But I was coming up to thirty-seven and I needed to pay some attention to my long-term prospects. I'd had a fantastic career as a player, spanning almost twenty years. I had reached heights no-one would have thought possible. I had played for some of the greatest clubs in the land. What was the best thing to do now? I could carry on at Wednesday but could anything get any better than the last two-and-a-half years? I was pondering all this when I got a call from a certain Mr. John Dennis.

Chapter Sixteen

IT'S JUST LIKE WATCHING BRAZIL

John Dennis, it turned out, was the Chairman of Barnsley Football Club. Barnsley, known as the Tykes, had for most of their existence been consigned to the lower divisions of the Football League. There was something about the club, though, that was appealing. The feeling was homely if a bit ramshackle. It was more like a family than anywhere else I had ever been. Barnsley had lived in the shadow of more famous Yorkshire clubs like Leeds and Sheffield Wednesday for ever. There were also any number of other smallish Yorkshire sides doing the same thing. Like them, Barnsley's roots are in the local community and they are as strong at Oakwell as they are anywhere in the land.

John was a local businessman. I think he made his money in the fruit and veg trade. When he rang me, Barnsley were in the renamed First Division but what in fact, before the advent of the Premier League, was called the second division. This was the summit of their ambitions before Dennis became involved with the club. John asked if we could meet. Now I had been offered a new contract by Trevor Francis that I was inclined to take. But I agreed to the meeting, out of courtesy more than anything else. I couldn't see myself playing in the second tier again, unless it was with a team with great potential, like Wednesday had been when I joined.

When we got together, Dennis told me he didn't want me solely as a player. He thought I would make a great manager and he offered me the dual role at Barnsley. I was taken aback. I had been thinking about management with Robbo for years but at the time of Dennis's approach we were both still players. I hadn't thought about being a player-manager. I was intrigued and pleased by John's approach, even more so when he said I was his first choice. It was a magnificent gesture. At the time, the only black manager in the professional game was Keith Alexander at Lincoln. My appointment would be more high-profile. I had been one of the first successful black players. Could I be the first successful black manager? It was a tempting thought.

When I was working on this book I contacted Barnsley's official historian, David Wood. He told me that Barnsley were known as an "all-white club". I hadn't known this at the time. "The fans were also notorious for making things tough for black footballers," he continued. "I don't know if there was an all-white policy on the part of the board but we didn't sign any black players after Winston Campbell left in 1986." So I not only broke the mould as far as black managers were concerned, I did it with a club who were living in the dark ages before John Dennis appointed me.

Whether I would have gone if I'd known that ... well, who can say? But good financial terms were on offer. John said there was not a lot of money for signings but they had the nucleus of a decent side. He told me that he could find the backing for a manager who could show potential. He wanted to take the club into the Premier League before too long. And he insisted that promotion should be achieved with the team playing attractive football, even if it took a bit of time. He didn't want to do a Watford or a Wimbledon and play long balls to big strikers. No, his Barnsley would – for good or ill – be known for watchable football. I have to admit I was flattered. I decided to give it some thought and talk it over with Debra.

As I've said, Bryan Robson and I had been discussing going into management for years. It was something we had talked about endlessly and we agreed that, if at all possible, we would do it together. I spoke to Bryan on the phone. He said he reckoned he had two years of playing left in him. "I think you should go to Barnsley," he said. "It will be a great learning process for you and we can team up when I retire in a couple of years. You'll have had all that experience by then." Debra, who had encouraged me to go to Wednesday in the first place, was also positive about Barnsley. She thought it was the perfect move at that time. And as it was just up the road from Sheffield, I could still keep my home in the Manchester area since the journey didn't take long.

Still, it was a big step. Was I ready to take on the task? The more I thought about it, the more I believed I was. Having played with such success down the years this was the chance to prove myself in another sphere. I pretty much talked myself into it and informed Trevor that I would be leaving. He tried to persuade me to stay, which was nice but he also realised that an opportunity like Barnsley might not come around for me again. And realistically, how long could I keep performing at a high level in the Premier League? I was sorry to say goodbye to Trevor and the players and they were sorry to say goodbye to me but it was time to move on.

I had a word with Danny Wilson. I wanted him as my assistant. He was really enthusiastic which helped cement my decision. I had already spoken to John Dennis and told him I would accept his offer provided he also took Danny on as number two. He immediately agreed and the new adventure began.

I wasn't quite prepared for the culture shock. I had spent my career at top clubs, all of which had great facilities. Of course I knew there was a different world on the other side of the tracks but the reality was something I was not totally prepared for. The dressing rooms were in a dreadful state, the training facilities were rudimentary to say the least and there weren't even any biscuits for the lads. I have to say that when I brought all these matters to the attention of the Chairman his response was always fantastic. He changed everything I asked him to, spending his own money in the process. Even the dressing rooms at Oakwell were upgraded. Well the home dressing room anyway.

The whole atmosphere of the place was friendly, like a close-knit family should be. There was never any hint of racism. Some of the back-room staff had been there for years. Nothing was too much trouble and John Dennis proved to be a wonderful Chairman. Debra was right. It was, in its way, the perfect job.

A great example of the family-type nature of Barnsley was Norman Remington. Norman, in his seventies then, had been at the club from the year dot and had done every job going. When Danny and I arrived he was the groundsman. One day in deep midwinter, when it was absolutely freezing, we saw him faithfully doing his best to keep the pitch in shape and decided it was time to offer him a new role. He was a lovely man as well as being a great servant of the club. It was something we really wanted to do. We made him kit man. He absolutely loved it, travelling with the first team and being part of things again. And the players loved him. We literally brought him back in from the cold, like you would with family.

In one respect, taking the job proved to be a baptism of fire. The previous management had accepted an offer to play in a pre-season tournament on the Isle of Man. It was the first time I had been in charge of a team, let alone a team on a trip away from home. I was a bit nervous. One night I sent the players to bed and was having a drink with Danny downstairs. Suddenly an official looking woman came into the bar.

"Who's in charge of the Barnsley footballers," she said, in a loud voice.

"I am," I replied.

"Could I have a word with you please?"

It turned out she was looking after a group of teenage girls who were staying at the hotel. They were young offenders, I think. Their trip had been paid for by the government to help in their rehabilitation.

"I've got a complaint," she continued.

"What kind of complaint?"

She came right out with it.

"One of my girls says that two of your players raped her."

I was staggered. Having obtained more details from the lady, including the identity of the players concerned, I told her I would immediately deal with the matter. I asked her to wait while Danny and I had words with the individuals named. My assistant and I were well prepared for football-related problems. But having to cope with something like this before we had really started on our management careers was not what we had expected. Nonetheless, it had to be confronted.

We went up to the room the two players were sharing and told them about the allegation as bluntly as we ourselves had been told. We wanted to see how they would react. Both Danny and I could tell from the expressions of complete and utter surprise on their faces that they knew nothing about any rape. Either that or they were great actors – which they weren't. They totally denied raping the girl in question and were adamant she had made the whole thing up.

Danny and I returned to the bar and reported our conversation to the woman downstairs. "My two players say there was no rape at all," I told her. She could have called the police there and then but she didn't. She was silent for a moment or two as if she had some inkling that the girl was lying. Then, instead of calling the police she and her staff decided to question the girl again. This time she asked us to stay in the bar while she enquired further. We spent quite some time worrying while we waited for her to return.

When she came back she looked grim. "The girl has admitted she made it up," she said. We breathed a big sigh of relief. So did the players when we told them. The woman looked uneasy and made an attempt at an apology which wasn't very convincing. Still, the tension that had been building up was relieved now the truth was out. The issue had been resolved in an hour or so. It could have been much worse for the guys involved if the girl had stuck to her story. If that had happened there would have been no way of keeping the police out of it. Once the police were summoned, the press would get hold of it and all hell would break loose. Luckily for the players, none of that happened. The next day it was made known to us that the girl's holiday had been terminated and she had been sent back to the mainland. It was a close call, that's for sure. But Danny and I had passed our first big test.

Expectations are not that high at a place like Barnsley. The fans have seen too many years go by without even a sniff of success for it to be any different. You can't compare working there in any way with the likes of Arsenal or Manchester United, where the loss of a couple of games on the spin is a full-blown crisis. Those clubs might as well be on a different planet. Nonetheless, John Dennis set targets and it was my job as manager to achieve them. Up until that point, Barnsley had always been a lower league club. The second (or new first) division was the highest they could realistically hope for in the short term. John Dennis wanted their position in the First Division consolidated and for the team to finish as high as possible. Mid-table was the minimum, anything higher a bonus. A couple of wins in one of the cup competitions would be welcome too. After that .... who knew? John dreamed of life in the Premier League one day. So a good campaign in my first season was expected to be followed by improvements year-on-year. It was a challenge on the budget we had.

Player-manager is not an easy role to get right. You tend to be harder on yourself as a player and not hard enough as a manager. You need the input of those around you. I was lucky to have had the experience of watching Trevor Francis because, apart from him, I had no experience of how a player-manager should operate. For instance, a big problem is the half-time talk. This is when the manager, who has been watching the match from his vantage point, really earns his money. Games are won and lost in the second half. The half-time talk can help the players consolidate a winning position or have a big influence on turning a game around if you are losing. How you approach the second half is the most important thing whatever the state of the game; even if you're losing 6–0. When you're playing, you have to concentrate on your own performance. You can't see the big picture so it's difficult to communicate anything meaningful to the players at the interval. In our case at Barnsley, Danny Wilson would normally have been expected to carry out the half-time talk. But he was also brought in as part player, part my assistant manager, so he couldn't do it either. We asked the long-standing coach, Eric Winstanley, to do the job. He did it willingly and made a useful contribution. But it was not an ideal solution, that's why Eric was not a manager.

I believed the existing squad of players, bolstered by myself and Danny, was almost – but not quite – good enough to do well in the division. Only two seasons before they had missed out on a promotion place only on goal difference. But that near-success had not been built upon. It was that failure, I think, which led to the departure of the manager, Mel Machin. After looking at them in training I decided that we needed to strengthen upfront. The Chairman found enough funds for me to secure the services of Andy Payton from Celtic to give us some goalscoring options alongside the striker, Neil Redfearn. Apart from that I left things much as they were.

I was right about the team in one way but wrong in another. When they were going forward they could play some great stuff, especially after Danny, Eric and I got them on the training ground. Andy Payton scored goals. The defence, however, was all over the place. Collective and individual mistakes cost us goals in game after game and we slumped down the table. These defects at the back surprised me. I couldn't leave myself out of the criticism although my own game wasn't too bad after I had adjusted to the difference between Division One and the

Premier League once more. We also had Gerry Taggart in the side and he was one of the most uncompromising defenders in the game. It was all very odd. Neither Danny nor I could put our finger on what was going wrong.

Gerry Taggart had been bought from Manchester City by Mel Machin in what was a very strange deal. Barnsley got Gerry on the cheap but if Barnsley sold him, City would get eighty percent of the fee. I got plenty of offers for Gerry, he was an outstanding defender, but I tried to stall them all because I knew that if we sold him, we wouldn't get enough out of our twenty percent to be able to buy a decent replacement.

During the first half of the season we lost five straight home matches and shipped thirty-eight goals in eighteen games. It was horrible and at one stage, after losing at home to Grimsby through a last-minute penalty, we dropped to twenty-first in the table. There were calls for me to be sacked. I knew now what Alex Ferguson must have gone through when it happened to him. But the Chairman stuck by me. He refused to listen to the critics and backed his judgment of me. That gave me the confidence to carry on.

While we were in the grip of those poor performances one of the senior players, Gary Fleming, came to see me. He said he thought that some of our problems stemmed from a poor attitude towards training on the part of the players.

"I reckon everything goes back to when the last manager was here," he told me.

"What do you mean?"

"Well, to be honest, boss, the players got to the point where they hated coming in for training."

"Go on."

"It wasn't Mel Machin himself, it was the coaching staff. They hardly ever had us doing stuff with the ball or working on different skills or tactics. They just had us running for stamina and practising how far we could kick the ball. That's pretty much all we did. It was horrible. Towards the end some of them (the players) wouldn't turn up."

I hadn't known about the training methods of Mel's coaching staff but from what Gary had said it appeared they had alienated the players to the extent that it had spilled over onto my watch. I talked to Eric Winstanley and he confirmed what Fleming had said in regard to the methods that were employed at the time. But he hadn't known about the players' reactions or how it affected them.

I spoke about the matter to Danny Wilson. We got together every day after training in a local pub and would analyse everything about what we were doing. We not only decided to put a new training programme in place but we would also change the team's style of play. On the training side, the first thing we did was to bring in loads of five-a-sides, which the players loved. Then we made sure the coaching staff laid off practising the long balls.

Under Machin, Barnsley played a sweeper system, which at first sight might seem at odds with what the training was trying to achieve. I couldn't pay too much attention to that, though, I had work to do. Danny and I had been brought up on 4-4-2 so that was naturally our preferred way to play. But we realised that this particular group of players were much more comfortable playing with a sweeper. Machin had instilled it into them. Switching them straight to 4-4-2 and expecting them to just understand its requirements had confused them. It was a lesson to me. Although you would think that a professional footballer can seamlessly switch from one system to another, this is not necessarily the case. Footballers need to have their role explained to them in great detail and they need to practice it again and again.

Danny and me decided on two major changes. First, we would revert to playing with a sweeper. Second, I decided to play less and manage more. I could still keep up with the younger lads on the pitch. But we thought the manager's briefings, especially the half-time talk, were more important. It couldn't be left to one of the coaches.

I began to see improvements in the team's performances. After Christmas, results started to go in our favour as well. The turnaround occurred when we scraped through the third round of the FA Cup against non-league Bromsgrove. The performance wasn't very good that day, in fact it was embarrassing. I thought Gerry Taggart got the winning goal but that just shows you what my memory is like. Recently I was out with Gerry for a night in London. He told me that, actually, it was Owen Archdeacon. Shows you how much I know. Whoever got the goal, we were lucky to win it and from there, confidence returned to the players and we strung together some good results. Not long after the Bromsgrove game, Andy Payton got the winner against Peterborough in our first home victory for three months. Gradually, Payton, along with Andy Rammell, began scoring more goals. The new work we were doing on the training ground was paying off. I could see the players enjoying it. At the business end of the season we won eight out of ten games and finished well clear of the drop zone in mid-table. We had reached the Chairman's minimum requirement.

It was around this time that an odd chant started to be heard on occasion from the fans: "It's just like watching Brazil," they sang.

Believe it or not, we played in a European competition that season. But we didn't play any European teams, which is of course a bit of a contradiction. It was in a weird tournament called the Anglo-Italian Cup, devised for teams in the second tier of each country's football leagues. The format comprised an initial group stage followed by semi-finals and a final. There were three teams in each group and they were only from your own country. So there was an English group and an Italian group. The winners and runners up went through to the knockout stage where they played teams from the other country. Then there was a final which might or might not be between an English and an Italian team. If it sounds mad, it was, and it didn't last for long before it died a natural death.

Unfortunately, the competition came in the first half of the season when we were at our worst. We played two games, against Middlesbrough and Grimsby. Very

Italian! We won one and lost one but finished bottom of our group on goal difference. So we never got to play any Italian side. I don't think anyone mourns the passing of the Anglo-Italian Cup.

Our improvement coincided with the FA Cup. We were drawn away to Plymouth in the fourth round. The Pilgrims were managed by my old Forest team-mate, Peter Shilton. Although they occupied a place in the division beneath us, Shilts had them playing well and they were pushing for promotion.

Plymouth took their good form into the game against us. Andy Payton put us ahead against the run of play but our opponents came back with two wonder goals. We were thankful to Gerry Taggart who came up for a set-piece and grabbed us an equaliser. The tie had to go to a replay, which would generate some money for the Chairman. An Andy Payton goal just before half-time won us the replay and set us up for a fifth round match-up away from home against Oldham.

Although Oldham knocked us out 1–0, Barnsley's mini cup run was the club's best performance in the FA Cup for some time. It gave the fans some much-needed cheer and the players new belief. The Chairman was pleased too.

All told, John Dennis was happy with our season. He didn't have much money to spend so we certainly couldn't buy our way out of trouble. He did what he could, though, and backed me all the way. At the end of the season he wanted to sit down with me and plan the next campaign.

By then, though, I had been having a number of conversations with Bryan Robson. Robbo had seen the writing on the wall. Fergie thought he had passed his sell-by date as a player. The time was right to leave, he said, because he had received a management offer. He wanted to know if I was still up for it.

He began to tell me about Middlesbrough and the club's new Chairman, Steve Gibson. Robbo was impressed with Gibson's ambitions for the club, which included, among other things, a new stadium which was already being built. That was a statement of intent for Robbo. He wanted a manager's job at a club whose ambitions matched his own. That club, he insisted, was Middlesbrough.

Was I up for it? You bet I was. At last it looked like the perfect opportunity had arrived. But I had an obligation to Barnsley, especially John Dennis. I talked about it with Debra. She didn't want me to take the Middlesbrough job. I don't think she was ever so against a move. Her arguments were that I was number one at Barnsley and would be number two at Middlesbrough. And she thought that even though we could continue to live in the Manchester area and I would be able to commute, Middlesbrough was much further away than either Sheffield or Barnsley. That meant I would spend even more time away from home. She liked the way I was treated at Barnsley and doubted whether this aspect could be the same anywhere else. She was also a bit worried about me and Robbo's drinking when we got together socially. Having said her bit, she was happy to leave the decision up to me.

I agonised for a couple of days but really my decision was never in doubt. I couldn't not go, if you know what I mean. However much I fancied finishing what I started at Oakwell, this was what me and Robbo had been talking about all these years. Reluctantly, I broke the news to John Dennis. He wasn't pleased but he wished me well. He also asked me to recommend my successor.

Chapter Seventeen

STARS IN OUR EYES

I enjoyed my time at Barnsley. It was a fantastic period and I thought the team responded to my methods and were definitely on the up. I would have loved to have worked with the players some more. I wouldn't have gone anywhere if anybody else but Robbo had been the one to ask me. I had a last conversation with John Dennis.

"The man you need to take my place is Danny Wilson, he can take this team forward."

John looked at me, scrutinising my face as if to see if I meant what I was saying or was just putting a word in for my old mate. I meant it alright. I couldn't see any manager being able to do as well as Danny could. I was pleased when John decided to give Danny his chance, it was exactly the right decision. Danny knew the players, he could provide some continuity from my period in charge and, I believed, he was good enough to be a success in the number one job.

Danny turned out to be the perfect successor to me at Barnsley. I cannot praise his achievements there enough. He took them into the Premier League with good football and the chants of 'It's just like watching

Brazil' ringing round Oakwell. There were no better times to be a Barnsley supporter than when the club got promotion then spent a season in the top division. Although that term in the Premier League ended in relegation, it was the best thing to happen to the Tykes in many a long year. Unfortunately, after relegation, finances suffered and John Dennis had to place the club into administration in 2002. Happily, a revived Barnsley are now doing well in the Championship. The fans will remember their adventure in the Premier League forever.

Robbo was full of praise for the set-up at Middlesbrough. A new stadium, the Riverside, was rising on the banks of the River Tees and would be the first major new football ground to be built in England for over seventy years. The chairman, Steve Gibson, told Bryan he intended to make Middlesbrough a top team. There would be big money for the best players. He had recruited Keith Lamb as Chief Executive. Lamb helped save the club when he worked for the administrators, who had been called in during Middlesbrough's darkest hour. The club were bankrupt in the mid-eighties and were forced into administration. They actually came within a whisker of folding completely. Now, thanks entirely to Gibson's efforts, Middlesbrough was a phoenix rising from the ashes. The club was a symbol of the new world of English football, ready for success with luxurious facilities and money to spend.

Responding to Robbo's invitation, I really had no hesitation in swapping Barnsley for Middlesbrough, despite

In the dug out with
United's new goal
scoring sensation Brian
McClair who went on to
score 24 goals in his first
season.

Leaping for a header with Kevin Moran, putting Liverpool under pressure, as Match
of the Day's Alan Hansen looks on. Man Utd. v Liverpool 1987.

Avoiding the sliding tackle.

Can you spot all the future Premier League managers?

Before kick off with my good friend Bryan Robson.

Goal celebration with David Hirst against
Blackburn.

All for the Wednesday cause.

"Big" Ron Atkinson talks tactics on the training ground.

Barnsley team photo 1993–94
Back row: L to R: David Currie, Adrian Moses, Gareth Williams, David Watson, Lee Butler, Jamie Robinson, Andy Rammell, Charlie Bishop. Middle Row L to R: Colin Walker (Youth Coach), Eric Winstanley (First Team Coach), Mark Feeney, Ian Bryson, Robert Hanby, Brendan O'Connell, Deiniol Graham, Gary Fleming, Mark Burton, Gerry Taggart, Wayne Biggins, Martin Bullock, Steve Stafford (Physio) Front row L to R: John Clegg, Owen Archdeacon, Andrew Liddell, Danny Wilson (Player Coach), Viv Anderson (Player Manager), Glynn Snodin, Nicky Eaden, Neil Redfern, Greg Morgan.

The Barnsley player manager in action!

I was only sent off once at Barnsley, but the cartoonist still found this sketch necessary!

Terry Venables, the master tactician, with Bryan Robson and myself pondering the Middlesbrough team selection.

Middlesbrough FC team management: Terry Venables, Bryan Robson and I direct from the sidelines.

Out for a duck!

Relaxing with my partner Nichole.

With, Charlie and Freddie, my boys.

I'm a huge fan of the Rolling Stones. Here I am with the original bass player supreme, Bill Wyman.

With a few football legends for the National Football Museum held at the Reebok Stadium 2007. In attendance were Bert Trautmann, Roy Hartle, Mike Summerbee, Jackie Charlton, myself, Frank Worthington, Bryan Robson, Phil Neal, Tom Finney, Alan Ball, Pat Crerand and Peter Reid.

Proudly collecting
my MBE with my wife
Debra and my eldest son
Charlie. January 2000.

Still winning trophies, with the
Manchester United Masters, at the Malaysia Cup 2009.

Debra's misgivings and the great relationship I had developed with John Dennis and the Barnsley fans. This was always what Robbo and I had agreed we wanted to do. Happy that I had done my very best for the Yorkshire club, I struck out for Teesside. In more ways than one, it was to prove a fateful decision.

Middlesbrough is a club with a long and proud tradition. However, when I went there they had never won a major trophy and had existed under the shadow of their fellow north-eastern clubs, Newcastle and Sunderland, for many years. Some success had come their way in the seventies when Jack Charlton was manager, but that first trophy had still proved elusive. They had some great players down the years, none more so than Brian Clough, who scored bagfuls of goals for Boro in the fifties. When I joined up with Robbo they had been suffering from the financial meltdown of the 1980s. Steve Gibson, however, intended to end all that. The fact that Middlesbrough still exists is down to Gibson. He is the founder and Chairman of a company called Bulkhaul Ltd., which transports dangerous substances such as liquids, gases and powders all over the world. He made his fortune available to the club, as a life-long fan would. Nothing was too good for his Middlesbrough.

Along with me and Robbo, we took the great Scottish defender Gordon McQueen with us to Boro. He had been a team-mate of Robbo's at Manchester United and both Bryan and I thought we could bring his experience to the younger players. After that, Robbo immediately set about breaking the club's transfer record, signing Neil Cox from Aston Villa for £1 million, the first time Middlesbrough had paid seven figures for a player. We also brought in Nigel Pearson from Wednesday to be our leader on the pitch. Amazingly, Manchester United let us take Clayton Blackmore on a free transfer. That was a real coup. I remained registered as a player and Bryan was player-manager. But while Bryan still wanted to play I didn't intend to make regular appearances. So it would be down to me to be Robbo's eyes and ears when he was on the pitch and handle the all-important half-time talk. In the unlikely event that we had a run of injuries, I would play. Otherwise I was now a full-time assistant manager.

When we arrived the team had spent one unsuccessful season in the new First Division, having been relegated from the Premier League the year before. Lenny Lawrence was the manager during that time and he resigned when it became clear that his methods were not working. Steve Gibson was a massive fan of Robbo's. He was prepared to back his judgment and give Robbo the chance to prove he could be a manager at a big club. He made it clear that Bryan was the only man for the job.

Our first season in management together – 1994–95 – was incredible and we stormed to the First Division title. We were the best team by far. A loan player we brought in, Uwe Fuchs, was particularly successful, scoring nine goals during the run-in.

Needless to say, the unlikely happened. Late in the season we suffered a spate of injuries and suspensions, particularly in the defence. So I was forced to make my full playing debut. We were away to West Brom and pushing for promotion. I was the grand old age of 39. How I managed to stay fit enough to appear in the first team at that age is beyond comprehension. Robbo also played in the game and he was the same age as me. I had a great game marking Andy Hunt and we ran out 3-1 winners. I was knackered afterwards, though, especially my feet and ankles. Robbo, on the other hand, couldn't get enough of the action. He was not only a player and manager for us, he also did some coaching with England. How he managed to keep it all together amazed me. It did mean, though, that I felt it my duty to keep an eye on him in case there were any signs of burnout.

Since the start of the Premier League, a play-off system of promotion had been adopted. For our first season at Middlesbrough, there was only one automatic promotion spot as the Premier League was once again tinkering with its format. This time the number of teams in the top flight was being reduced back to twenty. So four teams went down and two came up: The teams to be promoted were to be the winners of the First Division and the side that won the play-offs. Given our profile and the money Robbo and I spent, that one automatic place had to go to us. Some thought Wolves were favourites. They had also spent some big money and recruited ex-England boss, Graham Taylor, to be their manager. Like us they had a rich owner who was prepared to pay out on transfer fees and wages. But the lottery of the play-offs was not an option as far as Robbo and me were concerned. As things turned out, we blitzed the division and Wolves could not keep up with the pace we set. The expectations at Middlesbrough brought pressure but we were more than ready for the challenge.

Steve Gibson was in ecstasy as we clinched the First Division title. He saw it as his first objective achieved, right on schedule. What made Steve even happier was that we were going back to the Premier League with the Riverside ready to open for business. It would be a great showcase for the club. He wanted a team fit to grace the new stadium. He called me and Robbo together and asked us about our plans for the top flight.

In the close season, as we contemplated the Premier League, the work began in earnest. Robbo and Keith Lamb left me to look after team matters while they flew to Brazil. They went to see if they could persuade the Brazilian footballer of the year, Juninho, to come to the Riverside. We wanted him as our marquee signing. Steve Gibson agreed the £4.5 million transfer fee with Juninho's club and Robbo and Keith entered into talks with the player and his advisors. What clinched the deal, as would be the case time and again at Middlesbrough, was a combination of Gibson's money and Robbo's reputation.

Bryan wanted Juninho. He was convinced the little midfielder had what it took to be a major star in Europe and a massive performer for Middlesbrough. His plan was to build his team round the Brazilian. There was not much history of Brazilian players coming to England in those days and certainly none who achieved any great success. But Robbo loved the skills a player like Juninho showed on the pitch. He said from the outset, and I agreed with him, that Juninho was just the sort of player who could help produce the type of football we wanted to play. For his part, Juninho knew all about Bryan Robson even if he'd never heard of Teesside. His enthusiasm was obvious. When Robbo arrived home he was convinced he'd done the right thing. When I saw Juninho play, so was I.

We also bought Nick Barmby from Spurs for a massive £5.3 million. Barmby had been a really talented young-ster who had lost his way a bit with Tottenham. The size of the fee shows the regard in which he was held in the football world. We had to fight off a number of other clubs to get his signature. By now the town was jumping. Middlesbrough had suffered untold hardships during the eighties. Both the football club and the town itself were victims of a sharp decline in fortunes. Now, the football club were leading the way back. Our emergence was the talk of the country and the town was right behind us. It was a feel-good factor the like of which the citizens of Middlesbrough hadn't seen for years. For a time, Middlesbrough was the centre of the football universe.

In the meantime, both Robbo and I were spending more and more time on the club's business. Yet we both lived in Manchester with our spouses. The drive to Middlesbrough took at least two hours, often much longer. On occasion, Steve Gibson provided us with the use of a private plane, which made things a bit easier. But most of the time we either got home late or had to stay in hotels. Looking back I can see I was hardly at home for huge periods of my time at Middlesbrough. This in turn led to the bonds with Debra loosening that little bit more.

But back at the football club, we were on a roll. By October we were up to fourth in the Premier League. Surely we couldn't do a Forest – could we? But the football gods were not to be so kind. Our away form was not great from the moment we got back into the top division. We were sustained by our performances at the new Riverside. Moving there just as Juninho arrived was unbelievable. Crowds were flocking to the new stadium and, with an opening capacity of just over 35,000, it was proving too small to accommodate all those who wanted to attend matches. Steve Gibson had thought about this, and built into the design was the possibility of increasing the capacity year-on-year. In the first three months there we blew teams away with Juninho turning it on. But away from home, we were a bit of a soft prospect, and couldn't score goals. We only managed eight all season. This began to put pressure on us at home. After getting up to fourth we went on a terrible run and even our home form deserted us. Nonetheless, we finished a very creditable twelfth. As Middlesbrough's last season at the top finished in relegation, I think we all would have taken that at the beginning of the campaign.

It was the next season – 1996–97 – that football threw everything it had at us. What could happen did happen. First and biggest came when Robbo, Keith and me found ourselves in Turin. We were meeting with the management of Juventus, the European Champions and one of the world's greatest clubs. The meeting was held to talk about the possible transfer of an ageing Juventus forward, Vaili, to Middlesbrough as cover. We also wanted to establish a relationship with the Italians and we spoke to them about the business of football and where there might be any common interests between us.

After some initial small talk, we all congratulated them on their European Cup win. I decided to play the cheeky chappie, asking them "And how much will you sell us Fabrizio for?" This was a reference to the brilliant Fabrizio Ravanelli, one of the best strikers in the world and the scorer of Juventus's winner in the Euro-final. Instead of laughter at the obviously ludicrous request, the assembled Juventus management went silent before exchanging knowing glances. "Ten million pounds" came the reply. This was getting interesting. We couldn't believe our ears, really. Could it be true that the club was prepared to let someone of Ravanelli's stature go? It was only a joke question from me, now things had turned very serious indeed. We jumped in and immediately agreed their valuation, even if it was an outrageous price. We weren't about to let this opportunity slip away. The deal was done there and then.

There is no question that Ravanelli was shocked when he found out that Juventus were prepared to sell him behind his back. He could have rejected us out of hand; no-one would have blamed him for insisting on Champions League football at the very least if he were forced to leave. But again, Robbo's reputation held sway. And Steve Gibson made Ravanelli an offer he couldn't refuse. It made him probably the highest paid player in Europe. We now had the best from Brazil and the best from Italy lining up for Middlesbrough.

These days the great players from every country queue up to come to England. In the mid-nineties, when the Premier League was still in its infancy, that was not yet the case. We blazed the trail. Lots of the metropolitan media made fun of the sophisticated Italian coming to Teesside. But the truth is, just a short drive from the industrial landscape of the town there is some exquisite countryside and Fabrizio, when he came to visit, immediately fell in love with English village life. Having secured the great Italian, Robbo went for another Brazilian, the midfielder Emerson, who was playing in Portugal at the time. Once Emerson heard that Ravanelli had joined Juninho at Middlesbrough (and when he found out the size of the salary on the table), he couldn't wait to come to England. I think he was shocked when he saw Teesside. That's not what his image of England was. But he was still enthusiastic. We now had a team to really stamp our mark on the Premier League. And Middlesbrough, who had never won a League trophy or appeared in any Cup Final, were making huge waves in what was then still a very traditionally-minded Premier League. For Robbo and me it was the highest point in our managerial career.

Ravanelli was a revelation, scoring goals for fun and working as hard in training as anyone I've ever seen. The fans loved him, particularly when he pioneered the shirt-over-the-head goal celebration. Juninho also excelled himself and drew rave reviews. The media adored him.

They weren't so keen on Emerson but he was our best player on many occasions. Unfortunately, his manner made the press constantly question his commitment, which got on all our nerves I can tell you. We only had two problems with Emerson. The first was when he failed to return from a trip to Brazil on time. This was interpreted by the press as evidence that Emerson wanted away and it is true that his agent was hoping to engineer a move to Barcelona. Maybe he did find it hard in the north-east, but as a player he always gave it everything. And his failure to come back from Brazil on time was easily dealt with by our disciplinary procedure. I think Emerson was a great success. The other problem occurred one day as we prepared to go onto the pitch for a big Premier League game, I forget who we were playing. Bryan wanted a last minute word with the players and called them together. All were there except Emerson.

"Where is he?" Robbo enquired.

No-one knew. Some of us went off to find him.

I looked in the toilets, thinking that was the most likely place to find him. Maybe he was ill. Then something alerted my nostrils. It was tobacco smoke.

"Emer," I called. "Are you in there?"

I heard a few Brazilian-type grunts then Emerson appeared. He had been having a crafty cigarette. We didn't know he was a smoker. Although in years past smoking was common among footballers, our generation frowned upon it. As managers, both Robbo and I expected our players to be non-smokers.

"What?" he asked.

"The boss wants to talk to all the players, get in there and don't let me catch you having a fag again." He looked at me as if he didn't quite understand. But we never found him smoking after that.

It didn't help that the press were constantly speculating that our overseas stars hated life in the north-east and couldn't wait to move on. Even though these stories were a long way from the truth, the English contingent could never really be sure and team morale – or rather confidence – suffered as a consequence. We slipped down the League and found ourselves in a battle against relegation, to the delight of the cynics.

We would have won that battle but for a disastrous error of judgment on the part of all of us in positions of responsibility at the club. Coming into the Christmas programme we were struck down by the flu. The virus went through the whole squad like a dose of salts. Both Robbo and I caught it. So did the backroom staff and several directors. This wasn't just a cold or man-flu. This was full-blown influenza. I had never seen anything like it at a football club. We were going down like ninepins. And it had a really horrible effect on all who contracted it.

By the time we were due to face an away game at Blackburn we were really struggling to field a team. We sought permission to have the match postponed but this was not forthcoming. There was no national epidemic, it seemed to be a localised problem and the Premier League were unsympathetic. Meanwhile, on the day of the game, we lost even more of the few players who remained. Keith Lamb spoke on the phone to someone at the Premier League – I don't know who it was – and asked them what the penalty would be if we failed to fulfil the fixture. The word came back that we would incur a hefty fine.

On the basis of that phone call, Robbo and I recommended to Keith Lamb and Steve Gibson that we pull out of the game. Gibson authorised it. Quite why we did it on the basis of a phone call with nothing in writing I can't explain to this day, to be honest. Whatever, we didn't turn up to play at Blackburn. That turned out to be a big mistake.

The disciplinary panel took a very dim view of our actions. Failure to fulfil a fixture is a very serious offence in football. All the medical evidence in the world couldn't save us and as well as a fine we were docked three points. Never mind what we had been told in that phone call, it cut no ice. Those three points made the difference between staying up and going down. It was a terrible end to the season.

We appealed the decision and the punishment. At the appeal hearing we were represented by one of the most famous barristers in the country, the legendary George Carman QC, who was a big Manchester United supporter. Carman's fee was £13,000 a day (you think footballers are overpaid). The great lawyer couldn't believe the way the tribunal conducted itself. At one point he turned to Steve Gibson and said: "In a real court of law you would win your case hands down. But these people: they have their own set of rules and you will never win your case with them. I can tell."

At the time we felt we had been unfairly treated but with hindsight we really should have known better than to take such a major step as not playing a fixture on the basis of a phone call. It was just too big a risk. In our defence, I think we were all suffering from the effects of the flu. But still, it would have been better to recruit a bunch of lads off the streets than not play the game. Perhaps we had got ahead of ourselves. We had to take our share of responsibility for the fiasco. We certainly never thought for a moment that we would be docked points. Until it happened! Now, all our plans were in tatters. Not only would we have to start again in the First Division, we were bound to lose our stars. They would not be prepared to play in the lower league. We really would have to go back to square one. Although we managed to rally in the following two years, nothing was ever the same again.

To rub salt in our wounds, we lost the League Cup Final to Martin O'Neill's Leicester in a replay. We also got to the FA Cup Final but were well beaten by Chelsea. Before the League Cup Final the town was absolutely humming as we had become the first side in Middlesbrough's history to get through to a major final. Not only that, we were hot favourites. Not because we had performed better in our League campaign than Leicester – on the contrary, they finished way above us in the final table. No, it was the money we had spent, the stars we had in our team and our aura of success which made us odds-on (at the time of the final, we had not been relegated and most football-watchers thought we would survive). A very tight first game at Wembley seemed to be going our way when Fabrizio put us ahead in extra time. But Emile Heskey got a scrappy equaliser with virtually the last kick of the match and we had to go to Hillsborough for the replay. We were not very good that night and a solitary Steve Claridge goal won the Cup for Leicester.

Neither me nor Robbo were in a great frame of mind. Things on the field had collapsed. We would have to put in some serious hard work and regroup for the future. But there were other things collapsing in my life that would have more profound effects than anything on a football pitch could manage.

Chapter Eighteen

REAL LIFE - 2

Telling all of you who read this book about my football career, even the bad or controversial bits, is easy. No matter what, it's still just football, which is not real life. It's a game we have played and enjoyed since we were toddlers. Much as we love it, it is only a game. Being good at sport, however, doesn't necessarily equip you with the skills to deal with other things in life. For example, you have to be able to deal with the press, which is not an easy thing to do. I learned early on in my career that the attention you get from the media as a top player is intense and you can't do anything to change it. Maybe you don't want to, particularly when you are getting regular praise for your deeds on the field. There will always come a time, though, when you'll have to take some stick. That's the way it works. Some people handle that better than others. I like to think that I have always stood up for what I believed when I've been criticised in the media and refused to be intimidated. This was the case when there were calls for my resignation at Barnsley. But I've never challenged the right of reporters to do their job. Like in any field of work, some do it better than others. And some are more honest than others.

There are huge numbers of people who loved playing football when they were kids. For most, their lives take various courses and they go on to other careers. But the game remains a passion throughout their lives. They are interested in every story, every bit of gossip about the game they love. Those of us who progress to the ranks of the professional – whether we like it or not – become role-models for all who stay in love with the game they once played with their mates. That has produced a press that is hungry for any story, whether or not it has anything to do with football. And the scrutiny is getting scarier with every passing year. Ask John Terry. It's no good complaining about this. Footballers get paid well, receive the adoration of fans and generally live a blessed life doing what we love. That doesn't mean, however, that we are any good at anything else. We are expected to be experts on family matters, be brilliant at interviews in the media and to possess thrilling personalities. As the Americans might say: we can just play ball.

By the time I linked up with Robbo I should have been well aware of how the media operates. Not only had I been subjected to my fair share of positive and negative stories, I had also seen how any number of other players and mangers dealt with the intrusions that come with a high profile. What I wasn't prepared for was my personal life being splashed all over the newspapers. I still find it difficult, even now, to talk about it. But given that so much appeared in the press about my life during the time I was at Middlesbrough, I feel I would not be giving the reader a fair deal if I wasn't prepared to say something about what went on. I would not do this under normal circumstances and certainly not without the consent of some of the people involved. So I asked both my current partner, Nichole, and my former partner, Debra, what their thoughts were regarding me speaking about this part of my life. Both said they felt it should be included. They were even prepared to help with their recollections. That tells you what kind of people they are. They have both made a significant contribution to this book and I thank them for that.

As I have stated previously, by the time I went to Middlesbrough, my marriage to Debra was feeling the strain of events that had happened over the years. Our protracted attempts to have children and the consequences that came from them had a big effect on our relationship. It's not something you realise when it's happening because it occurs so slowly, but you can see it when you look back from a decent distance in time. The John Fashanu incident might have contributed to our problems but I don't think it did. It actually made us stronger as we fought against his misinformation, but the togetherness we displayed during that period only masked what, in the end, proved fatal to our marriage.

Outwardly, we presented a united front but really a distance had grown between us. The strain of trying for children and the bittersweet experience of Debra's pregnancy had taken their toll. Also, the footballer's lifestyle includes lots of time away from home. As a manager, more so. This can lead to a couple starting to drift apart. Absence doesn't make the heart grow fonder in my experience. There is no special pleading here. The kind of strains we suffered happen in many marriages up and down the land. Knowledge of that, though, doesn't lessen the impact when matters go wrong. Nevertheless, I would never have wanted things to turn out the way they did, with our personal lives plastered across the tabloids and the press-pack camped outside our house.

Everything came to a head after I took the Middlesbrough job. I wasn't seeing as much of Debra as before and, as I said earlier, the absences undoubtedly contributed to the problems. And she had advised me against taking the job in the first place, in part for that very reason. Robbo and I were spending an awful lot of time after training analysing every aspect of what was going on at the club. This wasn't anything new. We had always done it as players and I continued to do it with Danny Wilson at Barnsley. But with Robbo and me, those talks took up quite a bit of time. What was different was that at that moment in our lives we were also needed at home. There was also the task of going to other games to watch players. All this was compounded by a never-ending round of business meetings, reports to the Chief Executive, reviewing the progress of construction at the new stadium and dealing with the usual disasters that befall professional footballers. We had also resumed our drinking after work was finished for the day. I wouldn't say we were problem drinkers (although some might argue otherwise) but it did take up more time than it ought to have done. Perhaps we should have spent more of our hours relaxing with our families. On the other hand, if my life had not taken this turn, I would never have forged a new life with Nichole, nor would I have had the pleasure of another child.

Robbo and I often used to wind down at a restaurant, which had a night-club attached, close to the Riverside. That's where I met Nichole, who at the time was the club's manager. It was a busy and successful rendezvous, with a nice, relaxed atmosphere. It was always full and was a fun place to be. Nichole and I hit it off immediately. There was a connection and a chemistry between us and before long the inevitable happened. We started an affair that soon blossomed into a fully-fledged relationship. I had never been a womaniser – despite having every opportunity down the years – and didn't really know how best to deal with the situation. I am the first to admit that I could have managed it better than I did.

I am ashamed to say that I didn't tell Debra what was going on. I just couldn't. I don't know why. And anyway, it didn't become certain that Nichole and I would make a life together for some time after we started our affair. It was wrong of me not to deal with it there and then but now I can only hold my hands up, admit the fact, and apologise for the pain I caused.

As someone who had been schooled in the ways of the press over many years, I should have realised they would get hold of the story sooner or later. Who tipped them off, I don't know. These days it is impossible for anyone in the public eye to go to a restaurant, a club, a theatre or anywhere else for that matter, without being snapped by either the paparazzi or a member of the public's mobile phone. In my case I can only guess whether this was how the press found out about my affair with Nichole. The first any of us knew that the newspapers were onto it was when Debra got a knock on the door one morning to find two reporters there. I think they were from the Sunday Mirror or the Sunday People. They wanted to know what Debra had to say about the fact that I was having an affair with another woman in Middlesbrough. They had assumed she was aware of it. Debra, of course, knew nothing about it. Her surprise must have been obvious. She thought they were joking. When the reporters realised she was ignorant of my affair, it only served to whet their appetites even more.

Debra decided to say nothing further and got on the phone to me. I was with Robbo, I think we were driving. She was understandably extremely upset. Both Robbo and I tried to calm her down without much success. It was a shock for which I was totally unprepared and my reaction was at first defensive. I had no idea the media had been sniffing about. The reporters were clever. They had not yet approached me or Nichole at this point.

I denied it all at first. It was a silly thing to do. The game was up. I raced home to see what I could salvage from the mess but it was too late. After talking around the issue for what seemed like an eternity with Debra, I at last admitted my affair. Debra was stunned.

"Do you love her?" she asked.

I don't know why but this question threw me.

"No, I don't know," was my inadequate reply.

Nothing now was going to stop the media in all its

glory reporting what had happened. The papers had a field day, printing all manner of lurid stories. Once the floodgates were opened, we were swamped. Loads more journalists door-stepped our house in an attempt to get Debra to give them an interview. What they were after was a comment that sounded like a 'betrayed wife'. It wasn't very pleasant. She was in too much turmoil to respond to anything at that point. When she collected her thoughts she tried to give the press a wide berth. In fact she never gave them anything they could use against me, much to her credit in my view.

Meanwhile, two other reporters descended on Nichole's restaurant pretending to be ordinary members of the public. What they really wanted was to get a picture of her they could splash all over the paper. They claimed they had heard of the place from a friend and were there to see if it was a suitable club to hire for a private party they were organising. Nichole, not realising what was going on, was taken in by the deception. She showed them around like a good manager would when presented with a possible booking. She was happy to answer their questions. They even duped her into letting them take photographs – with Nichole included in them – on the pretext that they wanted to show their friends what the venue and its staff looked like. The photos, along with a highly-dubious article, duly appeared in the papers. This led to a deluge of reporters and paparazzi descending on Nichole. She, of course, had no experience at all in the ways of the press. The tactics they used were unbeliev-able. For instance, I had bought Nichole a watch for her birthday. When the newspapers got hold of this they published it in a way that sounded awful. 'Viv Anderson lavishes expensive jewellery on his mistress' was the spin they hit us with. It was a completely untrue interpretation but it sounded scandalous. The tabloids loved it; they couldn't get enough.

The thing is, Nichole and I were serious about each other. I think we both knew that. I was in love with her. But, at this stage, with this level of intrusion, we wanted to do the right thing. After a lot of soul-searching we agreed that I would try to patch up my marriage and we wouldn't see each other, at least for a time.

While Debra and I made a doomed attempt to save our marriage – we even went to New York for a holiday, staying at one of the city's finest hotels and flying back on Concorde – the press approached Nichole dangling huge amounts of money. It was on offer, they said, if she would tell her side of the story. As she resisted, the figure they were prepared to pay went up and up. Eventually, it reached over £100,000. It looked at this point as if the relationship between us might be over so it is not surprising that she was tempted. Sensing a foot in the door, the press put her under enormous pressure to kiss and tell. All the attention had made it ever more difficult for her to do her job and it looked like she would have to leave. This might have given her even more incentive to sell her story. But she refused to fall for the media's advances and that is something I will always be grateful to her for.

As for Debra, she also handled the difficult situation

with class. Of course there were times when she must have felt as if she wanted to take revenge on me for my infidelity and I wouldn't have blamed her if she did. I think she knew by then, though, even if I didn't, that the marriage was finished. When we returned from New York we just couldn't seem to relate to each other in the way we had in the past. Also, I missed Nichole. Eventually, Nichole and I began seeing each other again. Why I thought I could keep it secret after all that had happened I just can't say. When Debra found out she was, not surprisingly, angry. She decided to take drastic action.

It sounds funny now, and I suppose it was at the time, although I didn't think so. Debra ordered removal men to go to our house. She packed up all my stuff and when they arrived told them to take it to Middlesbrough's training ground and dump it there. We can laugh about it today, but can you imagine my embarrassment when, going through a serious training exercise with the players, this lorry turned up? It was unusual at the very least to see a removal van driving onto a football club's training ground. We thought it had got lost. Everyone stopped what they were doing and gave their attention to the truck. That's when the driver rolled down the window, stuck his head out and said:

"Is Mr. Anderson here?"

I stepped forward. "Yeah, I'm here," I replied, still not understanding what was going on.

"We've got your belongings here, mate. Where do you want us to put 'em?"

"What do you mean, you've got my belongings?"

"Your missus told us to move 'em."

"What?"

"Your missus, mate. And she said don't come back. Where shall I put it?"

I got the message.

So did the players. They looked at each other, then at the coaching staff. They started shuffling about. I thought I heard a stifled laugh. I wasn't going to live this down in a hurry. I had to store my things and arrange to get them taken somewhere else. At least the press weren't around to witness what happened. Thank heaven for small mercies.

I moved out of the house as quickly as I could and found my own place. Debra and I were now, without any doubt, finished. We went through a bit of a messy and drawn-out divorce. As this went on, Nichole and I resumed our relationship. We didn't set up home together at first. That came later, after Nichole became pregnant with our son, Freddie.

This period of my life was not easy for anyone involved. For that I take full responsibility. I caused a lot of pain, especially to Charlie, there is no question about that. I am sure there are millions of people out there who have been through similar experiences and suffer similar remorse. I am luckier than most in that everybody managed to do something the majority of people find impossible. They put aside the past, moved on and gave me the benefit of the doubt. That, at least, I think I deserved. Now, Nichole and I enjoy a family life I could never have thought possible when things were at their worst. I am pleased to say that Debra has also found a fantastic new partner, Geoff, with whom she is very happy. Nichole and I are proud to count them amongst our friends. We see each other regularly and Debra often helps out with Freddie. I am lucky indeed.

As I said at the beginning of this chapter, it has not been easy to tell this story. But even if at times it shows me in not the best of lights, I felt it had to be said. While it was all going on, of course, I had to continue working at Middlesbrough and, as the assistant manager, maintain a degree of detachment from the players. It was not so easy when that lorry turned up, let me tell you. Robbo gave me immense support throughout, as did a number of others. One thing I learned: when you are on top, as I was for so much of my life, everyone is your friend; it's only when you suffer adversity that you really know who your friends are. Again I was lucky in that plenty of people helped. And, if that wasn't enough drama for one lifetime, the roller-coaster ride that was my life was being mirrored in the affairs of the club which employed me. The unheard of was about to happen.

Chapter Nineteen

STRANGE DAYS

I couldn't believe my ears. In all my years in football I'd never heard anything like it. As far as I'm aware, nothing approaching Robbo's suggestion has ever happened in the game before or since, certainly not in England. And in the time Robbo and I had been discussing management, going back to our England and Manchester United days, we never considered a possibility like this.

"Run it by me again, Bryan," I said.

Bryan Robson spelled it out and even then it didn't really register. It didn't compute.

"I don't think I can go on like this, I just don't seem to be able to do it anymore," he continued.

"Of course you can, Robbo. If anyone can, you can. Look, we can get out of this, we really can. We've done it before. We just need to keep our heads and continue working hard."

But there was no shifting him. He never compromised as a player and he wasn't going to start now. There was something both tragic yet noble about what he was proposing.

"Have you told the Chairman?"

"I'm going to see him this afternoon. It's got to be

done, Viv. You know it and I know it. We can resign but that would leave the club in too big a hole and who knows what kind of manager they'd be lumbered with. I don't want to leave with us relegated. At least this way we know we'll have the best man for the job."

I tried to form an argument against what he was saying but all I could come up with was the comment that "he could sack us anyway."

"He is the best Chairman in the Premier League. No, make that the whole of football," Robbo said. "He's the best in the world. He stood by us when we went down for Christ's sake."

"I know, but ...."

After we were relegated, at the end of the 1996–97 season, Robbo and I survived in our jobs. At most clubs, relegation would have brought us the sack. But Steve Gibson was made of sterner stuff. I think he also recognised his own role in the three point deduction fiasco and, like the gentleman he is, didn't want to make Robbo and me the scapegoats. That alone shows the difference between him and the vast majority of football chairmen. Still, for all the mistakes of the backroom staff and the club's executives, there is no denying we should never have been in that position with the players we had. They were more than good enough to hold their own in the Premier League. Maybe getting to two cup finals did us no favours. Remember, Middlesbrough had never been in any final in the whole of their history. Everyone, I think, got carried away with the cup runs and we took our eyes off our main task – to prosper in the top division.

It broke our hearts that, because of relegation, we had to let what should have been the nucleus of a great side leave the club. That team should have gone from strength to strength. The two cup finals ought to have been the springboard for greater things. Instead, they were mill-stones round our neck.

Despite the ridicule heaped on us for buying Fabrizio Ravanelli, his signing put the Premier League in the frame to be counted as the best league in the world. It also put Middlesbrough right up there with the best of them. It set the template for so much that came after-wards. To the press we were gatecrashers. They said the great Italian had only come to Middlesbrough for a big pay day. But the same could be said for any high-profile transfer. They just thought that when so-called lesser teams had the audacity to think big, they were getting above their station.

I think the truth about Ravanelli can be seen in the fact that we sold him to Olympique Marseille for far more than we paid for him. As for Juninho, he was in great demand. There were any number of clubs all over Europe who came in for him. In the end we received more than double the amount we had laid out for the Brazilian, with Atletico Madrid stumping up over £12 million to take him to Spain.

Juninho loved it at Middlesbrough. So much so that he came back twice more, once on loan while Robbo and me were still at the club and later after Steve McClaren had taken over. With the departure of such world names as Ravanelli and Juninho, though, it was the end of an era. We had to re-examine our project and start all over again. To his credit, Emerson wanted to stay and prove himself to be a loyal team member.

Not that Steve Gibson and Keith Lamb were about to take things lying down. They were still prepared to spend big to bring the best players possible to the Riverside. Players who could get us back up at the first attempt and maintain the faith of the fans, who, quite naturally, were on the verge of being totally disillusioned. We recruited Paul Merson, who may have dropped down a division to play for us but whose performances were so good that the England manager, Glenn Hoddle, took him to the 1998 World Cup in France. He was the only player from the second tier to make it into Hoddle's squad. Merson was a brilliant playmaker and goalscorer for our team, helping to push us to promotion. Ravanelli for Merson wasn't such a bad swap. Paul did the same for Harry Redknapp's Portsmouth a couple of years later. Then there were players like the Australian goalkeeper, Mark Schwartzer, who still graces the Premier League to this day.

We only stayed in the First Division for a single season. Once again, we managed to stop the slide and get the team back to winning ways. We didn't win the division this time like we had in our first promotion season in 1994-95, but went up automatically in second place. The Premier League had finally sorted out its format and had brought in the system we know today. Forest won our division, having been relegated with us the year before. Again we were pleased to have avoided the play-offs. At one point between October and November we won five games on the spin, scoring sixteen goals and conceding just three. Emerson was absolutely brilliant during this spell. On the eve of a game against fellow high-flyers Forest, the Nottingham Post became one of the first newspapers to at last give Emerson the credit he was due, saying: "Perhaps the public rehabilitation of the complex Brazilian this season serves as an adequate symbol for the club's positive change of direction."

Our season got even better when we went on a run and reached the League Cup Final yet again. As a second division side, we were underdogs this time and playing against a resurgent Chelsea, who beat us 2–0 after extra time. Given that we started the campaign in such a depressed state, that term saw probably the very best of the resilience the Robson-Anderson management team possessed. We re-energised the side, gave the fans a memorable season, and in my view proved our capabilities to anyone who cared to look. In perhaps our most audacious coup to date, we also persuaded the greatest player of his generation to revive his career at the Riverside. Paul Gascoigne came from Rangers for over £4 million. Having spent time in Italy, he had surprisingly moved to Scotland. During his Scottish period he shone for England in Euro 96. It was a massive boost to bring him back to the English league, where he surely belonged. The fans loved him. He made his first appearance for us in the final against Chelsea, when he came on as a substitute.

Gazza was both brilliant and troubled by turns. As a fellow Geordie, prodigy and mega-drinker, Robbo was convinced he could get one last master-class from the England star. I agreed. It was a joy working with him. His level of skill was as high as anything I'd ever seen and his enthusiasm was infectious. The rest of the lads took to him immediately. Mind you, he was still daft as a brush.

I think Gazza would agree that he was not always fit in his time with us. He was also suffering from his drink-related problems and troubles in his marriage. He was hardly ever out of the headlines and that was something with which I could sympathise. However, he turned in some great performance for us and wherever we went, fans paid money to watch him. When he was 'injured', the whole squad suffered from his absence. In his time with Middlesbrough, it is my opinion that he more than repaid every penny the club invested in him. He became extremely depressed after Glenn Hoddle decided not to take him to the World Cup in France during the summer and I think that affected him more than anything else in his career. I don't think he ever recovered from the setback. He only made occasional appearances for us after that and before too long we sold him to Everton.

One game he did play in when we were back in the Premier League was an away match against Derby, which we eventually lost 2–1. From the moment the lads kicked off, Gazza was all over the place. When he passed it, he gave the ball away; when he tried to trap it, he put it out of play; when he went for headers, he was nowhere near the ball. It was a terrible display.

I looked at Robbo. He looked at me. I said to him, "What's he doing?"

"I don't know what he's doing," was Robbo's reply.

"We've got to get him off," I said.

Robbo looked into the middle distance. Then he said "we can't take him off. It's only fifteen minutes into the game. It will destroy him."

I went along with the manager's opinion for another quarter of an hour. Gazza didn't improve, in fact he got worse. He couldn't run, he couldn't control the ball, he looked as if he couldn't even walk.

"Get him off, Robbo, get him off."

Robbo nodded. We substituted him. It was only thirty minutes into the game. As he walked past me I went up to him and told him to get in the bath and I'd come and have a chat. Gazza looked spaced out. Dazed and confused would be a good description of his state of mind.

I went to find him and ask him some questions. "What the fuck were you doing out there Gazza, what's going on?"

"I don't know boss, I just can't get me act together."

"Were you out last night?"

"No, I promise."

I looked at him closely. His drinking was legendary. Could I believe him when he said he hadn't been out on the lash? It looked like he had been. But he was adamant he had drunk nothing alcoholic.

"What have you eaten?" I asked him.

"The chicken and beans like everyone else, that's all."

"Nothing else?"

"Nothing."

"Have you drunk anything?"

"No ... .well just some Red Bull, they sent me a crate. They want to know if I'll promote it."

"How many Red Bulls did you drink, Paul?"

"Six."

Now Red Bull contains the stimulant caffeine. Any more than two cans and you'll fail a drugs test. Gazza had drunk half a crate, one after the other. If you drink six in a short amount of time you can be completely disoriented, if you are an athlete. Paul was out of his head. He could hardly talk. He didn't sleep for three weeks. It's not surprising after all those Red Bulls. That's why he's daft as a brush.

When he got frustrated, Gazza did some silly things, both on and off the pitch. Remember that terrible tackle on Gary Charles in the 1991 Cup Final when he almost destroyed his career. While he was with us he got himself banned for three games following an elbow attack on George Boateng of Aston Villa. He injured himself at the same time and was out for about eight weeks in total. After that, the press wrote him off completely. There was talk of him being frozen out at the Riverside. I was having none of it. I told the press "Nobody is shutting the door on him. He's mad, not bad." I had no idea why Gazza sometimes lost it, it just happened when you least expected it – or sometimes when you did expect it. Paul didn't know why he did it either. No matter how much he tried to control himself, he was only storing up the explosion that would come sooner or later.

When we first went to Middlesbrough, the club had already been relegated and we started from a low-point for both players and fans alike. I suppose our latest experience of being relegated from the Premier League affected Robbo and me in many ways and when we got back to the top flight we were less prepared to take chances than we had before. The result was two seasons of reasonable but undramatic performances, finishing mid-table in both seasons. My biggest recollection during this period, and remember, this was when my personal life was at its most tumultuous, was winning 3–2 at Old Trafford, although I'd be hard-pressed to give you any details of the game. I'm told we were 3–0 up at one point but, to be honest, I can't remember it.

Having grown used to a comfortable position in the table, our fans now expected us to push on. I expected us to push on. Somehow we couldn't do it. On the plus side for me personally, around this time I received some unexpected good news. In the New Year's Honours List of 1999–2000 – the millennium – I was awarded an MBE for services to football. You would have thought I'd seen it all, what with European Cup wins and England appearances, but receiving that medal from the Queen was the proudest moment of my life. To be recognised by my country in such a way was extra-special. I even enjoyed the endless rehearsals of protocol before the event itself. We had to learn to bow so that we behaved properly in front of Her Majesty. To be the son of immigrants and now invited to Buckingham Palace to receive one of the nation's highest accolades was the stuff of dreams. Something to be cherished. Forever!

In the same Honours List MBEs were awarded to a number of England's 1966 World Cup heroes, who had somehow been forgotten when it came to dishing out the gongs. Nobby Stiles, Alan Ball, Roger Hunt, George Cohen and Ray Wilson were all recognised. I was so happy to receive my medal in the same list as those great performers. Other footballers who received recognition were Ian Wright (then playing for Celtic), the Wolves veteran Steve Bull and Mansfield's Tony Ford, who broke Terry Paine's record for the most number of games played, reaching the incredible number of 825. Henry Cooper and Stirling Moss were both awarded knighthoods.

During the following campaign the harsh realities of football came back to bite us. Far from pushing on, we were struggling again. As Christmas approached, we were odds-on for relegation. Our results were appalling from almost the moment the season began. After two years of consolidation this was unexpected. For some reason, we just couldn't get the team to function as we wanted. Whatever happened, though, Robbo did not want to put the club, and particularly Steve Gibson, through the trauma of relegation again. His solution, though, was extraordinary.

That was when Robbo and I had the strange conversation I referred to at the beginning of this chapter. He wanted to bring in another manager/coach to work with the players. He also wanted that person to be a big name. Not only had I never heard anything like Robbo's proposal before, I also understood that, whether it was successful or not, it spelt the end of the

road for us at Middlesbrough. If it ended up in relegation, we would be blamed and sacked anyway. If we
stayed up, it wouldn't be us who got the credit, but the
newcomer. But Robbo was adamant that he wanted to
do the unthinkable. He would take more of a back seat,
he said. He felt he had lost his powers of motivation, at
least for the moment. Maybe he had been around for
too long. Maybe I had failed to recognise the symptoms
of burn-out which I knew might be a possibility when
we first went to Middlesbrough. As defeat followed
defeat, Robbo seemed to withdraw into another world.
It was a place we'd never been before and not a very
nice one at that.

I have to say that in my opinion the answer Robbo
came up with was far from an act of weakness, which is
the way it was portrayed in the media. On the contrary,
it was an act of the greatest possible strength. Bryan
may have seemed to be in his own world – and television pictures of him in the technical area during games
reinforced this view – but he had actually analysed the
situation coolly and knew what was required. No matter
how unconventional it might be he would recommend
it to the Chairman. He was prepared to resign if necessary, but neither of us thought it would come to that. It
hardly needed saying that I would have gone with him
had he taken that decision. Instead, he convinced Steve
Gibson to open negotiations with none other than Terry
Venables, one of England's greatest managerial and
coaching talents of the modern era.

Robbo had worked under Venables when he was

England manager and rated him as one of the greatest coaches in the world. So did a lot of other people in the game. In addition, Venables was a household name, possessed charisma in bucket-loads and was someone who would command the respect of the players. Robbo believed the former England manager was the only man who could turn performances around and stave off the drop. He also knew Steve Gibson could afford to pay Venables's huge asking price: £1 million for half a season's work, no matter what the outcome.

This colossal amount of money caused considerable controversy, especially on Teesside, where many people had lost their jobs in the recent past, particularly in the steel industry. The popular view expressed in the pubs and working men's clubs, as well as on the local media, was that giving an already rich southerner such a massive pay-day was obscene. I had some sympathy with that view. But at the same time I knew what Venables could do and if that is what it took to get him, then so be it. The public naturally thought Gibson was already employing a team to carry out the job of managing the club. Us! So we came in for more than our fair share of the brickbats. There was a lot of local pressure on Steve, some of it pro-Venables, a lot of it anti. Gibson, though, continued to rate Robbo's judgment and he was still, at heart, a Boro fan who would do anything if he thought it would help the club. He agreed to pay Venables the money he demanded.

Robbo was proved right. I don't know how he did it

but Venables displayed all the qualities that had earned him success in the past and he saved us from relegation. Maybe it was simply the case of a new man with new ideas to freshen up performances. But I don't think it was just that. Terry had his own way with players. He could sum up their strengths and weaknesses after he had the merest glimpse of them playing. And he was rarely wrong in his assessments. He was also a breath of fresh air and brought all his experience and personality to bear on the situation. He was always jovial on the training ground yet he knew what he wanted from day one and he made sure the players delivered.

Our salvation was confirmed when we went to Arsenal and won 3-0, our best performance of the season by far. Terry loved putting one over on the Gunners. Whether or not Robbo and I could have achieved a position of safety without Venables, no-one will ever know. I like to think we could have. I'm not sure, even today, if I disagreed with Robbo's view or whether it was just so unprecedented it was difficult to take in. But we had genuine achievements to our name at Boro. I believe we had what it took to see the club through the choppy waters in which it found itself. But it wasn't to be.

Having survived - just - in the Premier League with Terry Venables at the helm, it was obvious that Robbo and I would have to be on our way. We had been at the Riverside for six great years. We had put the team in the limelight and, we felt, had taken it to the next level. We had reached three Cup Finals and left the club established in the top division. Steve Gibson was almost in tears when the time came but he knew as well as we did that the parting of the ways could not be put off. What concerned Bryan and I, of course, was what we were going to do next.

Chapter Twenty

LIFE AFTER FOOTBALL

When Bryan and I left Middlesbrough, we knew we had to take stock of our situation. But first, we needed to rest and re-charge our batteries after such a long time on the frontline. So we took some time out. I went on a couple of holidays, the first I had taken during the summer for twenty-odd years. Christmases and the July-August holidays are forbidden to the British footballer. After a while you almost forget what they are like.

Steve Gibson was more upset than either Robbo or me at our departure. We knew the score but Steve was strangely depressed about it all. For a time I thought the club might spiral down or Steve might lose interest. But, to give him his due, he came back stronger than ever with his commitment to Middlesbrough intact. I was pleased he managed to pull off what was then a bit of a coup. He enticed Steve McClaren from the assistant's job at Manchester United, where he was a key figure in the treble-winning season. McClaren – who is now most remembered for his ill-starred period as England manager – built upon what Robbo, Terry Venables and I had constructed on Teesside and took them to greater success than even we had managed. He won the club the first trophy in their history and got them to the UEFA Cup Final the next year. That was a truly amazing achievement which he is continuing with his new club, Twente Enschede of Holland. His time with England may have been a disaster but his record in club football speaks for itself.

Following our Middlesbrough experience neither Robbo nor I applied for any managerial jobs. It was a decision both of us took together. If anything was offered, we would consider it on its merits but we weren't going to chase another position. We had spent six tumultuous years on Teesside and we both needed to take a step back. Sometime later, Bryan was offered the manager's job at Bradford. He decided to take it. I was never going to go to there so in many ways; it represented the end of the road for Robbo and me. We had fulfilled our ambition of being joint managers of a great club with money in the bank and a Chairman who was prepared to spend it. We achieved substantial progress with Middlesbrough. When we went to Teesside the club had been relegated and was going nowhere. When we left, Middlesbrough were established in the Premier League – albeit with help from Terry Venables – had reached three cup finals and had brought some of the most exciting players in the world to the north-east. Whoever took over would have something solid to build on, far more than we did when we started. Steve McClaren was exactly the right man to take it forward. Did I want to do it all over again? I wasn't sure.

Far from being out in the cold, almost as soon as I left football I received offers of other work. I had owned a stake in an events company for many years and upped my role in its day-to-day operations, becoming more hands-on. I worked on hospitality packages at sporting events and on the creation and implementation of new events, such as a golf classic named after Norman Whiteside. In later years I formed a company with my old friend, Tony Woodcock. In partnership with the Jebel Ali Hotel in Dubai, we set up the Jebel Ali Centre of Excellence, a coaching facility in the sun. The centre came into existence after we took the owners of the hotel to Manchester United's training ground at Carrington and Arsenal's at London Colney, where they could see how football training works in the modern age. The centre now provides warm-weather facilities for a number of clubs and international teams, including Aston Villa, Blackburn and Portsmouth from the Premier League and the national teams of Russia, Ghana and Nigeria. Russian club sides come for their pre-season. In all, approximately ten or more teams use the centre every year at present.

These developments in my life meant that I did not miss the cut and thrust of daily involvement in the game nearly as much as I thought I would. I have really enjoyed the new challenges these activities have thrown up for me. It wasn't always like that for former pros.

The nineties was an era when the media, especially television and radio, were opening up. This led to far more ex-footballers being in demand by the broad-casters than had been the case previously. By the time I left management in 2001, there was a whole industry devoted to football. I did some work for Sky when I departed from Middlesbrough but I was soon poached by ESPN, which in those days was not available in Britain but was extensively broadcast to the rest of the world. Now, of course, the company is a major player in the negotiations for TV rights to the Premier League. I have been a regular on ESPN in the far-east for some years and was their main pundit in 2009 for the FA Cup Final and the Champions League Final. I also appear regularly on the in-house channel, Manchester United TV.

I enjoy the TV work and I think I've got a natural flair for giving my opinions in an interesting way, even if many of them turn out to be wrong. I was convinced, for instance, that United would beat Barcelona in the 2009 Champions League Final. I gave my views live to millions of viewers on ESPN. I thought Barcelona's injury problems would leave them fatally exposed to the likes of Ronaldo and Rooney. How wrong can you be?

My promotional work has increased through the years. I was appointed as an ambassador for the Victor Chandler betting empire, which entails attending sporting events around the world and giving my take on things to the company's clients. This year I teamed up with some high-tech guys to market a new, internet-based gambling product called Passoker. Designed by

John Carr, who is a systems designer for major auto-
mobile manufacturers, Passoker lets players bet in
real time on the next incident to happen in a sports
event as they watch it live on TV or their computer.

It works is like this: if the event is a football match,
it is split into its component parts. So as the game
progresses, the next incident will be, say, a throw-in, a
goal, a corner, a free-kick, a goal-kick etc. You can bet
money on what incident on the list of possibilities will
occur next. The odds are instantaneously reset after
every incident. You can bet against the house or other
players in a poker-style format. There is even a championship version of the game with prizes of sporting
memorabilia. By the time you read this, Passoker
should just about be on the market, in time for the
South Africa World Cup.

Another consultancy contract is with the Dubai-
based global transportation company, GAC. This
company is involved in a number of sports-related
activities. For instance, it is shirt sponsor of Crystal
Palace and sponsors one of the stands at Bramall
Lane, home of Sheffield United. GAC is also a logis-
tics partner to one of the world's leading Formula
One racing teams.

It is a different world from the one in which I first
started playing. Then, footballers had no capital behind
them or pension to see them through the long retirement
years. That was why so many opened shops, became land-
lords of pubs or looked for employment anywhere they
could find it. Many ended up with nothing. Even George

Cohen was forced to sell his World Cup winners medal to make ends meet. The unbelievable transformation since those times has opened up a whole new set of possibilities for players and ex-players. The hospitality industry, for instance, has been one of the fastest growing areas in all sport in recent times and large numbers of old pros earn a decent living from it.

When I won the European Cup for the first time with Forest my basic wage was eighty pounds a week. Sure, there were bonuses for winning but still we made about as much as a skilled worker in a car factory. This meant we felt close to the community who supported us. We were a part of it. Everyone knows that situation has been completely turned on its head since the inception of the Premiership and the Champions League. But things were changing before these two mega-competitions were established. In fact, the new order was the result of the changes rather than the cause. And I was right there when they happened.

By the time I left Forest there had been significant improvements to the negotiating position of players, especially at the top level. There wasn't yet total freedom of contract, that would come later, but neither could clubs any longer retain a player against his will once his contract had expired. The new club a player went to still had to pay a transfer fee but if the two clubs couldn't agree it would go to a tribunal to decide, as it did when I left Arsenal for Manchester United. No longer was it possible for clubs to completely control a footballer's playing career, telling them where they could or couldn't play.

This change gave players the confidence to promote their interests further. Our union, the Professional Footballers Association, under the astute leadership of Gordon Taylor, took up the long fight to gain true freedom of contract like every other worker. Before long the Bosman case gave us real freedom at last. We weren't asking for anything more than the conditions everyone else takes for granted. It is true that the money on offer these days to the best players is so huge that many ordinary people find it fundamentally wrong. But the vast majority of professional players do not make these massive amounts. They deserve to be protected. And they have every right to negotiate the best possible deal for themselves that they can.

After two European Cups, a League title and three League Cup Final appearances for Forest my pay had gone up but it was nowhere near the amounts on offer at bigger clubs, even those who were not winning things. My basic was around £250 a week by that time. There was also some bad feeling at Forest because towards the end of my period there, the players were disillusioned when expected bonuses did not materialise. Although my move to Arsenal was prompted by the need for a new challenge and a desire to experience life in the capital, I cannot deny that money played its part. Arsenal offered me double what I was getting with Forest. This level of payment allowed some footballers to leave the world of the factory worker I mentioned earlier far behind. We were starting on the road towards bigger rewards.

We were also examining things like private pensions. Change was in the air.

After three years at Arsenal, my wages reached about £1000 a week, which was a fortune compared to what I was getting before at Forest. I realise that this level of salary was outstripping by far the income that most people could expect from their work. But if the income generated within the football industry doesn't go to players where would it go? I don't think it would help to reduce prices for spectators or build better facilities. It would more likely be spent on even higher transfer fees than you see at the moment. Agents and greedy owners would take more money out of the game. It is, don't forget, players who bring crowds through the turnstiles, whatever the level of football.

The three most important reasons for improving the lot of the professional footballer are, in my view, these: first, you live and work with the possibility of a career-threatening injury every day; second, even if you avoid serious injury, your life as a professional player is over when you are in your thirties. It is difficult for anyone in a conventional job to understand the impact this can have. Most people start at the bottom, if you like, and over the length of their working careers climb the ladder of experience, success and remuneration. For an athlete, the opposite occurs. You can be on the scrapheap at 35. The third reason is historical: for decades, the footballer was little more than a serf. For years there was an income-ceiling of £20 a week – the maximum wage – which applied in no other area of business that I know of. Footballers – as most people are probably aware – were very badly treated by their employers, the clubs. They might, if they were lucky, receive a testimonial match in recognition of long service but even this morsel was at the discretion of the club's directors.

The long-time secretary of the Football League, Alan Hardaker, once said: "I wouldn't hang a dog on the word of a footballer." That tells you all you need to know about the attitudes of the time. Everything the modern player has gained has had to be fought for, often through the courts in the teeth of fierce opposition from clubs. All players in this country owe a debt of gratitude to those who paved the way, like Jimmy Hill, who fought for the abolition of the maximum wage, and Gordon Taylor, who single-handedly ensured that players' rights are taken into account at every stage and who raised the role of the PFA to unprecedented influence. There are those who might say that things have gone too far in the other direction, with players and their agents now too powerful. However, I make no apologies for the advancement of players' terms and conditions of employment and my small part in the process that brought it about.

Although every professional footballer's main motivation is a love of the game, it soon becomes clear that you have to take steps to look after your interests. This is particularly true when you have a family. You have to do everything you can for your loved ones in what is at best a precarious profession, where you are only as good as your last game and can be discarded before you know it.

Arsenal, one of the biggest clubs around, were paying good wages when I went to Highbury. As I said, they paid me far more than I could ever have received at Forest. But when I went to Manchester United, my pay packets went through the roof. Even though United were not, at the time, anything like the force they have since become, they still paid more than anyone else. They were always the glamour club. And I was in the top group of earners there. Only Robbo and Jesper Olsen were paid more than me. So you can see that during my time as a pro there was beginning to be a player revolution.

When the Premier League, soon to be followed by the Champions League, started in the nineties, they were the authorities' response to these and other changes that were occurring in the world of football. For example, along with player-power, the Chairmen and Presidents of clubs throughout Europe lobbied for competitions to be reorganised for their benefit and to the detriment of the smaller clubs. I doubt if a club like Forest could ever hope to win the Champions League today. All these changes came about in the wake of the players increasing their power. The consequence was that the new competitions helped the top players increase that power even more.

With the advent of the Premier League, far more of the world's best players began to come to England. To make this happen, the financial packages on offer had to be immense. I played a pivotal role in this development. Our quartet at Middlesbrough – Steve Gibson, Keith Lamb, Bryan Robson and yours truly – put together the team of Ravanelli, Juninho and Emerson. One had scored in the final of the Champions League just a few months previously to win the Cup for Juventus, another was Brazil's footballer of the year and the third was one of the most exciting prospects in the world. To bring such players to England was unheard of at the time: to bring them to unfashionable Middlesbrough was impossible.

In the main, even the biggest clubs in England could only attract good Scandinavians or East Europeans and continentals whose careers were coming towards their end. When Manchester United bought Eric Cantona from Leeds, the fee was modest, his wages not outrageous and because he was the wild child of French football he was seen as drinking at the last chance saloon. He had lost his place in the French team. Howard Wilkinson was one manager among many who failed to get the best out of him. Manchester United was his final throw of the dice. He turned out to be probably the most important signing of Fergie's career. Cantona's subsequent influence on United's destiny made Robbo and me realise that if we could entice Europe's best players we could make Middlesbrough a force to be reckoned with.

How did we do it? How did we convince these top performers to come to the Riverside? Well, as I think you already know, we raised the bar in terms of transfer fees. More important, we paid these players a king's ransom, far more than they could have earned anywhere else in the world. That's how far Steve Gibson was prepared to go in his backing of Robbo and me. Our plunges into the transfer market set in motion a game of catch-up by the big boys and smaller clubs alike. That meant that even journeymen Premier League players began to see their weekly pay reach the thousands of pounds level. After our outlay at Middlesbrough, the face of English football changed forever and it wasn't long before the Premier League began to be talked of as the most exciting league in the world. Its value to TV and to sponsors multiplied a hundredfold. New stadiums were built and the crowds went up every year. It is all a long way from my days as a teenager trying to break in to the Forest first team, when facilities for players and fans were primitive to say the least. I believe the changes, for the most part, have been positive developments.

But for all the talk of money, it is the game that means so much to all of us, players and supporters alike. I have called this chapter Life After Football but these days there is no life after football, really. For ex-players there is now more football to take part in than ever before. There has been, for instance, the emergence of veterans' – or Masters – tournaments going on all round the world to wildly enthusiastic spectators both live and on TV. I myself have recently appeared in a number of these events so you can see that even us old-uns can still draw an audience and play to a reasonable level ... provided the matches don't last too long. I captain the Manchester United Masters team all round the world and have appeared in tournaments from South Africa to Vietnam.

My most recent outing for the United old boys came in a tournament in Kuala Lumpur, Malaysia. The reason I am telling you this will become clear in a moment. The competition comprised various English sides, one a Premier League Select X1 captained by Ray Parlour. The other participants were Sheffield United, with Brian Deane still putting himself about and ... yes ... Liverpool. Another go at the old enemy. That's why I had to include it here.

We had the brilliant Andy Cole playing for us. It was good to see Clayton Blackmore again after knowing him both at United and Middlesbrough. In addition, we had Russell Beardsmore, one of Fergie's early youngsters who scored that great goal against the Scousers all those years ago. We had Paul Parker, another of United's great full-backs. Ronnie Johnsson and Jesper Blomquist made up our outfield, Frazer Digby was in goal.

For the dreaded Liverpool, who had made so many teams' lives a misery but whom I had managed to get the better of on the odd important occasion, there were some ominous names: Mark Walters, who could make mincemeat of the best full-back; the stylish Don Hutchinson; Michael Thomas, an old team-mate from my Arsenal days, who, after breaking Scouse hearts with that winning goal at Anfield in 1989 which took the title to Highbury, actually joined the club he had demolished; and last but by no means least, there was Mark Wright and Jason McAteer. We were all set.

The Liverpool veterans generally win most tournaments they enter, just like they did when they were regular players. This time, they faced us in the final. A magnificent match ended 3–3 and we went to penalties. We beat them in the shoot-out. Nothing could have given me greater pleasure than to triumph over them again, especially on penalties. It was a great moment when I lifted the trophy. My thoughts drifted back to that night in Nottingham long ago, in the first round of the European Cup. Against Liverpool! Liverpool the undefeated! Liverpool the best! Liverpool the destroyers of other clubs' dreams!

2–0!

The rest, as they say, is history.

POSTSCRIPT

Along with the whole nation I was absolutely delighted when England, under the watchful eye of Fabio Capello, qualified for the 2010 World Cup in South Africa. As the first black player to be capped by England, the choice of an African country, let alone one with such a history of racism, was a poignant reminder to me of what can be achieved with belief and commitment.

South African football has long been the province of the black majority in the country. Traditionally, the white minority favoured rugby and cricket. It was a pleasant surprise for all of us within the game that FIFA rewarded the reconciliation that has taken place within South Africa since apartheid came to an end. It brought home to me the full extent of the change the world has undergone since I first began to ply my trade as a professional footballer. Back then, you wouldn't have used football and South Africa in the same sentence. Now, the country is a football nation as well as a rainbow one.

2010 is truly a world event, the biggest sporting spectacular on the planet. By taking it to South Africa, football has given the South Africans the opportunity to show the world how far their country has come in the last two decades.

At first I was a bit worried that England would find it difficult to qualify. Our previous campaign to reach the European Championships under Steve McClaren ended in abject failure, as we are all too well aware. What was worse about our attempt to qualify for South Africa was that we again drew our nemesis from the Euro qualifiers – Croatia – in the same group. What I hadn't quite appreciated was the difference Capello would make. It shouldn't, perhaps, have been such a surprise. Hadn't I believed for years that managers make a difference? Wasn't this what Robbo and I had been discussing for so long? The trouble is, as every fan knows, when it comes to your country, it is easy to lose your sense of perspective. In the event, we qualified so easily that complacency is what we have to avoid.

Now that we are certain of participating in the next World Cup, I've had a chance to bring my experience and knowledge of the game to bear on the situation. I'd like to share my thoughts with you about how I think the South Africa tournament will pan out. I realise I'm giving you all a hostage to fortune here. At least anything I say can be checked against what actually happens. And my predictions are in truth no more likely to come to pass than someone sticking a pin in the fixture list. Still, you might be interested in my insider knowledge, offered to you here with no guarantees. If you want those, get Russell Grant.

How far can England go? That is the question all of us in this country are most concerned with. The last two World Cups have ended in quarter-final disappointment. Can we really expect to do any better this time round? Having seen World Cup campaigns from the inside I know what kind of things influence the outcome. Of course, tactical nous and motivational skill are very important. But there is more to it than that. As you settle down to watch the greatest tournament in the world, here is what I make of it all.

Well, I'm optimistic on England's behalf. I know the team has let us down in the past but I really believe it will be different this time. Fabio Capello will ensure there is no repeat of the WAGS debacle that occurred in Germany, when attention shifted away from the football and onto the shopping sprees of the wives and girlfriends. And the atmosphere he will create will be geared to winning. England could go all the way, you know. They should, in my opinion, make it to the semi-finals at the very least. Not that anything can be taken for granted. For England to do well, a number of things have to happen.

The first, and to me the most important requirement, is that Jermain Defoe is fit and firing. Although he has not always been first choice for Capello, I believe that will change. He can score goals at any level and if he is on his game, he will make the difference. Although the manager has often used Emile Heskey or Peter Crouch up front with Wayne Rooney, I think Jermain is our most natural goalscorer. To progress in a World Cup you need someone you can rely on to score you the goals you need. Gary Lineker was supreme in this role. When I played with him for England, the team just knew Gary could get you a goal, no matter what the circumstances. Having someone like that breeds a lot of confidence throughout the side. Rooney, Steven Gerrard, Frank Lampard and John Terry will be important in South Africa, obviously, but I think the key is Defoe. If he is below par for any reason, or not picked, I think we will struggle.

The hotels and facilities are also extremely important. Having been to two World Cups, I can tell you that boredom can be the biggest problem. You can't just take a stroll these days because of security concerns so you don't get to see much of the country you're in. Good relaxation time, however, is crucial. There have to be distractions and they must be relevant to today's young adults. You should also have old stand-by attractions like pool tables, dart boards, table tennis and video games. There must be lots for the players to do, because boredom actually causes fatigue, which is the last thing you want at a World Cup. You have to be ready for three games in a short space of time then be able to switch your focus onto the knock-out format. It is the manager's job to see that the players are fresh by the time each game comes around.

In terms of training, Capello will have a balancing act to deal with. Some of the players, particularly those from the most successful club sides, will have played a lot of games of high intensity throughout the year. Their season might not finish until the end of May if they are involved in the later stages of European competitions. This group doesn't need too much training, they need to be nursed along. Then there are the players who might have been out for some of the campaign, perhaps only playing 30 odd games at clubs whose season finished at the beginning of May. They may need more intensive training sessions. It is in these little things that Cups are won and lost.

Any team that wins the World Cup will have had a bit of luck somewhere along the way. Fortune, though, cannot be predicted. You just need a bit now and again. Remember, every team is there on merit and on any given day one of them could beat a so-called superior team or at least get a draw. It can happen. It has happened, too many times for comfort in England's case. I believe Fabio Capello will deal with all these issues better than previous managers. That is why I am optimistic.

In the group stage – which we really should qualify for without too many scares – we need to pay special attention to the USA. If we are not right on our game, they will beat us. Increasing numbers of the USA's players now operate in Europe, like Donovan Landon and Clint Dempsey in the Premier League, so they know how we play our game. The USA would love to put one over on the English, make no mistake. If we can perform to the standards we did in the qualifying competition, though, there will be no problem.

If you know anything about the remaining countries in the tournament, you will agree that none of them will fancy being drawn against England in the later stages. Of the countries who can win it, there are question marks against them all.

The European Champions, Spain, have a fabulous team that can play fantastic football. If Fernando Torres is fit, and their immensely talented midfield performs, their chances are sky-high. But can they raise themselves on the biggest stage of all when they have underperformed on so many occasions in the past? If they can, they must be favourites. But if they can't, the door is wide open for everyone else.

Argentina are an enigma. I think their chances depend on whether Lionel Messi can step up to the plate in the way the team's current coach – Diego Maradona – did back in Mexico 86. In the last World Cup, Argentina played some wonderful football early on but collapsed when it mattered. That could happen again if Messi doesn't perform. However, Messi is the World Player of the Year and that alone makes Argentina dangerous. I know they had difficulty qualifying for this tournament but that may make them hungrier. They may feel they have something to prove. In the end I don't believe they will have enough to win it but they will be nobody's fools.

Brazil are always a threat, we know that only too well. If we have to play them, we will find it difficult. They showed in the recent friendly against England in Doha that they are still a force. These days many of their best players are based in Europe and they have added extra dimensions to their game over the years. And you can never write off the most successful country in World Cup history. If England are to triumph, they will have to gain victory over Brazil somewhere along the line. Sometimes I think Brazil beat teams before they even get on the pitch. Their reputation can intimidate opponents.

If England face them, the players have to remember that this is not the Brazil of Pele or Zico. They are good but they are beatable.

As for the best of the rest, Italy are an ageing team and I don't think they will successfully defend their title. I don't mean to be dismissive but they were a bit lucky to win last time in my opinion. You always have to watch out for the Germans, every one of us knows that. They regularly seem to be in a state of transition but they always do better than you would think at the outset. The Germans are supreme at tournament-play. They will not be easily brushed aside. If we have to face them we have the players to win but ... mmm ... it's Germany ... I don't know.

This time round, I believe there is a possibility that an African team could do well. The accepted wisdom is that the African sides are not yet good enough. That view is maybe a bit premature. It would be fitting if one of them won it the first time the tournament has come to their continent. I don't think the hosts, South Africa, have any chance. Cameroon and Nigeria could cause upsets here and there but the African team with the best prospects is, in my view, Ivory Coast. I know they underperformed in the last African Cup of Nations but I don't think you can read too much into that. They possess one of the best goalscorers in the world in Didier Drogba. If he plays to his potential, Ivory Coast have a chance. I'm sure Drogba would enjoy facing England at some point. If that happens we will have to snuff out his menace, otherwise he will have a field day.

My last team to watch is something of a nostalgic and left-field choice. No-one who witnessed them will ever forget the exploits of North Korea in 1966. Their performances lit up the tournament, seeing off Italy in the process. The Italians went home to be bombarded with rotten fruit at the airport. It would be great to see that again. And when North Korea led a Portugal side featuring the great Eusebio 3–0, it seemed miracles could really happen. Eusebio, of course, dragged his team back into contention in that match on his own and the 5–3 win for Portugal is still one of the greatest-ever games in World Cup history. But no-one really knows the strength of the North Koreans. So my off-the-wall prediction is that North Korea will at some point in the tournament give us cause for celebration by upsetting one of their so-called betters.

That's my view of the 2010 World Cup. How much of it proves to be accurate remains to be seen. That is why the World Cup is such a fantastic tournament. But perhaps more important in the long term is how things are progressing in our quest to be hosts of the 2018 tournament.

As I wrote in the first chapter of this book, I have some reservations about the conduct of our bid. Looking at it objectively, we shoot ourselves in the foot far too often for our own good. There has been a lot of activity during the latter half of 2009 and I hope it pays dividends. I desperately want the World Cup to come here once again. I think you can see from the things I have written how committed I am. In the absence of a real plan to use the ambassadors, I concentrated on getting Nottingham selected as one of the host cities. This we managed to achieve, even though there is no stadium in the city at present that could put on a World Cup game. It has been a leap of faith on the part of the FA to accept that if England wins the bid, a new stadium will be built. The only shame is that Nottingham is the only venue in the East-Midlands to be chosen. When London could have three venues, Manchester two and there looks like being two in the north-east, it seems wrong somehow that our bid had to be at the expense of Leicester and Derby. The three cities of the East Midlands will always maintain their intense rivalry but in this case it would have been nice if the region – which has excellent hotels and great transport links – could have been awarded two venues. And the owners of the Derby and Leicester clubs have already invested in new stadiums.

The bid team for 2018 has undergone some changes since the avalanche of criticisms of its operations. The most notable has been the resignation of Sir Dave Richards, who runs the Premier League. His departure has not, in my opinion, been adequately explained. We are still on a knife edge and I don't yet believe we have got it right. With the decision coming up this December, all those things which I wrote about at the start of this book are still issues to be resolved. Will we win it? Maybe, by the skin of our teeth. A great performance in South Africa might tip the scales. I travel on football-related business all over the world and from what I've heard I have to tell you that for England, it's nowhere near a done deal.

As I have explained, much has been accomplished in the years since I began my life as a professional footballer. But unfortunately, racism does keep rearing its head. We have to be vigilant. We have to listen to ex-players who know more about this than anyone else. And racism must be tackled in those European countries like Spain who pay lip service to the cause but in effect do little to combat it and often seem to condone racist behaviour.

At the end of the first chapter, I wrote that around the time of my visit to Wembley for the launch of the 2018 bid, certain other things were taking place which affected me personally. This is what happened.

I have always been there for Nottingham Forest. When they have wanted reunions of the European Cup-winning team I have continually made myself available. The club has made huge amounts of money from the players who gave them the most successful period in their history. The same treatment, though, has not been forthcoming from the club to me and the other members of that history-making team.

The season 2008–9 marked the thirtieth anniversary of my ground-breaking debut in the England team. I was approached by a consortium who believed my appearance thirty years ago should be commemorated with an all-star charity football match. The event would celebrate the progress this country has made in overcoming racism over the last three decades. It would also show how England has led the way in the world of football.

The consortium contained some important names from the sports business. We received fantastic support from the PFA – from Gordon Taylor personally – and the anti-racist charity, Kick It Out, which would have been a beneficiary of some of the income.

A number of television channels were prepared to bid for the rights to screen the match, which told me that it would really resonate with people. It was a chance for the nation to feel good about itself and the changes that have taken place over the last thirty years in regard to racism. Sponsors were also queuing up to get involved. Players rushed to pledge their attendance. It was a no-brainer.

The FA offered notional support but didn't fall over themselves to get proactive. If you think about it, the FA could have used the event to promote the 2018 bid; they could have invited key FIFA delegates and shown them just how much this country has embraced multi-cultur-alism and fought racism over the years. They could have shown how England is in the vanguard of the anti-racist cause. It would have played so well with FIFA that their delegates would have been lining up to vote for England. Instead, the FA missed a golden opportunity by offering only lukewarm support and not spotting what everyone else could see. Everyone else, that is, except Nottingham Forest.

With all the backing we had, the only remaining issue was the venue at which the match would be played. Our first thought, you won't be surprised to hear, was Wembley, where my debut took place. Now, I thought that Wembley was under the control of the FA but it turned out that due to the way the stadium was financed, it is operated by a subsidiary company whose brief is to make as much money as possible in order to service the debt incurred when the stadium was built. The FA were powerless to intervene. As it happened, at the time we wanted to schedule the game, Wembley was due to have its pitch taken up so we were forced to look elsewhere. It still seemed odd that a game which had been received with enthusiasm from every quarter did not seem to register with the one organisation that could benefit the most from it: the FA.

Then we had a brainwave. Of course: it should be in my home town at the place where I achieved so much. The City Ground, Nottingham. I found out that the local council was establishing a sports facility for deprived kids from the inner city and I arranged for some of the proceeds from the match to go to the new building. In return, Nottingham Council offered their full co-operation and support.

It was a fantastic feeling for me to contemplate what it meant to hold the game in Nottingham. I have great affection for all the clubs I played for: Forest, the first and the most revolutionary; Arsenal, all class from top to bottom; Manchester United, the world's favourite club; Sheffield Wednesday, tradition, success and great football; Barnsley, just like a family; Middlesbrough, world stars, great fans, what a Chairman. I cherish all these clubs. But taking the match to my home town, where I grew up, where I had so many memories, was a very special idea.

We attended a meeting about the proposed event with representatives of Nottingham Forest. We came away with a handshake on a deal. For the club, Forest would get some much-needed income and be seen hosting a major event by a huge television audience. It would have been a great advert for the campaign for a new stadium and the 2018 World Cup matches that would come with it. The profile of the city and the region would immediately be raised. The consortium was to receive a reasonable – but not excessive – return on its investment, the designated charities would receive funds, while TV, sponsors and spectators would be participating in a massive, feel-good event. Fantastic!

Almost immediately, Forest began to shift their position. They wanted to impose impossible conditions, including taking over the administration of all charitable donations from the match. This included a demand that their own preferred charity – Childline – received a significant donation. Now, I've nothing against Childline, I'm sure it is a worthy cause. But this match was about celebrating the fight against racism and we had already put in place the charities which would benefit from the event, Kick it Out and Nottingham's facility for inner-city kids. Forest went on to make more inexplicable demands and continually refused to negotiate in good faith. I have no idea to this day why they changed their attitude after that handshake. As someone who has done more to put Forest in the top drawer of great football clubs than any of the current directors, I find their actions reprehensible. In the end, although we offered a number of compromises,

Forest's intransigence made it impossible for the game to go ahead.

I said at the beginning of this book, that we have come a long way, but we still have a long way to go. I think the events I've described surrounding the commemorative game illustrate that perfectly. It wasn't me who lost out. It was the charities, the game, the people, the club. Everyone lost the chance to celebrate our achievements as a nation.

Still, I remain optimistic, as ever. I prefer to dwell on what's gone right rather than what's gone wrong. For instance, I've given my criticisms of the FA in this book so it's only fair that I give credit on something the organisation is trying to get right. During the last couple of years the FA has been subtly changing the make-up of its disciplinary panels by bringing in ex-players who are closer to the modern game than the committee men who acted as judges in the past. I was one of the first to be asked to participate and I have now sat in judgment on a number of cases of alleged player or managerial indiscipline. It's ironic, given the times I was taken to task myself while I was a player. Maybe that's the point. I am the poacher turned gamekeeper. In my life I have to say that far more has gone right than wrong. I have played for some wonderful football clubs. I've had a fantastic career. It has been an incredible journey. I wouldn't have missed it for the world.

INDEX